PENGUIN CLASSICS

CONFESSIONS

SAINT AUGUSTINE (354–430), born in Africa, spent a decade in Italy, where he was baptized by the bishop of Milan, Saint Ambrose (c. 338–97). Returned to Africa, he was made the bishop of Hippo, a port city in modern Algeria, where he wrote such Christian classics as *The City of God*, *The Trinity*, and *Confessions*.

GARRY WILLS received his doctorate in classical languages from Yale and is now Professor Emeritus of History at Northwestern University. He won the Pulitzer Prize for *Lincoln at Gettysburg*. Recent books include *Saint Augustine* (A Penguin Life biography) and the *New York Times* bestsellers *What Jesus Meant*, *What Paul Meant*, and *What the Gospels Meant*.

To access Penguin Readers Guides online, visit our Web sites at www.penguin.com or www.vpbookclub.com.

SAINT AUGUSTINE

Confessions

Translated with an Introduction by
GARRY WILLS

PENGUIN BOOKS

PENGUIN BOOKS

Published by the Penguin Group
Penguin Group (USA) Inc.,
375 Hudson Street, New York, New York 10014, U.S.A.
Penguin Group (Canada), 90 Eglinton Avenue East, Suite 700, Toronto,
Ontario, Canada M4P 2Y3 (a division of Pearson Penguin Canada Inc.)
Penguin Books Ltd, 80 Strand, London WC2R 0RL, England
Penguin Ireland, 25 St Stephen's Green, Dublin 2, Ireland (a division of Penguin Books Ltd)
Penguin Group (Australia), 250 Camberwell Road, Camberwell,
Victoria 3124, Australia (a division of Pearson Australia Group Pty Ltd)
Penguin Books India Pvt Ltd, 11 Community Centre, Panchsheel Park, New Delhi – 110 017, India
Penguin Group (NZ), 67 Apollo Drive, Rosedale, North Shore 0632,
New Zealand (a division of Pearson New Zealand Ltd)
Penguin Books (South Africa) (Pty) Ltd, 24 Sturdee Avenue,
Rosebank, Johannesburg 2196, South Africa

Penguin Books Ltd, Registered Offices:
80 Strand, London WC2R 0RL, England

First published in the United States of America by Penguin Books,
a member of Penguin Group (USA) Inc. 2006
Published in Penguin Books 2008

7   9   10   8   6

Copyright © Garry Wills, 2002, 2003, 2004, 2006
All rights reserved

Portions of this book were published in volumes entitled *Saint Augustine's Memory*, *Saint Augustine's Childhood*, *Saint Augustine's Sin*, and *Saint Augustine's Conversion* (Viking Penguin)

LIBRARY OF CONGRESS CATALOGING IN PUBLICATION DATA
Augustine, Saint, Bishop of Hippo.
[Confessiones. English]
Confessions / Saint Augustine ; translated with an introduction by Garry Wills.
p. cm.—(Penguin classics)
ISBN 978-0-14-310570-1 (pbk)
1. Augustine, Saint, Bishop of Hippo.   2. Catholic Church—Bishops—Biography.
3. Bishops—Algeria—Hippo (Extinct city)—Biography.   4. Christian saints—Algeria—Hippo
(Extinct city)—Biography.   I. Wills, Garry, 1934–   II. Title.   III. Series.
BR65.A6E5 2006
270.2'092—dc22
[B]   2005049344

Printed in the United States of America
Set in Adobe Sabon

To Dan Berrigan

— *a Christian* —

Contents

Introduction   ix

BOOK ONE: Childhood   1
BOOK TWO: Sin   25
BOOK THREE: Manichaeism   39
BOOK FOUR: Friends   59
BOOK FIVE: Materialism   83
BOOK SIX: Milan   107
BOOK SEVEN: Neoplatonism   133
BOOK EIGHT: Vocation   159
BOOK NINE: Baptism   183
BOOK TEN: Memory   209
BOOK ELEVEN: Father (Origin)   255
BOOK TWELVE: Son (Form)   283
BOOK THIRTEEN: Spirit (Love)   311

Introduction

People who wander over a famous battle site—Gettysburg, perhaps, or the beach at Normandy—often have a sense of the momentous past lying under their humdrum surroundings in the present. One might well have that sense while strolling up to the vast Milan cathedral, crossing the piazza at its entrance. Deep under that surface a transaction took place, more significant than any battle scene, more than sixteen hundred years ago. To find the site, one must enter the cathedral, go down some steps almost hidden near its inner façade, and thread [one's] way through the church's architectural bowels to the buried foundations of an earlier cathedral. Cordoned off there is what looks like a polygonal wading pool.

At dawn on April 25, 387 CE, a group of people standing at the edge of that pool stripped off their clothes and went down into the water for a triple immersion. Among the men in the group were three Africans: thirty-three-year-old Augustine of Hippo, his sixteen-year-old son, Adeodatus, and his former pupil and best friend, Alypius, a man still in his twenties. Waiting for them to emerge from the other side of the pool, with a white robe to wrap each one in, was the bishop of Milan, Ambrose. The whole history of the medieval church in the West was latent in this event. The structure and governance of the Catholic Church would grow from Ambrose's dominance. Though not a pope himself, Ambrose was more powerful than any of the weak popes of his time, and later popes would aspire to his multiple roles, defying emperors, scourging heretics, making the cult of saints a principle of social order. And the teaching that filled the church thus structured would grow out of the many writings of Augustine. The two men were, even at the outset, yoked in a partnership despite differences in their temperaments and outlook, so even the strains and contradictions of the future were already presaged on that Easter morning.

Ten years later, when both Augustine and Alypius were bishops of their own African towns (in modern Algeria), Augustine would give an account of his journey toward that baptism. Other works of his would have a greater impact on medieval doctrine, but no other has addressed readers with more immediacy and intimacy than his *Confessions*. This effect is an odd one, since he speaks to us here through two formidable grids—a constant interweaving of biblical citations in the book's texture, and a highly artificial rhetorical idiom in the book's style. Writing through this screen of formal devices would normally distance the author from us, or from any spontaneity and directness in his own expression. But he uses both devices to travel down into himself, and to reach us on deep levels. In this translation I try to mark clearly both these grids placed over Augustine's language.

First, the biblical citations. Augustine, with his capacious memory, had the whole of Scripture on call in his mind, and he tried as a matter of religious commitment and psychological need to think in and through the sacred words. I signal the constant references and biblical vocabulary with single quotation marks around these phrases. It is important to keep the reader aware of this aspect of the text, to explain what might otherwise seem odd images, strange repetitions, or logical leaps prompted by the poetic or prophetic books of Scripture. Augustine reasoned by progressions of biblical symbolism. This constant citation of other persons' words did not estrange him from his own private identity, since he saw his life, at its deepest level, as a re-enactment of the cosmic drama traceable in the sacred writings.

His book is often treated as if it were an autobiography, but it is not. The narrative references to his own life end at Book Nine of the thirteen books. After assessing his own preparation for addressing the mysteries of Scripture in Book Ten, he devotes the last three books to the doctrine of the divine Trinity as that is adumbrated in the opening lines of the Book of Genesis. The *Confessions,* we must be kept aware, do not address us. They have an audience of One (or of Three-in-One), making them the longest literary prayer in our canon of great works. The traces of Genesis and of the Trinity run through all the earlier books, as Augustine searches them out in the workings of God's grace upon his life. This explains the many departures from literal facts as they were recorded in his earlier writings. The whole book is a theological construct, best compared with another construct that uses autobiographical elements, Dante's *Divine Comedy.* Like Dante, Augustine moves simultaneously both outward, exploring the revelation of God, and inward, letting that revelation affect and alter him.

Finally, the rhetoric. Augustine was a professional rhetorician before his baptism. Though he mocks that former role—calling himself a "phrase salesman" and "a peddler of glibness in the marketplace"—he kept all the tricks of his trade for sacred use. Purists have condemned this in him, rejecting his work as so many strings of artificial showiness. It is true that he loves and indulges himself in puns, alliteration, antitheses, jingles, anaphora, chiasmus, polyptoton, and other classical devices. Some of these are untranslatable. For instance, since *Paulus* means "little" in Latin, when he addresses the Apostle as *Magne Paule,* he is calling him "Large-Little." He is not merely quibbling, but referring to Paul's own modest claim that he was "the least of the Apostles," and referring to the paradox, often explored by Augustine, that human greatness comes only through humility—that God lifts up the man who lowers himself.

Though so complex an "in joke" as *Magne Paule* cannot be carried over into English, much of Augustine's wordplay can be imitated or suggested, and should be, since he did not think of these tropes as ornaments added to thought. He thought *by means of* rhetoric, just as he thought *by means of* scriptural texts, and for the same reason—both, he felt, reflected the mysteries of God. Since God is the Word (Logos, or Verbum), the hidden affinities and capacities of language were ways to trace the subterranean thought-connections of our own mind. When he addresses the child Jesus as *In-fans Verbum*—languageless language—he is putting the mystery of the Incarnation in an oxymoron as teasing as the thing being described. When he says that our duty toward Scripture is to "read, heed, and accede," he is saying that our triune response, in three acts that are different but the same, reflects how we are structured like the triune God being revealed to us. God is the Word. We are made in his image. We are words.

Augustine merged his two modes of thought, scriptural and rhetorical, in an idiosyncratic way. As used by him, the two do not tug against each other but are reciprocally reinforcing. Ciceronian amplitude (*amplificatio*), for instance, melds nicely with the verse form of the Hebrew prophets and psalmists, which was based on a two-line unit where the second line echoes the first. The result is a meditative rhythm, the self-reflection of phrases lingering and returning on themselves—a language of sighing replications—to induce in us a hushed inner attentiveness. The intense innerness of the *Confessions* comes from Augustine's conviction that God is to be sought within ourselves, not in outward preaching or observation. Since human beings are made in God's image, God can be understood by them only through self-observation, a deep probing of one's own makeup that has made some people call Augustine the father of modern psychology. Even Scripture, he believed, speaks within us, by God's direct inspiration. "I was outside myself, while you were inside me." He addresses God as "deeper in me than I am in me" (*intimior intimo meo*). His book calls us back into ourselves, to our own inner depths.

Citations from Scripture are here translated from the Latin texts Augustine used—African versions sometimes differing from the Vulgate Latin Bible used in the Middle Ages. Titles for the separate books, and subheads within them, are added to Augustine's text for the reader's convenience.

Confessions

Confessions

BOOK ONE

CHILDHOOD

I

HOW TO BEGIN?

1. 'Vast are you, Lord, and as vast should be your praise'—
'vast what you do; what you know beyond assaying.' Yet
man, a mere segment of what you made, strives to appraise
you—man, 'confined by a nature that must die,' confined by
this evidence of his sin, the evidence that you rebuff the overweening, yet man would still appraise you, this mere segment of what you made. You prompt us yourself to find
satisfaction in appraising you, since you made us tilted
toward you, and our heart is unstable until stabilized in you.

Then help me, Lord, to recognize and understand what
comes first, to call for you before appraising you, or to recognize you before calling for you. Yet how can one call for
what one does not recognize? Without such recognition, one
could be calling for something else. Or is calling for you itself the way to recognize you? Yet, 'how shall people call for
one they do not believe exists? And how are they to believe it
exists if no one proclaims it?'

Still, 'those who seek the Lord shall appraise him,' for by
seeking him they find, and by finding they appraise. I shall
seek you then, Lord, by calling for you, call for you by believing you exist; for you have been proclaimed to us, and it
is my belief in you that calls out to you—the faith that is
your gift to me, which you breathed into me by the humanity your Son assumed, taking up his mission of proclaiming
you.

2. Yet how 'shall I call for my God, the God who is my
Lord,' when it is precisely to me I am calling him when I call,
and what in me is large enough for God to enter? How can

he who made heaven and earth come into me? Is there anything in me that can hold you? Can even heaven and earth, which you made, and in which you made me, hold you? Or, since nothing that is can exist without you, do all things that exist hold you?

And since I too exist, how can I ask you to come to me, who would not exist if you were not already in me? Hell has no claim on me, not yet; and even there, you are present—so 'if I *do* go down to hell, there are you.' Thus I would not exist, my God, could not exist at all, were you not already in me. Rather, I could not be, were I not in you, 'from whom, through whom, in whom are all things.' Assuredly that is so, Lord, that is so.

Where *to* can I, already in you, call you to come? And where *from* would you be coming? Where *to* could I retire, outside heaven and earth, for God to come there to me, my God who has said, 'I fill heaven and earth'? **3.** Since, then, you fill heaven and earth, do they contain you? Or do you fill them, with a surplus of you left over, beyond their containing? Then where, once heaven and earth are filled, does the overflow of you go? Do you, who contain all things, need no container because what you fill is filled by your containing *it*? Any receptacle containing you cannot confine you—were it broken, you would not spill out of it. When your Spirit is poured out upon us, you do not fall down but lift up, you are not scattered out, but gather in.

But in filling all things, do you fill them with all of you? Or since all things cannot hold all of you, do they each hold its own part of you—all of them the same part, or each its own part, larger or smaller as they are large or small? Can there, then, be a larger or smaller part of you? Are you not entire everywhere, though nothing can hold the entire you?

4. Then what are you, God—what, I inquire, but simply God the Lord? 'What other Lord is Lord, what other God but God?'—highest, best, most powerful, all-powerfulest, most merciful yet most just, hidden far away yet very near, most beautiful yet most strong, most fixed yet most elusive, changeless in changing all things; neither young nor old, you give youth back to all things yet 'age the proud away insensibly'; active always, always at rest, you acquire without lacking, you support, fill, and protect; create, raise, and complete; seeking, though you have all; loving, yet not inflamed; jealous, yet not disturbed; regretful, without remorse; angry, without intemperance; you change event without a change of plan; acquiring what is at hand without having lost; never in need, yet happy at gain; receiving, without exacting interest on what is owed you; overpaid to be put in debt, yet none pay you with anything you did not, in the first place, give; you honor debts without owing, cancel debts without losing. And what, with all this, have I said, my God, my life holy and sweet to me, what can anyone say when speaking of you? Yet we must say something when those who say the most are saying nothing.

5. Who will help me find stability in you, help you come into my heart, to make it drunk with you, oblivious of my ills and hugging all my good to me, the good you are? Why do you matter so much to me?—pity me enough to let me say. Why, indeed, do I matter so much to you that my loving you is something you require, that you should be angry and threaten me with heavy punishments if I love not? Then can my not loving you be a slight thing? No, it cannot, to my sorrow! Tell me by your acts of mercy, God my Lord, what you are to me. Tell my soul, 'I am your rescue.' Tell me in a way that I may hear. My heart is all ears for it, Lord. Open them and tell my soul, 'I am your rescue.' I shall rush toward those words and lay hold on them. 'Hide not your countenance from me.' Let me die into you lest I die away from your countenance.

6. My soul is 'too cramped for you to enter it—widen it out.' It is in disrepair—restore it. It is filthy in your sight, I admit and recognize this, but who is to sanitize it? To whom before you should I call out, 'Cleanse me of my inmost sins, and outward promptings fend off from your servant'? I believe in you and that is why, you know, Lord, I address you. Have I not anticipated accusation of my own sins, 'and you freed my heart of impiety'? I do not 'take you into court,' you who are Truth. I would not deceive myself, not let 'my iniquity tell itself a lie,' so I go not to court with you. 'If you arraign our sins, Lord—Lord, who can stand the indictment?'

7. Yet let me enter my appeal before your mercy, let me, 'a thing of earth and ash,' appeal to you, since I enter my plea before your mercy, not before a fellow man, who might well mock me. Or do you, in fact, mock me? But even if you do, you will change your mood and pity me.

II

IN-FANS (SPEECHLESS)

What would I plead with you, Lord, but my ignorance of whence I came into this dying life, or should I call it living death? I know not whence I came, only that your merciful sustenance kept me alive when I did, as I learned from the parents who gave me flesh—the father from whom, the mother in whom, you made me (but not my memory) begin in time. It was your sustenance I drew from fleshly milk, since neither my mother nor nurses were filling their own breasts with it. You yourself dispensed this baby food through them, following the pattern, the gracious providence, you have embedded deep in nature. You provided that I should wish for no more than was supplied, and that those supplying it should wish to give me what you gave them. The wish to supply me came from the natural instinct you planted deep in them, so that doing me good did them good, a good they did not provide themselves but passed on from you, the source of all good, my God, my rescue at every stage.

This I came to reflect on only later, heeding the persistent call you issued through the inner and outer faculties you blessed me with, but then I knew only how to suck, to sleep when soothed, to cry when my body vexed me—this I knew, no more. **8.** In time I began to smile, only in my sleep at first, and later when awake—so it was said of me, and I believed it, since we observe the same thing in other babies, though I do not remember it of myself. Gradually I became aware of my surroundings, and wished to express my demands to those who could comply with them; but I could not, since the demands were inside me, and outside were their fulfillers, who had no faculty for entering my mind. So I worked my limbs and voice energetically, trying to signal out something like my demands, to the best of my little (and little availing) ability. Then, when I was frustrated—because I was not understood or was demanding something harmful— I threw a tantrum because adults did not obey a child, free people were not my slaves. So I inflicted on them my revenge of wailing. I have learned that babies act this way, from the ones I had occasion to observe, who, without having known me [as an infant], taught me more about myself than the nurses who did know me.

9.   See then how I lived on when my speechless stage had died away—unlike you, who live on always, with nothing of you dying away, since before all ages began, before everything that can be called before, you are, and are the God and Lord of all that you created, and in you are the certain causes of contingent outcomes, the unchanging origins that abide through all that changes, the eternal rationale for all irrational things that pass away.

Tell me, your supplicant, Lord, merciful to one needing mercy, tell me whether my speechless stage occurred after some other stage of me had died away. Was it just the time I spent in my mother's body—for I came to be told of that, too, and observed pregnant women myself. But was there something before that, my delight, my God? Was I, anywhere, anyone? I have no one who might tell me that— neither father nor mother, nor anyone claiming experience of such a stage, nor any memory of my own. Or do you smile, to mock me as I ask, you who tell me to praise you for what I know, and testify to that?   **10.**   I can bear you testimony, Lord of heaven and earth, returning praise to you for my origin and speechless days, though I remember it not, because you let man learn of his infancy from analogy with other infants, if not from women gossips who were there.

[So even without remembering] I was already in existence and had life, and I was striving, while still (just barely) speechless, to find a way of signaling my own meanings out to others. Where could such a creature come from, Lord, but

you? Can any such have framed itself, or found a conduit
through which existence and life could stream into him from
some other source than you, for whom existing is not one
thing, living another, since you are perfect existence, perfect
life? Perfect you are, beyond all change, and today does not
reach its end in you, yet it does end in you, since all days are
in you, nor could they have a course of transit not defined by
you. But your years never run out, your years are a single today; and our days, no matter how many—not only our own
but those of all before us—run their course through your today, are brought into being in it, find their identity in it; and
days still to come shall run their course through it, with their
own being and identity, while you alone are identical with
yourself, so every tomorrow to come, every yesterday gone,
is made in your today. What does it matter if one fails to figure this out? Let such a one be content to say, How could
this be?—so long as he finds in love what he does not figure
out, instead of figuring it out without finding you.

11.   Pay me heed, God. When one says 'How sad it is for
the sinner,' God takes pity, since he made the sinner (without
making the sin). Who is there to remind me of my sin before
I spoke?—'no one being clean of sin, not a speechless child
with but a day upon this earth'—who will remind me, will
any (even the tiniest) baby serve for me to observe what I do
not remember of myself, will it show me what sin I was committing at that age? Was it sin to work my mouth toward the
nipple as I cried? If I did that now, working my mouth not
toward the nipple but after food proper to my present state,
I would be derided and properly reproached. But though my
behavior then deserved reproach, I would not have understood if anyone issued it, the reproach would have had no effect, either from social pressure or personal acceptance. As
we grow up, we root out and relinquish such behavior. (People, I observe, when sorting out bad things to reject, do not
knowingly throw out the good instead.)

Or is this behavior allowable in terms of a baby's age—to
demand with tears what would harm it; to throw a tantrum
when not obeyed by servants and adults, by his own parents,

by any bystanders (however wise) not knuckling under to its whim; flailing away to hurt (if he could) those who dare disobey his own self-harming ukase? The harmlessness of babes is in their body's effect, not their mind's intent. With my own eyes I was a present witness at what we have all observed, a tiny thing's fierce competitiveness—how, though he could not speak, he made himself clear by his sudden pallor and the sour contortion of his features at a rival for the nipple. Mothers and nurses claim they can check the tantrum by some trick of their trade, treating as harmless a baby's effort to deprive another of the one food it depends on, though the milk flows abundantly for both. We put up with the tantrum, not because it does not matter, or matters little, but because the baby will grow out of it—as we see from the fact that no one will put up with such behavior in an adult.

12. You, God, who are my Lord, give life to the baby when you give it a body—we see how you articulate its sensory apparatus; fit limb to limb, giving beauty to its form; and coordinate all its instincts for self-preservation as a single thing. It is your will that I appraise all this, pay you, the highest of things, my testimony of song to your name, since this in itself, had you done nothing more for the baby, shows that you are all-powerful and kind, that no one else could do what you do—could, from your oneness, give each thing its degree of being; from your beauty give it shapeliness; from your law give it its rank in the creation.

Such, Lord, was the period when I was alive though I do not remember being so, a period for which I have taken on trust what others told me, or have guessed at my own behavior from analogy with other babies. However persuasive such analogy may be, I hesitate to count that period as part of my life in this world, since it is as wrapped in a darkness beyond recall as was the period I spent in my mother's womb—and if 'I was conceived in evil, and my mother sheltered a sinful me in her womb,' where, my God, I ask you, where, my Lord, was I, your servant, ever free from sin? Beyond that I say nothing of a time with which I recall not the faintest connection.

III

CHILDHOOD (SPEAKING)

13. What but childhood could I enter by advance beyond my speechless stage? Or is it better to say that childhood entered me, displacing the speechless stage? Yet my speechlessness did not depart—where else could it have gone?—though it was no longer with me. As soon as I began speaking, I could no longer be speechless, but a speaking child. I remember speaking, though I learned only later *how* I came to speak. It was not by the teaching of my elders, arranging words in some prescribed order, as when I learned grammar. All by myself, using the brain you gave me, my God, for want of getting each thing I wanted from each person I wanted, when my screams, my noises random and random flailing of limbs, did not convey the desires within me, I began to use my memory to pull in what I desired. Whenever people named something, and used the same inflections when indicating that thing with their bodies, I would take note and store in memory the fact that they made the same sound when they wanted to indicate that thing. It was clear they wanted to do this from the physical action that is a body language for all humans—facial expressions, glances, or miming actions that, linked with vocal inflections, convey an intention to get or retain, repel or evade something. The words I heard, used in their right way in different grammatical settings, and recurring over time, I steadily accumulated and, wrestling my mouth around these sounds, I expressed what I wanted. With these tools for enunciating what I wanted, I plunged deeper into the storm-tossed lives of those around me, where I was shaped by my parents' direction and the pressures of my elders.

14. God, you who are my God, what pitiable things, things that made me ridiculous, did I undergo when the goal marked out for me as a boy was to follow advice that would make me a success, would give me an orator's facility for gaining human fame and a wealth that deludes its slaves. For this was I sent to school and taught grammar; and though I could not see what use there was in that, I was beaten for not being eager in its pursuit—a custom praised by our elders, since men living long ago laid out the painful course we must be forced down, adding more to the work and suffering that was already our lot as sons of Adam.

But I came across, as well, people who prayed to you, and they made me, in my small way, aware of you as a vague high being beyond my sensible experience, one who could, nonetheless, hear me out and bring me help. Thus, even as a child, I ventured on prayer to you as my support, my place of shelter. Tongue-tied words I faltered out, using my small voice with no small intensity, to be spared being beaten in class; and when you did not grant me my prayer (not yielding to my false values), my elders, including my parents, laughed off my beatings, not wishing me ill, though a large and weighty ill the beatings were for me.

15. Is there, Lord, anyone so brave, so resolute from love of you (aside from mere natural obduracy), is there, I say, anyone so steeled by love for you as to make light of the rack and tearing instruments and other tools of torture (things people all over the earth beg with great terror to escape) and to laugh at those stricken with terror at the tortures, as much as parents made light of the torments we children underwent from our teachers? I did not lack any of the panic, or lack any desperation in begging to escape blows—though it was only my lack of attention to reading and writing and performing the assignments given me that was to blame. I had no excuse from lack of memory or talent, which you made sufficient for my age; I simply loved games more, and I was disciplined by those who had their own games (since *gain* is the game of adults). So children's games are punished by their elders, and no one gets worked

up for the punished, the punishers, or both, unless some cal-
culater of advantage should *approve* my being beaten for a
child's games since the games slowed my rapid advance in
the education I could use for viler games. Who, in these
terms, was worse—my teacher, who writhed with bitter envy
when caught in a solecism by a fellow pedant, or I, when I
resented losing my ball game to a fellow player?

16.   This is not said to deny my sin, Lord, you who both
correct and create all things in nature, but can only correct
[not create] sins—it was a sin to defy the edicts of my parents and those teachers, since I later put to higher use the education those people, from whatever motive of their own,
made me acquire. I did not disobey them to do something
better, but from a love of games—I longed for lofty triumphs
and fantastic tales that tickled my ears and made them itch
for more, making my eyes sparkle bright and ever brighter
with excitement at the public games, the play of adults. Those
who put on such shows are clothed with a high dignity that
parents wish for their children; and they gladly let those children be beaten if attending shows hinders their education,
which can gain for them the status to put on shows themselves. Look on all this, Lord, with a forgiving eye, and free
us now that we call on you, freeing as well those who do not
call yet, that they may call and you may free them.

17.   Already in my boyhood I was taught about the eternal life promised us through the Lord's lowliness reaching
down to our haughtiness—I was signed already with his cross,
seasoned with his salt, when I left the womb of my mother,
who turned fervently to you. And you saw, Lord, how I,
while still a boy, almost died from a sudden attack of chest
fever—you saw, Lord and guardian, with what emotion and
belief, with what reliance on my own mother and the mother
of us all, your church, I begged for baptism in Christ your
son. The mournful bearer of my mortal body cared more,
from her pure heart's faith in you, to deliver me into eternal
life than she had to bear me into this one. She made quick
arrangements for the rites of my ablution in the saving mysteries, with my testimony to you, Lord Jesus, for forgiveness

of my sins. Only, instantly, I recovered—so my cleansing was put off, on the assumption that I would surely be tainted as I grew up, and the taint, after such a cleansing, would be greater and more perilous.

I already had faith, then, as did my mother and all our household, except my father, who, though he was not yet a believer himself, did not deny me the protection of my mother's devotion, that I should believe in Christ. She made it a point to say that you, not he, were my father, my God, and you helped her in this way to prevail over her husband, staying subservient to him though superior to him, since in this she was obeying your demands.

18.   This is my request, God: I would know, if you will let me, why I was put off, why not baptized; was it for my own good to be given free rein to sin for a while, or was I not, in fact, given free rein? Why even now is it everywhere dinned into our ears, when this or that class of men is discussed, that we should Let him carry on, since he is not yet baptized, when we do not say about physical health, Let him further damage his body, since he is not yet given his health. How much better would it have been for me to be healed on the spot, so that care might be taken of myself by me and by mine, that the healing given my soul should be preserved in your preserving ways who gave it—how much better indeed. But mighty storm-waves, and many, were foreseen rolling over me after my childhood, and my mother, understanding this, preferred to commit to the waters' workings my unshaped clay rather than a self already reshaped.

IV

SCHOOLING

19. Yet even before my testing time as a young man, even in my childhood, I resisted education and despised those pressing it upon me, though they pressed anyway, and good was done me though I myself did no good. I would have learned nothing if it had not been forced on me, and no one deserves credit for what is forced on him, though the thing itself be creditable. Nor did those forcing me deserve any credit, since the credit is all yours, my God. They did not realize—as they forced learning on me to sate insatiable yearnings for penurious wealth and infamous fame—what different uses I would make of it. But you, 'who keep count of our every hair,' put to my use the useless efforts of those forcing me to learn, and used my resistance, which merited the beatings, as a punishment for me, so little in size, so large in sin. Thus you get the credit for those who earned no credit for what they did to me, and I got the punishment I deserved for resisting what they were doing, for what you have decreed is fulfilled when sin becomes the soul's own punishment of itself.

20. Why I loathed Greek lessons, when I was plunged into them at an early age, I have not to this day been able to fathom. I took fondly to Latin, not indeed from my first tutors but from those called teachers of literature. The basic reading, writing, and numbering in Latin I considered as dull and irksome as any aspect of my Greek lessons—the explanation of which must be sin and the aimless life of 'fleshly whims that stray off without returning.'

Actually, the basic lessons were the more valuable ones,

just *because* they went by rule, letting me acquire and retain the ability I still hold to read any book I come across, or to write exactly what I want to say—things more useful than the strayings of some Aeneas that I was forced to memorize while forgetting that I was astray myself, better certainly than my tears for the perished Dido, who killed herself from love, while I, the truly pitiful one, was dry-eyed to my perishing, my God, from loss of you.

21.   Who is more pitiful than a pitiable man without pity for himself—one who weeps for Dido, dead because she loved Aeneas, but not for himself, dead because he failed to love you, God, my heart's enlightener, the feeder of my soul's inner hunger, the vital principle breeding depth of thought out of my intelligence? I [not Aeneas] was the abandoner, the faithless lover, and my faithlessness earned the world's Bravo! Bravo!—since love of the world is abandonment of you, and the world cries Bravo! Bravo! to keep its own in line. For all this I had no tears, only tears for Dido, exploring with the sword her utmost doom. So I, in flight from you, explored the utmost depths of your creation, 'earthy and to earth returning.' If I had been forbidden to read this tale, I would have lamented the loss of what made me lament, so crazed are those who think belles lettres nobler than the rudiments of reading and writing I had to learn.

22.   Now, however, may my God cry through my soul, your truth assuring me That is not the case, not at all—basic learning was far better. Assuredly I am readier to forget, now, the strayings of Aeneas and all his sort than to lose my ability to read and write. Ceremonial draperies are hung at the school door, but they are not so much veils of honor for the esoteric as blinds for the erroneous. And let no phrase peddlers or purchasers scorn me, an escapee from their thrall, while I give you my soul's willing testimony, since I accept the correction of my strayings, I long to tread your righteous ways. If I should confront them with the straightforward question whether the poet spoke true when he claimed that Aeneas went to Carthage once upon a time, the uneducated will admit they do not know, while the educated admit it is not true. But if I ask how to spell Aeneas' name, all those who know how to read will give the right answer, honoring the agreed-on conventions that establish the alphabet. Similarly, if I ask what would make life less bearable, to forget how to read or write or to forget those poetic imaginings, we know what anyone in his sound mind will say. So it was sinful of me to prefer airy trifles to the solider rudiments—or, more accurately, to loathe the latter and love the former. The singsong One and one make two, two and two make four was detestable to me, but sweet were the visions of absurdity—the wooden horse cargoed with men, Troy in flames, and Creusa herself ghosting by.

23. Then why did I loathe Greek literature, which has tunes for the same kind of tale? Homer knew how to weave the same spells, just as pleasantly trivial, yet he repelled me as a boy. I suppose Greek boys would feel the same about Virgil, if they were forced to con him as I conned Homer. It is hard, very hard, to pick up a foreign language—for me, this dashed with bitterness all the sweet Greek nonsense. I was ignorant of the words, and violent threats and acts were used to make me learn them. Once, admittedly, still in my speechless state, I knew no Latin words either. Yet I applied myself to learning them, without intimidation or coercion, surrounded as I was by nurses who coaxed, adults who laughed, and others fond of playing with a child. The Latin words were learned without others' punitive insistence that I learn. From my own heart's need I went into labor to deliver my thoughts, which I could not have done without a stock of words, picked up not just from tutors but from anyone who spoke with me, and in their ears I completed the parturition of what I felt within me. Unfettered inquisitiveness, it is clear, teaches better than do intimidating assignments—which assignments, nonetheless, chasten random inquisitiveness within rules, your rules, God, imposed even in the beatings of teachers, as in the trials of martyrs, those healing pains that draw us back from the sickly pleasures that might drift us off from you.

24. 'Hear, Lord, my cry to you,' lest my soul prove too weak for your discipline, lest I prove too weak to bear testimony to all your merciful dealings with me, by which you drew me from my vicious bypaths, outdazzling with your allure the attractions that misled me, so that I may love you more worthily, hang on to your hand with a whole heart's energy, as you 'carry me out of trial to the final goal.' You see, Lord, my king and God, I would use whatever I learned as a child for your service, whatever I speak or write or enumerate—since you disciplined me when I was learning trifles, and have forgiven me the sin of taking my delight in them; for I learned some useful words even from trifles (though I might have learned them from less trivial sources, as is the safer way for children to proceed).

V

CONFORMING TO A DEFORMING SOCIETY

25. Cursed be you, Society, onstreaming—who can stand against your tide never stemmed, your torrent carrying Eve's sons out to the vast sea's peril, where even those who ride on the Wood barely survive? Was it not from you, Society, that I learned how Jove is both thunderer and adulterer? He could not really be both, but he was portrayed as both, so that real adultery could be indulged with fictitious thunder serving as its pimp. What gowned rhetorician can take it seriously when his fellow, who breathes the same court air, says: Homer in his fictions made gods behave like humans, but I prefer for humans to behave like gods? Well, in fact, Homer did create fictions precisely to give divine sanction to human vice, so vice would not seem vicious, and those indulging it could claim to be following the example of gods on high, not of lowliest men.

26. Into you, you hellish river, men's children are thrown, to learn such things for a price, and a great ceremony is made when they display what they have learned in the forum, the very place where the teachers' state fees, superadded to the private fees, are posted. And the river, pounding against these rocks, roars out: This is the reward for learning literature, for acquiring the eloquence needed to plead persuasively and argue well—as if we could never have encountered the phrases *showered gold* or *lap* or *trick* or other words put together in one place by Terence, if he had not put on stage a vile young man taking Jove as a model for his act of rape. The man gazes on a mural presenting the device by which Jove tricked a woman, ejaculating himself as showered gold into her lap. Just see how the youth works up his lust, as if by heavenly injunction:

> If ev'n this god, who thumps heaven's temples so
> With crashing noise, showers also down so low,
> Can lowly I not follow where he goes?—
> You bet, and have great fun, too, heaven knows.

Vocabulary is surely not acquired more readily by means of obscenity, but *this* vocabulary makes obscene acts more acceptable. I indict not the words, which are 'choice and precious vessels' in themselves, but the wine of error poured into them by teachers drunk with it, who beat us if we do not drink with them, and we cannot appeal to any sober arbiter—not that I did not drink it gladly, my God, I recall that fact clearly before your gaze, I was wretch enough to enjoy it. That, indeed, is why I was said to be a promising child.

27.   Let me say, my God, something of the talent, your gift, that I dissipated on various forms of nonsense. I was called to a contest that destabilized my mind between praise hoped for and embarrassment or a beating feared: I had to recite the speech of Juno as she raged in anguish over not *fending off Troy's king from Italy.* I had learned that no Juno ever said that, but we were compelled to follow poetical strayings into unreality, paraphrasing in prose what was set down in verse. The child who best adapted the emotions of rage and anguish to the status of the imaginary queen, fitly decking her thoughts out in words, was given the prize.

What of value was it to me, my God, my true life, that my recital was praised beyond the multitude of my fellows in age and study? What was this but drifted smoke? Was there no other way to develop my talent and my speaking voice? Honoring you, giving honor to the words of your Scripture, would have 'trellised up my heart's young tendrils,' not raveling them out in vain exercises to be the rotten prey of birds. So many ways we find to honor the dark angels.

28.   It is not surprising that I was swept along in folly away from you, my God, and wandered abroad, when the role models I was given were ashamed if they were caught describing their own good behavior in ungraceful or ungrammatical terms, but luxuriated in men's praise if they could describe their vicious acts in choice words well fitted together, flowing with easy and elegant phrases. Do you, Lord, 'long patient, very merciful and true,' look on all this in silence? And will your silence never end? Already you are drawing from such an immense abyss the soul that longs for you, that thirsts to be satisfied by you, whose heart tells you, 'I have sought your countenance, it is your countenance, Lord, I shall seek,' for to be far off from your countenance is to be in a murk of feelings. It is not by walking or by any locomotion that one moves off from you or comes back to you—the younger son of the parable did not call for horses or chariots or ships, nor soar off on visible wings, nor trudge along on foot, when in a distant land he prodigally wasted what you, mild father, had given him on departure. Mild when he left, you were milder when he came back destitute. To be in a lustful murk of feeling, therefore, is what being far off from your countenance means.

29. Look on, Lord God, and, as you look, with patience look at how carefully men's sons honor earlier speakers' conventional arrangements of letters and syllables, while they neglect your eternal arrangement for eternal salvation—so that if one who is taught or teaches the rules of speech should, against the norm of pronunciation, drop the *h* before *human being,* he is more censured by human beings than if he, a human being, should, against your rule of love, hate any other fellow being—as if another human being could hurt him more than does the hate he directs at that human being, or as if a man could inflict on a foe some wound greater than he inflicts on his own heart by letting it hate. The rules of grammar are not as deeply inscribed as the morality of Scripture, which says: 'Treat another as you would be treated.' How hidden you are, God, 'housed on your heights,' who alone are great, cloaking in penal darkness all criminal desires, when you look on while a would-be champion orator stands before a judge, with a crowd looking on, and lashes his opponent with a boundless hate, yet is cautious not to say something ungrammatical, like *between he*— and he does not care that the rhetorical storm he is working up may sweep his victim off from life.

30. I, wretch, was even as a child abandoned to Society, left at the edge of the arena where I was to contend, where I was more afraid of committing a solecism than concerned, if I did so, with my envy at any who did *not* commit it. I tell you this, and testify, my God, that this kind of praise was what I sought from those whose approval was my goal in life. I did not realize in what a maelstrom of ugliness 'I was being swept off from your gaze.' What could be fouler than the way I earned disapproval even from the worldly with my endless lies told to pedagogue, to teachers, to parents, so I could indulge my love of games, my passion for trivial plays, for re-enacting them with ludicrous clumsiness?

I also sneaked food from my parents' cupboard or table, to pamper myself or to give to others, who exacted this price for letting me share their delight in the games they played. And, once in the game, I often maneuvered to overcome others by devious means, overcome myself by a blind urge to win—yet I was a stickler for the rules, too, and savagely denounced any other's infraction of them I uncovered, even when it was the very infraction I was guilty of; while if *I* was caught out and denounced, I would throw a fit rather than admit it.

Is this the innocence of children—how can it be, I ask you, Lord, how can it, my God? Is it not a natural progression, from one stage of life to the succeeding ones, to move from playing for nuts and balls and sparrows, under pedagogues and teachers, to playing for gold, estates, and slaves, under governors and kings, and to move from beatings in school to criminal sentences? You, then, praised nothing but a child's small stature, as a symbol of humility, dear king, when you said 'Heaven's kingdom is for the like of these.'

31. I must, however, still give thanks to you, Lord, highest and best maker and ruler of this universe, had you given me only the life of a child; for during that time I existed, I experienced sensation, I preserved myself—by an echo of your mysterious oneness, out of which I came to be—as I maintained a single control over everything my senses delivered to me, and my first slight hold upon slight truths gave me satisfaction. I tried to avoid fallacies, my memory developed, I learned to wield words, I was shaped by friendship, I shunned being hurt or losing hope or being fooled. What, in this animate life of mine, was not admirable, worthy of praise? All of these were your gifts, God, I did not endow myself with any of them—and the sum of these good things was myself. My maker is good in himself, and my only good, and I hold him high for all the good that was in me even as a boy. Only sin was my own, when I sought joy, glory, and truth not in him but in things he made, in myself and other creatures, thus sliding off toward pain, dejection, and error. Still I thank you, you my delight, my pride, my trust— I thank you, my God, for your gifts to me, may you preserve them, thus preserving me, so that everything you gave me may grow and be improved, and I shall be with you, whose gift it is that I exist.

BOOK TWO

SIN

I

SEXUAL OFFENSES

1. I am determined to bring back in memory the revolting things I did, and the way my soul was contaminated by my flesh—doing this not out of love for those deeds but as a step toward loving you. I move toward you this way because I would love to love you. I bring back up to expression the bitterness of my vile wanderings so you may sweeten them, you my sweetness never deluding, sure sweetness ever delighting. You gather me from my own scatterings, after I have torn myself from your unity and fallen apart into multiplicity. At the time of my young manhood, when I burned to be engorged with vile things, I boldly foisoned into ramifying and umbrageous loves, while my inner shapeliness was withering—I was decomposing before your eyes while in men's eyes I was pleasing myself and 'trying to please them.'

2. Where did I find any satisfaction then but in loving and being loved? But I did not observe the line where mind meets mind. Instead of affection's landmarks drawn in light, earthmurks drowned in lust—and my erupting sexuality—breathed mephitic vapors over the boundary, to cloud and blind my heart in clouds and fog, erasing the difference between love's quietness and the drivenness of dark impulse. Quietness and drives were mingled chaotically within me, battering my impotent maturity on the anfractuosities of desire and dousing me in a maelstrom of offenses. Your ire impended over me, but I was unaware of it, deafened by the clattering of my mortal chains, a deafness inflicted by my soul's loftiness. I wandered farther from you, as you played out the leash—I was full of outflingings, effusions, diffusions, and ebullitions of illicit loves, as you maintained your silence. You, the joy I was so slow to hear, said nothing as I ranged farther out from you—I, loftily downfallen, actively paralyzed, sowing arid and ever more arid sadnesses.

3. Who might have brought within boundaries my misery, turned to some purpose the evanescent beauties of extreme experience, and set a clear limit to their deliciousness, that the stormy waters of my youth might have seethed up only to the shoreline of marriage? But could I have limited myself to sex used only for begetting children, Lord, as your law commands? (Yet it is you who make images of our mortality, able to soften with your gentling touch the thorns not allowed to grow in Eden, since your omnipotence is never far from us, however far from you we are.) In any case, I might have pondered more carefully your voice out of the clouds saying, 'They [the married] have all these cares of the flesh, which I would spare you.' Or 'Better for man not to lay hand to a woman,' or 'The man who has no wife expresses concern for God, and wants to please him, while the man with a wife expresses concern for worldly matters, because he wants to please his wife.' Had I listened to your words with greater attention, then with greater anticipation I might have welcomed your embrace as one 'castrated for heaven's reign.'

4. Instead, I frothed along in the wake of my driving passion, having left you to range beyond all the limits of your law, though not beyond your scourge's reach—for who is beyond that? You had not in fact left me, but showed a pitying severity. You dashed with bitter repinings my forbidden joys, making me seek joys with no repining, which I would never find apart from you, Lord, apart from the way 'you affix your pain to precept,' and 'heal with a wound,' and 'slay us that we may not die' by loss of you.

Where did that leave me? 'In distant exile from the comforts of your dwelling' during this sixteenth year of my age, when I surrendered with ready hand all rule over my self, turning it over to mad cravings condoned by our debased humanity but condemned by your law. My family did not care to divert me from my mad course toward marriage. They cared only that I might acquire rhetoric and sway others with my words.

5. It was in this sixteenth year that my studies were interrupted, when I was brought back from Madauros, the nearby town for which I had first left home in order to study grammar and rhetoric. My father was saving up funds to send me farther off, for study in Carthage, a project better suited to his aspirations than to his acquisitions, since he was a townsman of slender estate in Thagaste. Why do I bring this up? I do not bring it up to you, Lord, but in your presence I bring it up to my fellows, my fellow human beings—those, at any rate, however few, who may chance upon this book. And why to them? That we may express together, I and my readers, 'from what depths we must cry up to you' (though what could come closer to you than the testifying heart and 'a faithful life'?). An instance is this man, my father, whom all were extolling since he squandered money beyond his means to finance his son's education in a distant place. Admittedly, many wealthier men made no such arrangement for their children, but this father could not be bothered with my cultivation in your eyes, nor with my chastity, so long as I should become verbally fertile—futile, rather, without the tending you provide, God, my heart's gardener skilled and true.

6. So, in this my sixteenth year, in an idleness caused by my father's impecunious state, with no school to attend, I began again to stay with my parents, and the thorns of my own drives, with no one to weed them out from around me, shot up above my head. So much was this true that when my father saw in the baths that my childhood was gone and I was clothed with unstable young manhood, he mentioned this to my mother, overjoyed with anticipation of having grandchildren by me. It was the intoxicated joy with which the world forgets you the creator, to love in your place what you created, drunk on the invisible wine of desires deflected from you and declined toward the depths. But you had already begun to hallow 'your own temple' within my mother, laying

the foundation for 'your holy habitation' there, while my father had only recently become a candidate for baptism. She
was jolted 'with holy apprehension and trembling' that I,
though also not baptized, would be set on the crooked paths
that men tread when 'going away from you, not toward you.'

7.   Can I, alas, have the nerve to claim that you were saying nothing to me as I strayed from you? Were you in fact saying nothing at that time? Then whose if not yours were the
words you drummed into my ears through my mother? But
they did not sink into my heart, to make me act. She wished—
and I recall deep within me how urgently insistent was she—
that I would refrain from all illicit sex, but especially from
relations with a married woman. Her warnings seemed old
wives' tales to me, too embarrassing to be taken seriously. But
these warnings came, without my knowing it, from you—
I thought you were saying nothing, while what she said proved
that you were not silent after all. It was you I scorned in
scorning her—I her son, 'the son of your servingwoman, and
myself your servant.' In my ignorance I blundered on, so
blinded that it shamed me to be less shameless than my fellows. I listened as they boasted of their deeds, and the more
perverse the deeds, the more pride they took in them, not only
orgasmic over orgies but over publicizing them. What could
more deserve vilification than such villainy? Yet I actually became villainous to *avoid* vilification—where I could not
match them in admission of foul ways, I feigned deeds never
done, preferring to be thought more outrageous than con-
formist, more dissolute than respectable.

8.   These, then, were the fellows I strolled about with on
the streets of Babylon, in whose 'filth I wallowed' as if in
'cinnamon and precious ointments.' My invisible enemy was
treading me down there, to agglutinate me 'to its underbelly,'
taking in one who wanted the taking. The mother of my
flesh, though she had 'escaped from the center of Babylon,'
still lingered in its territory, and despite her advice to me on
continence, in response to what she had heard from her husband, she did not try to check (if she could not repress) my
pernicious and potentially fatal conduct. She did not try this

because she feared that her ambitions for me would be thwarted by a wife. This had nothing to do with her ambition for my future life with you, but with the ambition she and her husband shared for my career in rhetoric, he because he thought nothing about you and nothing sensible about me, and she because she calculated that the traditional course of rhetoric would do me no harm in itself and might help me to serve you—or so I suppose, reading my parents' motives as well as I can. The reins were therefore loosed on me, to be tossed about, with no moderating discipline, by random influences. Deep fog sealed me off from the bright sun of your truth while I 'fattened as it were on my own evil.'

II
PEAR THEFT

9. Robbery is undeniably punished by your law, but also by the law written in men's hearts, which not even their own evil can efface—for what robber will calmly submit to being robbed? Not even a wealthy robber will submit to one pressed by want. Yet I desired to commit robbery, and did it. I was driven by no deprivation—unless by a deprivation of what is right, a revulsion at it, while I was bloated out with evil. I stole things I had much more of, and much better. I wanted the stealing, not the thing stolen. I wanted the sin.

There was a pear tree near our vineyard, laden with fruit not enticing either in appearance or in taste. In dead night, after prolonging our pranks in the streets, as was our noxious custom, we malicious young punks steered our way to the tree, shook down its fruit and carted it off, a huge load we did not want to eat ourselves but to throw before swine—or if we ate some of it, that was not our motive. Simply what was not allowed allured us. Do you see into my heart, God, see a heart you can take pity on in its degradation? Then let it tell you, this heart you see into, what I wanted as I tried to do a wrong without reason, having no motive for wrongdoing but its very wrongness. The act was ugly, and that is what I loved in it. I was in love with my loss, with my own lack, and not because I loved the lack itself. My soul was perverse, was disarticulated out of its basis in you, not seeking another thing by shameful means but seeking shame itself.

10. Admittedly, the beauty of physical things is appealing (gold, silver, and the rest), and we sway to what touches the flesh or affects any of the senses by its fitness to them.

There is a dignity in worldly respect and in the power to order others about or to subdue them (which makes us so ready at redress for wrong). Yet to gain even these good things we should not give up you, God, nor wander from your law. Life in this world has its enticements because it accommodates us to its order, patterned to beautiful (lower) things. Disinterested friendship, for instance, is a sweet linking that brings separate souls into harmony. Sin arises from this, and from things like this, only if a disordered fixation on lower goods draws us off from better and higher goods, and thus from the highest good of all, you, my God, your truth, your law. For no matter how delightful these lower things are, they cannot match my God, who made them all, since he delights the just man, and is delight itself for those 'who keep their hearts in order.'

11.   When the motive for a crime is sought, none is accepted unless the eagerness to get goods of the lower sort just mentioned, or to avoid their loss, is considered a possibility. For they *are* beautiful, they *do* please, even if they must be abandoned for, or subordinated to, higher and more fulfilling goods. A murder is committed. Why? To get another man's wife or wealth, or to snatch at the necessities of life. Or for fear that someone would deprive the murderer of such things. Or from a sense of wrong burning for redress. Who murders with no motive but the mere murdering? Who would credit such a motive? Though it was said of one deranged and brutal man that he was evil without motive, yet a motive was given in the same passage: to *keep hands or hearts from losing their edge* for lack of practice. Ask him, Why keep up this practice?—so that by this training in crime he could take over the city and reap honors, dominion, and wealth, escaping legal intimidation and other obstacles placed in his path by *an exiguous family estate and a criminal record*. So even Catiline did not love his crime for its own sake but for the objects to be gained by it.

12.   But what could I, pitiful I, have found lovable in you, my robbery, my midnight deed of the sixteenth year of my life? There was no beauty in you as such, as robbery. Do you in fact exist, for me to address you? There was beauty in the pears I stole, insofar as they were made by you, the most beautiful of all things, who made all beautiful things, you the good God, and the supreme good and my true good. Still, I had plenty of pears that were better, and these I stole only to be stealing, since I threw them away once they were stolen. I dined on the crime itself, which is what I wanted to savor. If I tasted any of the pears, it was the crime that had flavor for me. At present, however, I still need to know exactly why robbery was an object of desire. As a robbery, it has no beauty of its own. It lacks not merely the [moral] beauty of fairness and foresight, or the [human] beauty of intellect and memory and sensation and animation, or the [physical] beauty of things like the stars, patterned in their [airy] places, or earth and sea, teeming with offspring renewed by those born to fill the place of those dying—no, robbery has not even the maimed and shadowy beauty that some sins pretend to.

13. Pride, for instance, feigns loftiness (though you alone are high above all). And worldly designs aim at honor and glory (though you alone deserve to be honored and glorified eternally). Naked aggression is meant to instill awe in others (though who is more awesome than you, whose power can neither be usurped nor diminished, not at any time or anywhere, by any means or anyone). The intimacies of the sensual are meant to express love (though nothing is more intimate than your love, and nothing can be more securely loved than your truth, surpassing all shapely or shining things). Transgressive knowledge feigns a zeal for wisdom (though you alone have the deepest knowledge of everything). Willful ignorance would pass for simplicity, and dullness for innocence (though nothing can be found like your simplicity, and what could be more innocent than you, who let others punish themselves by what they do). Sloth affects to seek serenity (though where can true serenity be but in the Lord). Self-pampering would be called fullness and satisfaction (though you are fullness, endlessly replete with a delectation that never fades). Wastefulness throws over itself the shadow of generosity (though you are the most lavish provider of all good things). Stinginess wants to have many possessions (though you are everything's owner). Envy contests supremacy (though who is more supreme than you). Anger wants vindication (though who vindicates more justly than you). Cowardice recoils from any surprising or sudden menace to what it loves, and prepares for its repulse (though what can surprise you, be sudden to you, or deprive you of loved things, since you protect them entirely). Melancholy pines for lost things by which it was comforted, and wants to have them back (though you are the one who loses nothing).

14. That is how the soul 'plays your unfaithful lover,' abandoning you, seeking pure and luminous things that are not to be found except by return to you. All men mount a grotesque imitation of you when they set you at a distance in order to exalt themselves above you. Yet even in this mimicry of you they indicate that it is you, the creator of all nature, they would be, and they cannot extract themselves from that nature. So how, by the love of my own robbery, was I imitating you—in, admittedly, some grotesque and twisted way? Was it a delight in breaking your law, though only in feigned ways, where I could not openly overbear it—was I, that is, enacting a prisoner's maimed freedom, breaking rules where punishment did not reach, in a shadowy pretense at being able to do anything I want? In this I became your servant [Adam] who 'flees the Lord and courts shadow.' What rottenness is here, what living enormity, what a downward plunge into death—to be allured by what was not allowed, just because it was not allowed.

15. 'What can I offer back to the Lord' for the fact that what my memory recalls my soul no longer fears? Love I can offer back, Lord, and gratitude and 'testimony to your name that you have forgiven me' my wrong and malicious acts. I give credit to your favor and pity that you have 'dissolved my sins like melting ice.' Your grace I credit, as well, for all the wrongs I did not commit. Is there any crime I might *not* have committed, who could love a crime without motive? Yet that, and all else, you have forgiven, both what I did under my own initiative and what under your leadership I did not do. What man honestly aware of his own frailty can attribute any chastity or innocence to his own control, as if he has less need to love you because he does not need your pity as much as those whose sins you forgive when they return to you? Anyone called by you, who answers your call, who avoids the sins that I am remembering and confessing, should not mock me if my illness was healed by the same physician who kept him from falling sick—or, more properly, from falling into so deep a sickness as mine. He should love you not merely as much as I do, but more, when he sees that the one who has stripped me of my sin's symptoms kept him free of such symptoms.

16. 'What was I seeking at that time, in my pitiable state, that it now shames me to recall?'—what, especially, in that robbery where nothing but the robbery was what I loved, where the robbery itself was a nothing, and I so much the more pitiful [for wanting nothing]? But there is this to be said: alone I would not have done it—I call up again my state of mind on that point—there is no way I would have done it alone. So I must have loved a partnership with my fellows in the theft. Can I say, then, that I did love something else beyond the theft? Not really, since the something else was also a nothing. For what else could that [partnership] be called in reality? (And who can help me understand this but the one 'who sends light into my heart' and 'divides it from the shadows there.') What is this robbery my mind is nagged into questioning, discoursing with it, contemplating it? I could have done it, even alone, if all I wanted was the pears, to eat them. If that were the real motive, my urge to take them would have required no friction with colluding fellows to make it catch fire. But since I cared nothing for the pears, what I wanted was to commit the crime in partnership with those sharing my sin.

17. What was my reaction to this situation? Admittedly it was a low and skulking one, and I was in woeful condition to entertain it. But what, precisely, was it? 'Who can understand what is wanting?' This was a prank. We chortled inwardly to be fooling those who thought us incapable of such an act—they would stoutly go on rejecting the idea. Why then [if I were so unlikely a culprit] did I want to do what I would not have done alone? Is it because no one laughs by himself? Well, normally one does not, even though laughter does occasionally overcome isolated individuals, men with no company at all, when some truly far-fetched sight or thought strikes them. But this act was not [like that] one I would ever have done alone, never would I have done it—that is my strong recollection in your presence, my God. I would not have robbed on my own, where *what* I robbed was not alluring but *that* I robbed. I would not have robbed at all had I been robbing alone. How infectious, then, is this affection, the mind's inexplicable swerve, the way laughter and pranks become a readiness to harm, a willingness to inflict loss, without any compensating gain, no sense of a wrong being requited! Someone has but to say, Let's do it!—and feeling shame becomes one's only shame.

18. Who can untie this knot of intertwining contradictions? It is obscene, I want no thought of it, no view of it. You who are justice, your innocence both beautiful and proper, these are what I want, with candid eyes and a fullness never filled. Only with you are perfect repose and a life without turmoil. Who enters into you enters his Lord's joy where he shall know no fear and shall possess in the best way the best. Yet I slipped away from you into my wanderings, my God, my young manhood skewed off from your stability, and I became my own terrain of deprivation.

BOOK THREE

MANICHAEISM

I
CARTHAGE

1. I reached Carthage, all that *cartage* of criminal loves sizzling about me. Without love to this point, I was in love with loving. Unaware of my own needs, I resisted what would make me less needy. I wanted something to love, since I was in love with loving, but I did not want to reach it along the Path that springs no traps. I was starved of that inner food that is you, my God; yet starvation did not make me hungry, since my system rejected spiritual nourishment— I was not fed with it, and the more I starved, the more would nourishment make me queasy. My soul, sick and covered with sores, lunged outward instead, in a mad desire to scratch itself against some physical relief. These were soulless rubbings, where no love was to be found. Sweet as were loving and being loved, sweeter still was the taste of the loved one's body. I fouled the springs of pure love with the dregs of lust, muddying its clarity from the depths of my sexual drive. Brutal myself, and lacking honor, I nonetheless peacocked myself as an urbane sophisticate. Desperate for love, I became its willing captive. How good it was of you, 'my God who pities me,' to dash this sweet thing with bitterness, since—however loved I was, and secretly happy in that bondage, pleased with its entrammeling embraces—I was also tortured with the burning 'iron bludgeons' of jealousy, distrust, fear, wrath, and quarreling.

SHOWS AND STUDIES

2. Stageplays made me ecstatic. They bodied forth my own plight and fed my fires. Why does man happily watch unhappy scenes of woe and anguish which he would never wish on himself? Yet he is not only willing to derive unhappiness from these spectacles, but to make that unhappiness his pleasure. What could be more paradoxical than this, that the more he empathizes with the unhappy, the more he comes to resemble them? An object of pity if he were unhappy himself, he gets credit for a pitying heart when he looks on others' unhappiness. Yet what is the quality of pity given to made-up actions on stage, where one is not moved to help the unhappy, but to enjoy their unhappiness? In fact, the actor of such fictions gains more applause the unhappier he makes his audience; and if historical or mythical plots are acted and cause no unhappiness, the playgoer stalks out, annoyed and panning the play. Make him unhappy, however, and he sits enthralled, pleasurably weeping.

3. So even unhappiness can be cherished. Is this because, though no one wants to be an object of pity, showing pity somehow pleases, and unhappiness, as the necessary condition of pity, is what we cherish? Now pity is a rivulet deriving from pure love, but through what channel and whither flowing? Must it, of necessity, flow into the 'roaring stream of bubbling pitch,' the weird seethings of blackest sexual drive, deviated willfully from the calm of heaven into churning and precipitous courses? Then must we reject all pity? Not at all—some unhappiness can be cherished. But be on guard, my soul, against impure motives for the pity—keep guard against it, with the guidance of my God, 'the God of our fathers, in every age to be praised and held above all things.' I am still moved by pity, but not as I was in the theater. There I shared in the lovers' enjoyment of their illicit affairs (though they were merely mimed in a stageplay) and I also shared their sadness if they were parted, in a kind of pity for them. I savored both the joy and the sadness. But now I pity the lover more when he is happy in his sin than when he feels afflicted by the deprivation of harmful gratification, losing his wretched joy. My pity is now more genuine—it takes no joy in loss.

Though one can admire a proper charity that condoles with the unhappy, yet a deeper compassion prefers that there should be no cause for the unhappiness in the first place. Only if benevolence were malevolent—a clear impossibility—could true pity wish people to suffer so they could be pitied. That some suffering is appropriate does not make it lovable. You, God, the lover of our lives, show a pity that is far purer and less mixed in motive than ours, since you cannot suffer any sadness. 'Who of us can say that?'

4. But I, pitiable at the time, was drawn to such unhappiness, and sought occasions for it. My delight was the greater if someone's nonexistent suffering were acted out by a performer—who pleased me more, the more tears he made me shed. No wonder that I, a sheep of your flock escaping your care, broke out in a filthy mange. Such was my attraction to being unhappy—a superficial thing, since I did not want to *be* suffering, only to *see* it. Yet hearing these dramatized falsehoods affected me like a shallow abrasion of the skin—further irritated, as by the itching of a scratch, it became running sores, inflamed and pustulant. Could this life of mine, my God, be called a life?

5. Yet high above me, never deserting me, hovered your pity. With sin I was depleting myself as I sought transgressive knowledge, steering myself from your way into mine, going deeper into infidelity and the devil's disguised rites, to which my actions were an offering. All the while I was under your lash—and I dared, even within the walls of your church, while your holy rites were being celebrated, to enter into a lustful transaction deserving the soul's death. Your pummelings for this were heavy (but not as heavy as my guilt), but they came from your vast pity, my God, my only refuge from what afflicted me so sorely. From you I was traveling far off, with neck too proud for the yoke, preferring my path to yours, preferring my kind of freedom—that of a fugitive.

6. My fashionable studies were supposed to make me formidable in legal pleading, the less honest the more honored. Men are blind enough to boast of being blind—as I did when I led my school in rhetoric, glad in my pride and preening giddily. Yet I was quiet, as you know, Lord, and withdrawn when it came to subversions by "the Subversives" (a low and fiendish name they took to show how with-it they could be), with whom I mingled, ashamed I was not shameless as they were. I was in their company, glad at times to be their friend, though I shrank from their subversions—for they preyed on the timidity of unpopular students, harrying them with unprovoked mockery to gratify their own humor. What can be more fiendish than this? They justly laid claim to subversion, or rather to perversion, diverted as they were by fiends who used their mockery and befuddlement of others to mock and befuddle them.

III
HORTENSIUS

7. In such company I, in my immaturity, was studying works of rhetoric, in which I hoped to shine for a fiendish and empty purpose, to indulge my pride. In the normal course of these studies I reached a book by a man known as Cicero, whose tongue all praise, not his heart. This book, however, urges philosophy upon the reader—it is known as *Hortensius,* and it changed my life. It transformed my prayers to you, O Lord, and changed the character of my strivings and hopes. Vain aspirations it made, all at once, contemptible. I pined for a deathless wisdom with a churning of my heart I could hardly believe, and I 'roused myself' for a return to you. I no longer read this book to acquire a speaker's polish, which I was supposed to be purchasing with my mother's assistance (I was only eighteen and my father had been dead two years)—I did not value it for its effect on style, since I was moved by what it said, not how it said it.

8. How on fire I was, my God, burning to lift my wings from earth toward you, though I still did not know what you were planning for me. 'Wisdom is yours,' and that is what the Greek word *philosophy* means—the love of wisdom, which that book had kindled in me. True, some use philosophy to mislead men, putting on error a cosmetic rouge of imposing, enticing, or ennobling language. But this book singles out and refutes almost all such deceivers from the author's time and before. It demonstrates the saving wisdom of your Spirit, as spelled out by your good and faithful servant [Paul]: 'Be on guard against philosophy and empty beguilements, as men and worldly forces hand them down, not as Christ does, in whom every attribute of divinity is corporally lodged.' These admonitions of the Apostle I was unfamiliar with at the time, as you know, my Lord. All I had to stimulate me was the book's advice that I not subscribe to a particular sect or other, but only to whatever wisdom I could strongly love, search out, follow, adhere to, and embrace—that is the language that struck me, set me on fire, and made me glow. Even in this blaze I balked at one thing, that there was no mention here of Christ, the name of my rescuer. By your mercy, my innocent heart had devoutly drunk in that name with my mother's milk, and stored it deep within, so that nothing, however learned or elaborate, could entirely carry me away if it lacked that name.

9. I undertook then a close scrutiny of the holy Scripture, to ascertain its worth. But I found at once that this was neither patent to the haughty nor plain to the lowly. It gave at the outset some meager return, but withdrew at the next step into heights and mysteries veiled. I was not qualified to enter here, or to proceed with reverently bowed head. What I can say now is not what I felt then, as I looked at Scripture. It seemed trivial next to Cicero's majesty. My own loftiness was unfitted for its humility. My gaze reached no inner meanings. One must become a child to grow up again with the Scripture, and I was above such childishness. Pride made me swell to a big man in my own eyes.

IV

THE MANICHAEANS

10. So I descended into comradeship with the pride-maddened, the sensualists, the prattlers, whose words spread the devil's nets and mixed a trapper's lime made up of garbled versions of the names of Jesus Christ and the Supporter—names always on their lips, sounds and noise on their tongues, without meaning in their hearts. *Truth, Truth* was their byword, of which they told me much, though no truth was in them. False was all they told me—not only of you, who *are* the truth, but about the makeup of the world, which you created. About the latter I must trump whatever true things philosophers have said with your love, Father, the highest good of that order and its supreme beauty. Truth, Truth—how the inmost fibers of my soul pined for you, as you were invoked in frequent and multiple ways, by their oral instruction or their many extensive writings. The books were platters for serving up, to my hunger and thirst for you, the sun and the moon as substitutes for you—things you made, beautiful things but not you, not even the highest of your creatures, since intellectual creatures rank above material ones, no matter how luminous in the sky. And my hunger and thirst were not even for the highest of your creatures, but for you yourself, for the truth in which there is 'no alteration or dimming by change.' In place of these they dished up the gaudily pseudo-real. It were better, indeed, to be devoted to the real sun, which is at least evident to the eyes, than to their projections from what the eyes see. Yet I fed on the latter, thinking they were you—tentatively, since they did not taste like you (and they were not) and they did not satisfy me. They left me hungrier.

Dream food at least resembles what one sees when awake, however unable it is to nourish the dreamer, who just dreams it. But these figments did not even slightly resemble you, as I know now by your help, since they were mere projections from physical reality, not physical reality itself—not those actual bodies (whether in the sky or on land) that we see with the body's eyes, just as birds and beasts see them. Those bodies are more real in themselves than are our mental images of them. Yet even our mental images are more real than grand vague things we project from them, which have no existence at all. Yet on those nonentities I was feeding, unfed.

You, my love, from whom my frailty draws strength, you are not the starry bodies we can see, nor any higher things we see not—you who placed them there do not even prize them supremely. How distant from you, then, are the constructs I accepted, conjectured from non-existent bodies. More real are the images we take from bodies that do exist; and more real are those bodies than our images of them, though the reality of bodies is not yours—nor, for that matter, of souls, which animate bodies and are superior and more intelligible than bodies. You are the soul's animator, and life's vivifier, living of your self without alteration, and making my soul live.

11.   Where were you then if not near me, even though I was 'far from you in exile,' not even sharing [as the prodigal son did] in the slops as I slopped the pigs. Even poets' songs and flights of Medea are more nourishing than the [Manichaean] Five Elements, varying in hue according to the Cave of Darkness from which each issues, and having no real existence but in their power to slay those believing in them. I could at least sing for my supper when reciting Medea's flight, which I no more believed in when I sang it myself than when others did. But those false theories I believed, alas. I went, alas, step by step down toward hell's region, thrashing about and seething without truth, seeking you (I testify this to you, who pitied me when I testified not) but seeking not with the mind's reason, by which you singled me out from the beasts, but with the body's senses. All the while you were more in me than I am in me—yet far off above my highest reach—while I blundered outward toward the typological woman in Solomon, 'the shameless reckless woman seated on a chair at her door, saying: Prefer bread secretly eaten, and drink water sweetened by slyness.' She snared me, since I was outside myself, taking in only what my carnal eye saw, trying to draw sustenance from what it fed me.

12. Truth was elsewhere, though I did not know it, real truth. I was so taken with my own acuity that I fell for the tricks of fools when they asked me where evil comes from; or whether God is confined in a body with hair and fingernails; or whether men could be counted holy who had several wives, who committed murder, who sacrificed animals. In my ignorance, these questions befuddled me, and I thought I was pursuing truth as I fled it.

I did not realize that evil does not exist of itself, but is a lack of good—short of the point where the lack erases existence altogether. How could I see this when my eye saw only the body and my mind saw only a construct? Nor did I realize that God is spirit, without parts of his whole having their own length or breadth or weight. Any part would weigh less than the whole. If spread everywhere, such a body would still weigh more or less in any spatial segment of it, and each part could not be everywhere, as with the spirit, as with God. But [apart from what God is] I was ignorant, even, of that within us which makes us exist, and I did not know how Scripture could speak true when it said that we exist as an image of God.

V

THE MORALITY OF THE PATRIARCHS

13. Nor did I realize that true holiness is an interior disposition, not guided by social norms but by the all-powerful God's stringent ordinance, which adapts the standards of different times and places to the conditions of the times and places while remaining unaltered itself, everywhere and always, not differing in this time or that, this place or that. Thus can Abraham, Isaac, Jacob, Moses, and David be holy, all of them commended in God's word. Those who call them wicked are inappropriately applying 'the test of a day,' measuring the standards of the entire human race by their own segment of it—as if one unacquainted with the armorer's fitting of parts to the body should try to protect the head with a shin-guard, or the shin with a helmet, and then complain that the armor was ill made.

Or as if a merchant should be peeved because, on a day with a special ban on sales in the afternoon, he cannot sell his products as he wishes, when he might have done so in the morning.

Or as if one should complain that everyone in one habitation does not have the same rights everywhere because a slave in charge of wine cups is not allowed to handle other parts of the service, or what is done behind the barn is not admitted into the dining room.

Such men, hearing that holy men of the past were permitted some things that are not permitted now, resent the fact that God could order one thing for those in the past, another for the present, allowing for different circumstances in the past though both are subordinated to a single justice—just as, in the case of one man on one day in one household, you see a person properly doing what would be improper for another, or see things often done in the past that are not allowed in the present, or actions allowed or encouraged in one spot but forbidden and punished in another. Does this mean that justice is fickle and inconstant? No, but it does not apply in the same way to all times, because they *are* times. Men, whose 'life is brief,' object to what goes on in distant times and cultures, which they cannot analyze because they have not been in them, while they acquiesce in present distinctions of person, time, and place when these affect a single man on a single day in a single household.

14. I was ignorant of these distinctions, blissfully unaware of them, though they struck my eye wherever I looked. Even when composing poetry, for instance, I could not use any metrical foot wherever I wanted. This foot fit here and another one there, even in the same line—yet there was not a different rule of art for each of these differences. One rule prevailed in them all. Could I not see how one rule of justice prevails—though in a far higher and subtler way—in the lives of good and holy men? It is unaltered itself, though it does not apply to all times in the same way, but orders each circumstance in the way appropriate to it. Blinded myself, I mocked the holy fathers for responding to their condition as God led and bade them, and thought they could not be prophets of the future as God revealed that to them.

15. Is not the rule universal 'to love God with a single heart, a single soul, a single mind, and love our neighbor as ourself'? And are not sordid acts against nature universally detested and punished, as the Sodomites were? No matter how many commit such sins, they would still be criminal, falling under the divine ban on such male couplings. Our proper bond with God is violated if we taint the nature he has given us by sexual perversion. A different prohibition applies to outrages against the behavioral norms established in each society, by civil contract or social custom, according to its standard of acceptable conduct. These norms cannot be willfully defied, either by a member of the society or by a visitor to it, since any part of a society offends if it refuses to be adjusted to the whole.

When, however, God's rule is different from a people's contract or custom, then God's rule, even if not earlier in force, must prevail—must, even if not earlier acknowledged, be observed; or must, if observance of it has lapsed, be restored; or must, without earlier status as law, be legislated. If a king, after all, acting where he legitimately rules, commands something new, something never commanded before by him or his predecessors, he must still be obeyed, provided he observes the constitution of the state. In fact, *not* to obey him would violate the constitution since it is the general rule of societies that kings must be obeyed. Even more clearly must the command of God be instantly obeyed, since he is the ruler of all his creation. Lesser authority yields to greater, and his is the greatest authority of all.

16.   Also forbidden are the crimes of personal injury, whether by word or deed. There are many varieties of each— to kill a foe out of revenge, to hold up a traveler out of greed for his property, or to ward off a perceived danger out of fear. The less fortunate may, from envy, harm the more fortunate, as the fortunate may harm real or potential rivals in their fortune. Or one may just take a sadistic pleasure in pain, whether by watching the agony of gladiators or by belittling and insulting others.

These are the kinds of things that swarm under the three headings of sin—the drives for domination, or for transgressive knowledge, or for sensual gratification. They can be committed singly or two together or all three. They pit evildoers against your ten-strung harp, my God most high and gentle—against the Ten Commandments, three for offenses against you, seven for those against our neighbor. Yet what outrage can affront you, completely pure, what crime harm you, entirely invulnerable? You actually punish men for the harm they do themselves, because in sinning against you they are 'fooled by vice' into acting against themselves. They either damage or cripple the nature you created and set rules for. They either carry allowed acts to extremes, or push what is not allowed into the unnatural. Or they rave in their minds and their speech against you, 'kicking at the prod.' Or, emboldened by any breakdown of social restraint, they gladly exploit factions and feuds to do whatever they want, indulging predilections or aversions. This is the result of abandoning you, the font of life, the single true creator and ruler of the cosmos, when a self-engendered pride treats some part of things as if it were the whole. A dutiful lowliness leads back to you, as you burn away evil habit, 'kindly to those who testify to their sin' and 'hearing the prisoners' sighs.' You strike off the chains we forge around us, if only we lift not the proud thrust of our pretended freedom, if only our greed, wanting more, does not risk losing all, loving the little that is ours more than the everything you are.

17. Aside from sordid and aggressive acts, or any other evils committed, there are the sinful lapses of those striving for virtue. The lapsed must, on the one hand, be denounced by true judges, who hold to the standard of perfection; and, at the same time, they must be encouraged with hope of progress, like shoots that will grow into fruitful stalks. There are, besides, things that are cognate to the sordid or the aggressive yet are not themselves sinful, since they defy neither you nor the fellowship of man—as when one amasses a store of goods to support himself in accord with his condition, and may not be driven by greed. Or when a properly constituted authority is strict in punishment, and may not be sadistic. Many things subject to human contempt have the seal of your approval, while what is praised wins your condemnation, since the outer aspect of a deed is not the same as the inner intention of the doer, affected we know not how at a specific time.

But should you emit out of the blue an unexpected and unprecedented command—were it something you forbade before, were no explanation given for the fiat at the time, were it counter to the moral code of a particular society— would we not have to obey without demur? A society is only just insofar as it obeys you. Our blessing is to know that you are the one in charge. Those who serve you do everything either in accord with the demands of the present or to prefigure the future.

18. I did not realize all this when I laughed at your patriarchs and prophets, making myself a laughingstock in your eyes by laughing at them. I was the one insensibly being drawn, step by step, into such puerile beliefs as that a fig whimpers when picked off its mother tree, which sheds milky tears for it. And if one of the elect should eat the fig—after someone else, of course, committed the sin of picking it—after getting it into his guts, he would burp out angels or, better, throw up bits of god, belching prayers the while. These bits of the high true god would have stayed imprisoned in the fig unless freed by the teeth and viscera of the elect persons. This is what I, in my pitiable state, had come to believe—that more pity should be shown to the fruits of the earth than to the human beings for whose sake they came to be. If some hungry non-Manichaean should ask for the fruit, his eating it would be seen as giving the divine morsel a death penalty.

VI

MONNICA'S DREAM

19. Yet 'from your heights you stretched your hand out over me,' and drew my soul up out of this dark abyss, since my mother, your servant, was crying more abundant tears than mothers would cry for a dead son. She knew that I *was* dead, from the 'faith you breathed into her.' You heard her, Lord, heard her and heeded her tears, so freely flowing from her that she moistened the ground beneath her as she prayed. You heard her and she was so comforted by a dream that she agreed to stay and live with me and share my household table, which she had initially resisted out of her disapproval and detestation of my damnable heresy. In the dream she saw herself standing on a leveling-balance made of wood, along which a youth approached her with a jocund and amiable smile, while she was sad, 'was broken by her sadness.' He asked why she was so sad and daily weeping—asking less, as is God's way, to learn than to teach—and she said that she lamented my damnation. As a comfort, he directed her to 'look up and see' that where she stood, so would I—and when she looked, there I was, standing by her on the same leveling-balance. How could this be unless 'your ears were at her heart' in your goodness and omnipotence, you who care for each of us as if we were your only care, yet have the same care for all?

20. When she had told me her dream, and I tried to interpret it as saying that she should not give up the possibility of joining me, as opposed to my joining her, who but you instructed her to say, no, it was not said that where I stood, so would she, but where she stood, so would I? I testify, Lord, to what most impressed me at the time, as much as I can recall of the moment by often mentioning it after—that my plausible interpretation of her dream did not faze her a bit. She saw at once the real point, which had not occurred to me before she spoke. This comment, which you prompted in her while she was awake, affected me much more than did the dream itself, which gave this good woman in her current distress some promise of future consolation. Yet I spent almost nine more years deep in the dark muck of error, trying often to climb out of it but sliding farther back in, to thrash there—and she all the while, this chaste widow, with the kind of piety and sobriety you treasure, though she had been given hope, did not grow less earnest in her tears and sighs, never slackening in her grief at every moment of her prayer, as she lamented my plight before you. Her prayers were steadily making their way to you, while you left me for the time to toss and re-toss in the dark.

21.   Meanwhile you gave her another sign, as I recall—I have forgotten much, and much I am omitting, in favor of things I want to testify to more urgently—this sign you gave her through a priest, a certain bishop reared in the church and familiar with your Scripture. When this woman asked him to grant me an interview, to refute my errors, weaning me from evil and winning me for good (for he was in the custom of doing this with selected persons), he refused, with a wisdom I came later to appreciate. He told her I was not yet ready, dizzied as I was with heretical innovations, and (as she had reported to him) making the inexperienced giddy with my quibbles. He said: Leave him alone (all but praying to the Lord for him)—he will discover from reading where the error lies and how evilly he acts.

And he told how his own misled mother had committed him as a boy to the care of Manichaeans, almost all of whose writings he read, and even copied as their secretary, before finding out on his own that he could no longer adhere to them—though no one had argued with him or given him contrary evidence. That was how he escaped them. Even though he told her this, she would not give up, but kept at him with her requests and copious tears, saying he must see me and refute me. Annoyed by this pestering, he told her: Be off and get on with your life—the son of such tears as you are shedding will never be lost. These words—she often told me in recounting the incident—she had taken as heaven speaking to her.

BOOK FOUR

FRIENDS

I

TEACHING

1. During the nine years I have mentioned, I was one of those misled and misleading, deceived and deceiving, at the mercy of assorted lusts—with a public life teaching the arts which claim to be liberal, and a private one given over to heresy—publicly arrogant; privately superstitious; in both lives empty. Publicly we chased after the bauble fame, after applause in the arena for poetry contests, for crownings with a flimsy garland and the puerilities of the stage—with no check on our lusts. Privately, we sought cleansing from such filth by serving food to those called our elect or holy men, whose digestive workshops would fabricate angels and gods for our liberation. These were my pursuits, carried on with my friends, the deceived with their deceiver.

Let the haughty laugh, who have not been struck down for their own good, humiliated by you, my God; yet I shall testify before you to my own disgrace, to honor you. Aid me in this, I pray you, help me follow in memory now the anfractuous path to my infractions then, offering this up as a sacrifice of thanksgiving. Without you, what am I but the captain of my own ruin? And what am I, in my better state, but 'a child nursed with your milk,' feeding on the food that never fails? And what is any man whosoever if he is but a man? Let the high and mighty laugh at us, while we the low and helpless give our testimony to you.

2. In those years I was a professor of rhetoric. Vanquished myself by the urge for gain, I took pay to show others how to vanquish verbally. Yet you know, Lord, that I preferred honest pupils (as honesty was understood then), and I taught them without guile the guileful arts—not hoping that they would convict the innocent, though they might occasionally save the guilty. Distantly you saw me, God, slipping on a greasy surface, but with a spark of honor still visible through my thick murk—the honest way I taught the ones who were 'intent on empty things and learning to lie.' I had in those years a woman who could not be called my lawful wife, since my wild desire and lack of forethought had found her—but she was the only one, and I was faithful to her bed. My life with her taught me the difference between the restraint of the marriage pledge, formed for the sake of offspring, and a lustful sexual arrangement, where any children born were unintended (though bound to be loved if born).

II

VINDICIAN

3. I remember as well entering a poetry contest in the arena, how a seer asked what I would pay him to guarantee my winning. I told him his ghastly rites were hateful and ugly, I would not let even a fly be killed to bring me a crown, be it of imperishable gold—he meant, you see, to slaughter animals sacrificially and win demonic help for me with these offerings. Not that I turned him down from the purity that comes from you, 'my heart's God,' since I had no concept of you to love, acknowledging as I did no higher beings than bright celestial bodies. Was it not a 'whoring away from you' to be awed by such made-up things, to 'trust untruths and give the winds grazing'? I would not let animals be sacrificed to demands for my sake, yet I was sacrificing myself to that heresy—for what is it to 'give the winds grazing' but to feed oneself to devils by one's falsehood, for their derision and delight?

4. I was still willing, by my standards, to bank on those mountebanks called astrologers, since they sacrificed no animals and did not ask demons to tell the future. Yet true Christian piety rejects and abhors this art in its entirety. So it is right for me to testify to you, Lord, and pray, 'Have pity on me, heal my soul, since I have sinned against you,' and not to exploit your indulgence as permission for further sinning, but to keep in mind the Lord's voice saying: 'Now you are healed, sin no more, to suffer nothing worse.' The astrologers try to obliterate this saving truth when they say that the inescapable cause of sin is lodged in the stars, that Venus determines this, or Saturn does, or Mars. Thus man, mere flesh and blood and conceited putrescence, cannot be at fault—the creator and arranger of the stars in heaven bears the blame. Yet who can that be but our God, our sweet fountain of justice, who 'assigns responsibility to each according to his acts,' and 'does not spurn the heart that is contrite and lowly'?

5. There was a wise man there [Vindician], a skilled physician prominent in his profession. In his duties as proconsul, he put the poetic crown on my diseased head, but not as my healer—only you are the physician for what ailed me, 'you who reject the proud, but grant abundance to the lowly.' Yet this elderly man, for all that, was not entirely unhelpful to me. By your direction, he gave a degree of healing to my thought. We became friends, and I hung intently on his every word—while not a polished writer, he was sharp and profound in conversation. When he learned from our talks that I was poring over horoscope tables, he advised me in a kind and fatherly way to give them up, not to squander on such idiocy the time and effort needed for more useful work. He told me he had learned enough astrology in his youth to make it his occupation and earn a living by it— after all, if he could understand Hippocrates, why not the astrologers' writings? But he gave it up in favor of medicine, for one simple reason—it was all a fake. He was too honest to make his living by fooling others. He said: You have in rhetoric a profession that will support you, you are pursuing this nonsense as a hobby, not a matter of income—all the more reason to take my advice, since I made the deepest possible study of something I thought would be my sole livelihood.

But why, I asked him, do so many things predicted come true? The only answer he could give was that sheer force of coincidence plays a large role in the course of things. If a man picks up the work of a poet, some passage may strike him as magically appropriate to his own situation, though the poet had entirely different things in mind as he composed. It would not be surprising, he said, if some deep prompting in the mind, emerging from the unconscious, should resonate with the reader's situation and outlook, by coincidence, not by consultation.

6. Through or by his words you were leading me, and I retained in my memory what I afterward put to a personal test. But for the time neither he nor my dear friend Nebridius, a very good and chaste young man, could persuade me to give up astrology, much as they ridiculed this whole business of foretelling the future. They had less weight with me than the astrological tomes, and I had not yet found the certain proof I had been seeking to demonstrate without a doubt how forecasts thought to be true had occurred casually or by coincidence, not by the experts' consultation with the stars.

III

A FRIEND'S DEATH

7. When at this time I began to teach in the town where I was born, I formed a friendship with one very dear to me because of our shared interests. We were the same age, each in the prime of our young manhood, and we had known each other since boyhood, when we went to school together and were playmates. But he was not my friend at that time— nor, even later, was ours a true friendship. For that, you must meld friends together in a closeness sealed by their love for you, a love 'suffusing our hearts by the Holy Spirit sent upon us.' Yet our tie was a sweet one, warmed by the views we shared—including the damnable religious fairy tales my mother lamented in me, since I wrenched him from the true faith, to which he in his youth was only lightly attached. He joined me in my heresy, and I could not be disjoined from him. But see how close on our backs you were as we fled you, you the punishing God and the fountain of pity, who twist us around toward you in surprising ways—for you took him away from this life when we had been friends scarce a year, in a friendship sweeter than anything I had known in life.

8. What individual can 'adequately praise what you have done for him' individually, as when you acted for me 'in the depths unplumbed of your decrees'? As he was convulsed with fever, lying insensible in a lethal sweat and given up for lost, he was baptized without knowing it. That did not bother me—I was sure he would prefer what he had received from me when conscious over what was done to his unconscious body. But I could not have been more wrong.

When he revived and was strong enough, I spoke to him as soon as I could (and I could as soon as he could, since I never left his side, and we were entirely open with each other). I made fun of his baptism, expecting him to laugh along with me at what had been done to him when he was incapable of knowing or feeling anything. But he had been told of his baptism, and he recoiled from me as from a foe. With a stunning new independence, he warned me never to talk like that again if I wished to remain his friend. I was taken aback and disoriented, but I suppressed my feelings till he should be restored to his full faculties, confident I could bend him to my will at that time. But he escaped my mad designs and found safety in you—a fact that would comfort me later. In a few days, while I was not present, the fevers returned and he died.

9. With this grief my heart 'was steeped in shadow.' Look where I would, I saw only death. My own town tormented me, my home was haunted by sorrow. Whatever I had done with him became, without him, an extreme torture. My eyes darted everywhere to find him, and found him not. Any place that did not hold him I hated for not telling me, as it had when he was missing in it before, that he would be coming. I became a conundrum to myself, asking my soul 'why, in its anguish, it was whirling me about.' The soul had nothing to answer. And if I urged it to 'have hope in the Lord,' it remained inert—rightly, since the man it had lost was more real and cherished than that wraith it was asked to rely on. Weeping was my only comfort. It alone took the place of my friend, 'my soul's delight.'

10. Those trials, Lord, have now receded, and time has salved my soul. Can you who are truth tell me, if I place my heart's ear near your mouth, why weeping is a comfort to the sad? Or have you, who are present everywhere, distanced yourself from our misery, since you are self-contained, while we are thrown from trial to trial? Yet if we cannot carry our plaints to your ears, we have not a rag of hope to cling to. So tell me how sweet flowers are plucked from bitterness when we wail and weep, sigh and plain? Do we derive our comfort from the hope that you will hear us? That may be true for prayers, which have the aim of being answered, but not for mere grief and mourning over loss of the sort I experienced, since I did not hope that you would bring him back, nor did I ask that with my tears. I simply mourned and wept, miserable to be missing what made me happy. Can it be that weeping, bitter in itself, is comforting as an alternative to the horror of dwelling on our former joy?

11. But why dwell on this? This is not the moment for complaint but for testimony to you. I was sad, but sad is every soul overcome by love for what must pass, whose loss tears part of the soul away with it, but where the sadness existed even before the loss. In my case, I cried bitterly, and found relief in my bitterness. I was sad, but I hugged my sad life closer to me than I did my friend, not wanting to be sad, but preferring life, even with sadness, to him—doubting, therefore, that I could do for him what Orestes and Pylades did for each other in legend (if we can believe it), preferring to die together, since living on singly was for each of them worse than his own death. Somehow or other I was feeling the very opposite of that. My weariness with life was weighty, but so was my fear of death. The more I loved my friend, the more I hated and feared as the most obscene enemy of all the death that had taken him from me—it seemed about to gulp down all of humanity, as it had him. So at least I felt at the time.

You see me, my God, see my heart, see what is in me. You see what I am remembering, my hope, you who cleanse the uncleannesses I felt, lifting my eyes to you yet 'keeping my feet from the snares laid for me.' I was astonished to see other people living after he no longer lived whom I had loved as if he could not die, and I wondered how I could still be living when my alter ego no longer did. Well was it said of a friend that he is the soul's other half. My soul and his I considered one soul in two bodies—so my life was unbearable, to live with only half of our soul, but my death was terrifying, perhaps to see his remaining half of soul die in me whom I so much loved.

12.   To love a man as more than a man—what craziness! How stupid to be a man and resent the condition of man—as I did. I seethed, gasped, cried, was distraught without sleep or plan. I grappled my soul to me, lacerated and bleeding as it was, resistant to my grappling. Yet I could not see where I could set it free. I could not soothe it with pleasant groves, with shows or songs, with sweet-scented bowers, well-furnished banquets, pleasures of bed or boudoir, or finally with books or poems. Everything disgusted me, even the light of day. If a thing could not show me him as he was, it was hateful and repulsive—better my groans and tears, which alone gave me semi-relief. But when that relief was intermitted, a huge weight of woe crushed me. I sensed that it could be lifted and ameliorated only by you, but I neither could nor would look to you, since you were nothing real and reliable in my mind. My heresy—those projected unrealities—was my God. If I tried to put any weight on them, they crumbled, they disintegrated about me. I was my own land of lament, impossible either to inhabit or escape. How could my heart escape my heart? How flee from me? Would I not hunt me down? Yet flee I did, from my hometown. In places he had never been I would not keep expecting to see him. From Thagaste I went back to Carthage.

IV
OTHER FRIENDS

13. Time does not stand still, it unreels itself. Its passage impinges on the senses which strangely affect the mind. 'Day by day' it came and went, and its coming and going seeded in me new things to expect or remember. Little by little it restored me to joys of the kind I used to experience, as my mourning relaxed its hold. New sorrows did not directly follow, but new reasons for sorrow. Why, after all, had that sorrow pierced me to the very marrow but that I was pouring my soul like water into sand by loving a mortal man as if he could be immortal? Yet I was trying to restore and revivify myself with this very solace of friendship, lavishing on it the love I owed to you. I prolonged the giant imposition and long self-deception, and in their faithless embrace 'my ears itched' for what was confusing my mind—so my heresy did not die along with any of my friends.

Yet some things about those friends entranced me—conversation and laughter and mutual deferrings; shared readings of sweetly phrased books, facetiousness alternating with things serious; heated arguing (as if with oneself) to spice our general agreement with dissent; teaching and being taught by turns; the sadness at anyone's absence, and the joy of return. Reciprocated love uses such semaphorings—a smile, a glance, a thousand winning acts—to fuse separate sparks into a single glow, no longer many souls but one.

14. That is what love of friends means. It makes us feel guilty if we do not reciprocate another's love for us, and hope for a return on our love—not as a matter of sensual gratification but of wishing another good. No wonder then that there is grief for the friend who dies—a darkness of sorrow over all, the heart melting to tears as the sweet becomes bitter, the life lost to death making others' lives a kind of death. But 'happy the one who loves you,' and loves his friend in you, and loves his enemy because of you. One never loses a loved one in the person who loves all and cannot himself be lost—and who is that, God, but our God, 'who made heaven and earth' and 'fills them both,' making them by filling them? You are lost only if left, and where does 'leaving you, fleeing you,' take one but from you to you, from you serene to you wroth? What place is outside your law with its punishment—'your law that is truth,' the truth that is you?

15. 'Lord of powers, turn us around, show us your face, and we are safe.' Turn where it may, so long as it turns not to you, the human soul is mired in its own sorrow, even if the mire is made up of beautiful things, things detached from you and detached from the soul—yet what can exist but by coming from you? Things rise and sink, and begin to be by rising, then progress toward being all they can, and when they have become all they can, they grow old and perish, though some things perish even without growing old. So when they rise and begin to be, the sooner they reach full being the sooner they rush on toward non-being. Such is the limit of their being, set by you, since they are parts of a universe whose parts are not simultaneously all in being. The entirety of things acts by the passage and replacement of the parts that make it up—just as we speak by the passage of meaningful sounds, which would not form a sentence if one word, its syllables sounded, did not yield to the next word. May my soul praise you for these succeeding things, God, who created them all, without my being mired in any, stuck to them by a sensual love for them. For these go their way and cease to be, and the soul is torn from them with sick longing, for it wants them to continue being so it can rest in what it loves in them. But there is no resting in things that will not stay. They flit off, and what meaning can be absorbed from them by the physical senses? Who really takes them in even when they are present? The physical senses are

sluggish precisely because they are physical—that is their
limit. They are fit only for the task allotted them—which is
not to halt things in their transit from certain beginning to
certain end. They heed your word, in which they are created,
decreeing their passage 'from here to there.'

16. Be not giddy, my soul, nor block your heart's hearing with a clangor of giddiness. Heed, as do those things, the
word, its voice calling you back to him. In him alone is there
a place whose calm is never disturbed, where love is never
abandoned unless it abandons. Earthly things, you see, all
pass away and are replaced by others, and their succession of
parts makes up this lower universe. But God's word says:
Whither could I withdraw? There make firm your habitation, my soul, there give back all your goods. Tired of all
falsehoods, give over to Truth what Truth has brought you.
Nothing will be lost to you. What is decayed in you will be
repristinated, all your symptoms cured, your raveling out restored, made new, rewoven into your fabric. And when the
failing body descends, it will not take you with it but will
stand with you and perdure beside the ever standing and lasting God.

17. So why, soul, veer toward the flesh? Steer where it
must follow. What the senses show you is but part of the entire physical realm, which you do not see as a whole when
you are being gratified by its parts. The senses are rightly
limited by punishment and react only to the parts; but if they
were fitted to comprehend the whole, you would speed by
the transitory present things, to take a greater joy in their
completion. It is by such physical sensation that you hear
what we say, and you do not want to stop at one syllable, but
to speed them on, so that, other syllables having passed, you
may grasp the whole sentence. So it is with every whole made
up of parts, where all the parts cannot be present. The parts
would be more pleasing if we could take them all in together,
not singly. But better still is the one who made all the parts,
who is our God, who is not transitory, since nothing can succeed him.

18. If material things please you, 'praise in them God' and steer yourself back to their maker, lest your pleasures displease. If persons please you, let God be loved in them, since they too are evanescent unless steadied by his support, they come and are swiftly gone, to be seized while you are able and taken to him along with you, telling them: Him let us love who made all these things, and who is not far from us. For he did not make and then leave them. They not only came from him but remain in him, and where he is, all savors of the truth. He is inward to the heart, even as it roams from him. 'Re-enter your own heart, you who are dissemblers of it.' Cling to him who made you. Stand with him and never fall. Rest in him and have full peace. Is your path anfractuous? Where is it taking you? What is good in your love is from him, and good and easy is the way to him. But hard it will be, for good reason, if you love things derived from him as deprived of him. Why try over and over to trudge paths that are taxing and impeded? The ease you are seeking is not where you seek it. You seek what you seek and it is not there. You want a happy life where there is only death. It is not there, and how could there be a happy life without life?

19. Our 'life itself came down to us,' assumed our death, and 'made death die' by the fullness of his life, in thunder calling us back with him to the mystery of his coming. For he came from a virgin's womb, where mankind was wed to him, mortal flesh, to end mortality. Thence 'he emerged as a bridegroom from his chamber, towering in strength to run his race.' He 'did not hold back,' but called as he ran, in his words, in his deeds, in death, in life, 'in descending, in ascending,' calling us to go back with him. He withdrew from our sight, to make us 're-enter our heart' and find him there. He took himself off, yet here he is. He would no longer stay with us, yet would not leave us. He returned to what he never left. For 'the world was made by him,' he was in the world and 'came to the world to rescue sinners.' To him my soul testifies, and 'he heals it whom it offended.' 'How long, my fellows, will your hearts be heavy?' Fallen in life, can you refuse to rise up and live? But where shall you rise if 'on the heights you have delivered your own heavenly judgments'? Lower yourself that you may rise and reach God. For you fell in rising against God. Tell others to 'weep in the valley of weeping,' for that is what you say to them, by the Spirit's prompting, if your speech is ablaze with love.

V

BEAUTY AND DECORUM

20. Of all this I was unaware. Infatuated with beauty of a lower order, I touched bottom. I told my friends: How can we love anything but the beautiful? What, then, is a beautiful thing, or beauty itself? What entices and satisfies us in what we love? Can anything compel us that is not beautiful and fitting? And as I pondered this I distinguished between physical beauty (a thing complete in itself) and the fitting (accommodated to something outside itself—as our limbs fit our body, or as our shoe fits our foot). And this concept so penetrated my mind that I composed a heartfelt work, *On Beauty and Decorum*—in two or three books, I believe; but only you know, God, since it disappeared. I do not know how I lost track of it.

21. What impulse, my Lord God, led me to dedicate that work to Hierius, Rome's orator? I had no personal acquaintance with him, I was just taken with his splendid reputation for learning, and with what I had heard of his speeches, which impressed me. Actually, I was more taken by what others thought of him, by the way they lavished praise on him, how struck they were that a Syrian fluent in Greek should become not only a star orator in Latin but a philosopher of the first rank. He was praised and admired at a distance. Can a person, just by mouthing praise, touch another person's heart? Of course not. But enthusiasm kindles enthusiasm, and praise can cause admiration when the praise is believed to be heartfelt—arising, that is, from a true appreciation.

22. So then I assessed men by others' estimation of

them, not by yours, my God, who never mislead. But why did I admire Hierius, not some celebrity charioteer, not some man famous for fighting animals in the games—why did I have a quite different and more serious regard for him, the kind of regard I would desire for myself? I did not envy actors their notoriety or popularity, however I might praise and admire them—I would, in fact, prefer obscurity to such notoriety, and obloquy to such popularity. What explains the different emotional assessments one makes of different types and callings? Why do I admire in another what I must detest in myself (or I would not shun and be repelled by it)? I am dealing with another man, not a fine horse, which can be admired though one would not become it, even if one could. That is not the same as admiring in an actor what I would not wish for myself, since we share the same humanity. Why should I reject for myself what I applaud in another, who is as much a man as I? Man is a great abyss. Though you 'number the hairs of his head,' missing none, yet the moods and attractions of his heart far outnumber the hairs of his head.

23. I admired that orator as I would be admired myself, giddy pride leading me astray to be 'buffeted by every wind.' Yet there was some subtle guidance by you in this. Why, that is, do I know for sure now, as I testify to you, that I admired him because men praised him and not because of the qualities they were praising? I know it because my admiration would not have been kindled and kept alive if men had despised instead of praising him, and had passed on this contempt and scorn in their reports of him—though the facts about him, or the man himself, were no different, just the attitude of those giving report of him. See how listless the soul lies when not supported by the solid truth. It is blown abroad and twisted about, turned and re-turned, by whatever gabble the light-minded bother to puff from their lungs, to cloud the light and obscure the truth, though it be staring us in the face. It was my great concern that this man should notice me and my book. I would have glowed had he praised it, but his disapproval would have struck me to my heart, empty as it was, and void of your consistency. As for me, I dwelt on what I saw in my own work, *Beauty and Decorum,* which I had dedicated to him. I was lost in an admiration no others could share.

24. I did not see yet that the clue to this whole subject is the workmanship by which you alone, the all-powerful, 'make everything that deserves admiration.' My mind fumbled through physical bodies as I defined beauty and decorum, distinguishing the former (pleasing in itself) from the latter (pleasing by its juxtaposition with other things). I illustrated this with physical examples. I treated the mind as well, but I could not see the truth about it—I was still denying that there could be incorporeal realities. The force of fact smote me in the eye, but I turned my mind with a wince from incorporeal things to lines and colors and palpable large bodies. Since I could not find such physical things in my mind, I thought I could not find the mind itself.

I was drawn to the peace I found in virtue, and repelled by the rancor I found in vice, attributing the former to unity, the latter to division. Unity was the sphere of the ordered mind, of real truth and the highest good, while in division I thought I saw some status of the disordered mind, of the highest evil as a reality, having not only a state of its own but a life as well. Yet this could not exist unless it 'came from you, my God, as all things come.' I called unity the Monad, pure mind without gender, and division I called the Dyad, pure anger to hurt and lust to despoil. It was my ignorance speaking, since I had not grasped or been told that evil has no reality of its own and mind is not the highest and changeless good.

25. As aggressive crimes occur when flawed passions rage unchecked and wild, and sordid crimes occur when the appetite for sensual gratification is indulged, so mental crimes occur when error and false theories taint the soul. This was the condition of my mind when I did not realize that light must come to it from another source than itself, that it must *share* in the truth because it cannot *be* the truth. You, Lord my God, 'light a lamp for me to bring light into my darkness.' For 'we all partake of your fullness,' since you are 'the true light, giving light to every man who comes into this world.' In you 'there is no alteration or dimming by time.'

26. I was striving up toward you yet 'pushed back by you,' with a taste of mortality in my mouth, for 'you rebuff the proud'—and what could be prouder than the mad claim that my nature was divine, like yours? I was subject to change, a point made clear by my very effort to acquire more knowledge, to improve my condition (from what must be an inferior one). Still I preferred to think you also must be changeable rather than to think I could be different from you. That is why I was pushed back, why you repulsed the cocky lift of my verbose head, as I played with fictive physical entities and I, fleshy, criticized things of the flesh, 'a spirit on the loose, nor reoriented toward you.' I plowed on and on, deeper into what did not exist, either in you or me or in the bodies I dealt with. These were not real things created in your Word's truth, but things confected from my foolish thought about bodily things. My argument to your lowly ones [Christians]—my unrecognized countrymen, from whom I was in unwitting exile—was this glib one, missing the point: How can a soul made by God go astray? I did not want to hear the counter-argument: How could God himself err? For I claimed that your unchangeable nature was forced to err in its constrained particles, rather than testify that my changeable nature erred unforced, and that this error was itself my punishment.

27. This was my plight at the age of twenty-six or twenty-seven, when I wrote that book, hugging to me my own conceptions of the physical world, which filled my ears with their outer noise while I was trying to hear your inner music, my sweet truth. By dealing with beauty and decorum, I was trying to lift myself up and listen to you, gladdened by the glad call of my spouse, but I could not—the noise of my errors pulled me outside myself, while the weight of my pride sank me below myself, where you could not grant me 'news of real happiness and joy,' so my bones could not be lifted up because I had not lowered myself.

VI

ARISTOTLE

28. How can I boast that when still twenty or so I read on my own and understood a book by Aristotle I happened across, the one known as *Ten Categories,* whose reputation awed me with a vague sense of the formidable and intimidating? My rhetoric teacher at Carthage—and other scholars of repute—had puffed it, giddy with pretentiousness. When I compared notes with friends, who told me they had grasped the book only with the help of the best scholars, not only describing but diagramming its concepts, they could add nothing to what I had already grasped on my own just by reading the book. Its teaching on substances seemed obvious to me—man, for instance, and his various aspects: his configuration, his stature (how many feet high), his relationships (as to a brother), his country, his birth date, his posture (standing, sitting), his clothing (shod, in armor), what he does, what is done to him, however he is affected by the numberless aspects I have given by way of example, or by the category of substance itself.

29. How can I boast of knowing this when it impeded me? It made me treat the ten categories as applicable to everything, even to your wondrously simple and unique nature, as if greatness and beauty could be predicated of you as they are of a corporeal body, whereas your greatness and beauty are yourself. Greatness and beauty are not the same as the body of which they are predicated, since that body can become less great or beautiful and still be a body. So all I thought of you was a falsehood, not the truth, fabled from my sad state, not founded in your joy. What you had commanded applied to me—that my 'earth should bear thorns and thistles,' and I should 'obtain my bread by toil.'

30.   How can I boast that I read every book I could find on the arts and sciences, and understood them all, while I remained the worst slave to my own desires? Reading them gave me pleasure, though I was blind to the source of whatever was true or solid in them. My back was to the light that lit them as I faced them. Thus my face, even as it saw what was being lit, was itself in shadow. I mastered rhetoric and logic, geometry, music and mathematics, easily and without the need for an instructor—a facile mind and fine judgment come, you know, from you. But since I did not offer them up to you, they worked more for my bane than my benefit. I took pains to hoard most of my heritage under my own protection, not 'committing myself bravely to you.' I 'left you for a far place,' where I squandered my heritage in trashy longings. How can I boast of good things badly used? I was not even aware that the arts and sciences are acquired with difficulty by the most dedicated and intelligent people, until I tried to teach them, and found that the quickest students were simply the least slow in trying to follow me.

31.   Still, what is there to boast of in that, since I still considered you, my God and my Truth, to be a physical being of great size and splendor, and myself a particle of that body? What a perversion. Yet such was I. I do not blush, my God, to call on you and give testimony to your pity for me, I who had unblushingly given witness to falsehoods about your nature, 'with canine snarls against you.' How can I boast of mastery in the arts and sciences, by which the knotty meanings of those books were teased out, when I was twisted about in my wandering from true piety into pestilent irreligion? Or how can your lowly ones regret their slower minds when they did not 'go into far exile' from you? 'Fledglings in your church's nest,' they drew sustenance from true teachings and 'grew wings of love.' Let us, Lord our God, take hope 'under your hovering wings.' Protect and carry us. You will 'carry little ones through to snowy age.'

When our steadiness is from you, we stand fast. When we try to steady ourselves, we stumble. Our own good flourishes in you. Aversion from that good is perversion, so give us conversion to it, lest our fortunes be inverted. Only in you does our own good flourish flawless. 'For you are you.' We need not fear return to a place no longer there after our lapse. Our home—which is your eternity—did not collapse because we left it.

BOOK FIVE

MATERIALISM

I

MATERIALISM

1. Receive the offering of my testimony, 'the handiwork of that tongue' you created and have prompted 'to testify to your honor.' 'Heal my bones' that they may cry, 'Who, Lord, is your like?' One testifying to you does not reveal what is happening within him. The closed heart cannot close you out, nor the frozen surface resist your hand. You thaw the surface, either in pity or in wrath, and 'none can find shelter from that heat.' Let 'my soul praise you' in love for you, and 'testify to your mercies' in praise of you. All your creation is vocal and unceasing in your praise, all 'spirits through their own mouths,' all animals and objects through the mouths of those beholding them, so that our soul may rise from its sluggishness, leaning first on the things you have made and then passing on to you, who 'made it all for our wonder,' to reach the place of renewal and true perseverance.

2. Let malcontents stray on in their evil ways—you have your eye on them and pierce through their darkness. Even with them, all things are good, though they do evil. Yet how can that harm you? Can they disgrace your reign, whose justice is intact from high heaven to the lowest creatures? 'Where, for that matter, can they be gone if they go from you?' Is there a place you will not find them? They depart only from seeing that you see them, and 'in their blindness they bump into you,' since 'you do not give up on anything you have made.' They 'bump unjustly into your justice thwarting them,' fleeing the gentle you, bumping into the severe you, and falling into the punitive you. They cannot see that wherever they go you already are there, not shut up in some other place. No one but you can be present to those absenting themselves from you. Turn they then about, to seek you, since you did not abandon them, your creatures, when they abandoned you, their creator. Turn they back, and you are already there in their hearts, hearts that testify to you, cast themselves upon you, weep in your bosom for 'their hard wandering.' You gently 'wipe away their tears,' as they take more comfort the more tears they shed. For it is you, Lord, not any man made of flesh and blood, it is you who made them and are now remaking them in consolation.

II

THE PHYSICAL SCIENCES

And where was I, Lord, in my quest for you? You were there before me, but I had left myself behind and could not find me, much less you. **3.** It is the twenty-ninth year of my age that I now indict under God's scrutiny. That is when a Manichaean bishop called Faustus, 'the devil's chosen snare,' reached Carthage. Many had been trammeled in his sweet verbal nets, with which I, too, was impressed. But I found nothing sound on the points I most wanted clarified by him. I looked not at the ornamented vessels being served by this Faustus [Fortunate] famous in his sect, but at what nourishment was in the vessels. I had been told that he was known for the range of his knowledge and especially for his familiarity with the arts and sciences. Now, I had been reading widely in the philosophers and turning over in my mind what they said. When I matched them against the large imagined claims of the Manichaeans, I found them more successful in 'explaining the universe (though without exact knowledge of its Lord).' For you, Lord, though vast, 'look to the lowly, and hold aloof the haughty.' To 'crushed spirits' you bend down, while the proud seek you in vain, able as they are by transgressive knowledge 'to count stars and sands,' to chart the heavens' bodies and trace their transits.

4. You gave them the faculties, and the skill in using them, that can accomplish these things. They predicted, years ahead, eclipses of the sun and moon, partial or total, down to the day and the hour, and their calculations turned out right. They have published the results of their findings, where people can now read them and predict the year, the month of the year, day of the month, hour of the day, and degree of eclipse, whether of sun or of moon. When their predictions are confirmed, ignorant onlookers are stunned, and gape with astonishment. Learned ones, however, celebrate and are themselves boosted up, to stray in irreverent pride from your light into their darkness. They can see shadow in the sun's future but not in their own present, since they do not reverently consider from whom they acquired this skill in investigation—or if they see that you made that skill, they do not offer it back to you for its preservation. They make no burnt offering of their effort at self-creation, do not smother their high flights of pride like so many birds, their fishlike transgressive knowledge swimming deep in murky depths of the abyss, their lusts ranging like beasts of the fields, that you, God, 'a voracious fire,' might burn away their mortal concerns, transforming them into immortals.

5. Ignorant they remain of the Path, 'your Word, through whom you made' the things they measure and their own measuring ability, both the senses that show them what to measure and the mind that does the measuring—from your 'wisdom that is beyond measure.' Your Only-Begotten 'is made our wisdom and vindication and sanctification,' who took on the measure of a man and measured out the tribute to Caesar. Ignorant they remain of the Path by which they can lower themselves from their own heights to his lowliness, so they may rise up to him by way of him. Ignorant of this Path, they fancy themselves shining high amid the stars when they have 'plunged to earth,' their 'hearts darkened with folly.' Themselves giving true accounts of the cosmos, the maker of the cosmos they do not seek with reverence. Therefore they find him not—or if they acknowledge a maker, they do not 'honor him for what he is and show their gratitude to him.' Rather, 'absorbed in their calculations,' busy with praise of their own wisdom, they confer your attributes on themselves; or, turning things upside down, give you their traits, fashioning their untruths as the true God, putting idols shaped like perishing men or birds or animals or ser-

pents in the place of the imperishable God. This makes truth a lie, and worships creatures instead of their creator.

6.   Whatever truths they had uncovered about your universe I accepted, since I found method in their calculations, in their predicted times, in the visible star patterns. These points I contrasted with what Mani had so extensively written on them in his endless raving, and I found there no methodical account of solstices, equinoxes, eclipses of the sun or moon, or similar things that I read of in works on the arts and sciences. Yet belief was demanded in Mani's sayings, whereas rational method was used in the secular calculations, and evidence capable of visible proof. The contrast was glaring.

7.   Can we say, then, my Lord and my God of truth, that you favor the astronomer? Far from it. Let him know all that can be known of that science, but not know you, and he is lost, while blessed is the man, ignorant of astronomy, who knows you. And should one know both it and you, he is no better off for the former knowledge, since only in you can he be blessed—'seeing you for what you are, he praises and is grateful to you, and is not absorbed in his own calculations.' That man is better off who securely possesses a tree, and is grateful for what it bears, even if he does not know exactly how high it is or how broad it spreads, than is the man who measures the tree and has an exact count of its branches, but possesses it not, and knows not nor loves the one who made it. It is 'the man of faith who reaps all the treasures of the world,' who is 'rich in possessing nothing' if he be close to you, whom all things serve. Though he be ignorant of the wheelings of the Great Bear and its phases, is he not happier than one who charts the heavens, counts the stars, and weighs the elements, but knows nothing of you, who 'arranged all things by measure and number and weight'?

III

MANI'S "SCIENCE"

8. Who put up this Mani, of all people, to write about things not required for understanding true reverence? You have told man, 'Reverence is wisdom.' One could understand everything about astronomy without understanding wisdom— yet Mani, who did not know astronomy, had the sheer gall to teach it, making it even clearer he could never understand wisdom. It is an empty thing to certify one's own knowledge of astronomy, even if one possesses it; but it is an act of reverence to give you testimony. This is not a distinction Mani observed in the vast corpus of his writings. How, after he was refuted by those with a sound understanding of astronomy, could he be trusted in matters more difficult to understand? He had no low opinion of himself—he tried, in fact, to persuade others that the Holy Spirit, the Supporter and guide of your faithful, dwelt with full teaching authority in him. So when he was caught teaching nonsense about the heavens and stars, about the solar and lunar courses, things irrelevant to religious doctrine, he made it clear that he was violating true religion by having the crazy nerve to spread not only his ignorance but his deceit, sanctioning it with an appeal to his divine personality.

9. When I come across one or other of my fellow Christians ignorant of astronomy, believing what is not so, I calmly look on, not thinking him the worse for mistaking the place or order of created things, so long as he holds nothing demeaning to you, Lord, the creator of all those things. But he is worse off if he holds that his error is a matter of religious faith, and persists stubbornly in the error. His faith is still a weak thing in its cradle, needing the milk of a mothering love, until the youth grows up and cannot be the plaything, any more, of every doctrinal wind that blows. But one who ventures on the role of teacher, of leader and ruler of those under his spell, whose followers heed him not as a man only but as your very Spirit—what are we to make of him when he is caught purveying falsehoods? Should we not reject and despise such madness?

Yet I had not, at this point [before Faustus' arrival] settled definitively one point—whether his explanations of the waxing and waning length of days and nights, or of their relation to the eclipses of sun and moon, and other such phenomena, could be reconciled with what I had found in the books I read. As long as they might, it would be possible for me to suspend judgment between contending possibilities. I could maintain a belief in his reputation, based on his purported holiness.

IV

FAUSTUS

10. Through the nearly nine years I had been wandering in error as a hearer in the Manichaean sect, my piety kept me on expectant tiptoes for the arrival of this Faustus. When other Manichaeans met along the way could not answer my questions, Faustus was the one, they assured me, who could resolve the problems, and any greater ones I might propose. He would do so point by point as soon as he arrived and heard me out. When he came, I did find him a gracious fellow, facile and talkative, repeating what they usually said but far more engagingly. Yet what help for my thirst was a deft waiter bearing a fancy chalice? My ears were already tired with what they offered, nor was it improved by fancier presentation. Elegance did not make it truer, nor was the man himself wiser for his handsome face and ready words. He was puffed to me as the ideal of judgment and wisdom, but only by poor judges of such matters, by those who simply loved to hear him talk.

I realize there are men who refuse to accept anything as true if it is presented with studied polish. But you had been telling me something else, in your subtle and indirect ways—something I took as coming from you, since it was true and there is no other teacher of truth, wherever or whithersoever derived. This, then, is what I learned from you, that nothing is true just because it is beautifully phrased, nor anything false because haltingly sounded out. Conversely, nothing is true because awkwardly phrased, nothing false because voiced grandly. As food is healthful or unhealthful without regard to the refined or base tableware it is served in, so are

wisdom and folly independent of the words, studied or un-
studied, used to express them.

11. The eagerness I had felt for Faustus' arrival made
me welcome the impact and style of his converse, the ease
with which he expressed his every opinion in just the right
words. I was impressed as others were, and more than most
I praised and promoted him. I was irked, it is true, that in
large gatherings I could not raise my problems with him and
thrash them out in the give and take of argument. But even
when I was able, with some of my friends, to spend some
time with him where an exchange of views was appropriate,
and where I could raise points troubling to me, my first testings of him showed a man untested in the arts and sciences.

He knew, of course, the basics of grammar and rhetoric, as
commonly taught. He had read some of Cicero's orations
and a small sampling of Seneca's works, along with several
poets and the writings of his sect (those composed in good
Latin). From the conditioning of daily discourse he had
pieced together a style which careful management and natural charm made gracious and captivating. Am I remembering
this fairly, my Lord God, the judge of my mind at the time?
My heart and 'awareness are open to you,' who were even
then affecting me inwardly by your hidden guidance, thrusting my false views back into my face, where I could see and
hate them.

12. After it became clear that he was ignorant of the
arts and sciences in which I had expected him to excel, I lost
hope that he could expound and clear up the points that
were troubling me. A man could be ignorant about those
points and still be truly reverent, but not if he were a
Manichaean, trained by their books in lengthy mythical accounts of the heavens and the stars, the sun and the moon. I
no longer considered him capable of the nice analysis I was
eager for, to tell me if the Manichaean accounts would bear
comparison with the methodical calculations I had read elsewhere, to show me they were correct, or at least equally
probable. Nonetheless I raised some problems with him,
at least as a matter of discussion. It was not a task he was

willing, in his ample humility, to shoulder. He realized it was beyond him, and he was not ashamed to testify to the fact. At least he did not resemble those men I have had to endure in great numbers, ready to teach me at great length by saying nothing. He had a certain openness, if not candid toward you, canny enough about himself. He was not too ignorant to see his own ignorance, and knew enough not to get trapped in arguments where there was no breaking through or backing down. I rather liked that in him. The modesty of a mind testifying to its own limitations is a more admirable thing than the scientific matters I was pressing him to know. Such was the quality he showed me whenever I brought up an abstruse or demanding question.

13. With my ardor to study Manichaean writings now dashed, I did not expect to learn much from other teachers after their most "fortunate" man showed me his quality in response to my deepest concerns. Yet I fell progressively into his company because of his literary interest in the works I was teaching my students there in Carthage. I read with him any works he wanted to hear or that I thought appropriate to his stage of learning. But the better I knew him the less did I desire to go deeper into the teachings of his sect, as I had intended. I did not entirely renounce it, since I had found nothing better, and I was content to abide for a while where I chanced to find myself, until something better appeared. Thus the very Faustus who was a deadly snare to others began, without his realizing or intending it, to loosen the ties that had trammeled me—though it was actually your hands, my God, making sure by secret provision that my soul would not be lost. In the endless prayers tearfully poured out, day and night, from my mother's very lifeblood, you were arranging things for me by your mysterious dispositions. This was your work, my God, since 'the Lord guides man's every step and he determines the path.' What hope is there for man's rescue but by your hand remaking what you first made?

V

ROME

14. You were the one who made me think of going to Rome, to repeat there what I had been teaching in Carthage. My own reasons I shall willingly testify to you, since your guidance from on high and mercy from near at hand deserve our study and praise. I was not drawn to Rome by any promise held out by friends of earning higher fees or gaining greater reputation there (though those had great attraction for me at the time). No, my main and almost sole motive was the report that the young were more serious there, more quiet in their submission to instruction. Unruly bands did not burst into the classroom of a teacher not their own, and no student attended unless enrolled. In Carthage, by contrast, students disgracefully run wild. They feel free to crash into any class and with crazy grimacing destroy the order imposed for the students' benefit. With stunning obtuseness they inflict great damage, doing things punishable by law, were they not accepted as common practice. But this just makes them more pitiable, leading them to think they are allowed what your eternal law never allows, as if they could escape punishment for their acts when those blind acts are the very punishment they inflict on themselves, far worse than anything they do to others.

As a student myself I had not added my rowdiness to that of others, but as a teacher I had that very rowdiness inflicted on me. Better to go where knowledgeable people assured me this did not occur. But it was you nudging me, 'my hope and my share in the land of the living,' to leave my land for 'the rescue of my soul,' goading me to tear myself away from

Carthage. You held out to me the attractions of Rome, using as your instruments men [Manichaeans] who love a dying life, which makes them act madly on promises that are empty. You used their perversity, and mine, secretly to lead me on, while those who upset the tenor of my life were blind and those drawing me away had 'a mere worldly wisdom.' I went from where my sad plight was real to where my hopes for happiness were unreal.

15.   The reason for my leaving here and arriving there you knew, Lord, without revealing it to me or to my mother, who wept violently over my departure and followed me to the seashore. But I tricked her as she clung to me forcefully, asking me to stay or to take her. I pretended I was waiting for a friend to arrive on a favorable wind. That is how I fooled my mother—this of all mothers—and slipped away. Even here you spared me, keeping me with my tainted and vile burden from drowning in the waters of the sea, to bring me to the waters of baptism, by whose laving the rivers of tears from my mother's eyes would be dried, after being poured out to moisten the earth where she wept before you. Since she would not go back without me, I persuaded her to stop the night at a chapel of Saint Cyprian near our anchorage. That night I made my clandestine departure, without her. She was left behind to weep and pray.

What, my God, did she pray for me with all her tears? To prevent my departure. You did not grant her this, since you with deeper wisdom attended to the core of her concern, that you would make me what she always prayed I would I become. So the wind blew, the sails filled, the shoreline dropped from view, leaving her in the morning crazed with her loss. She assailed your ears with complaining and moaning which you heeded not. You were driving my desires on to the extinction of those desires, and you were wielding a flail over her carnal affection. Like any mother, but more urgently than most, she desired my presence, unaware of what joy you would contrive for her from my absence. Unaware of this, she was all tears and outcries, and her anguish proved her still a daughter of Eve, seeking with groans what she 'brought forth with groans.' Nonetheless, after denouncing my deception and cruelty, she took up again her prayers for me as she went back to the home she lived in, and I went on to Rome.

16. There I fell at once under the lash of physical illness. I was 'descending to the underworld' with all the sins I had committed still upon me, those against you, against me, against my neighbors—sins numerous and grave, added to original sin's bondage, which makes us 'all mortal in Adam.' None of these sins had been forgiven me yet in Christ, nor had he 'by his cross broken though the enmity between us' built of my sins. How could that cross break through, when I still believed it a wraith? The death of his body was as unreal in my view as the death of my soul was real. But since the death of his body was in fact real, the life of my soul was unreal insofar as I believed not in that death. As my fevers increased, I was on the verge of expiring, of perishing. And had I died, where would I have gone? Where but to the fire and torture merited by my sins, according to the truth of your just order for the universe? She did not know I was sick, but she was praying for me while absent from me. But you, omnipresent, were there with her, hearing her prayer, and were with me, taking pity on me, that my body might recover while my heart was still deranged in irreligion. I did not call for baptism even in this perilous state, proving that I had been better in my youth, when I demanded it from my mother's piety, as I have recalled and testified. Since then I had gone backward and now thoughtlessly laughed off your healing counsels. Yet you saved me at this point from the death of my soul with my body. Had you not, what a deep wound, incurable, would have been inflicted on my mother, she whose total dedication to me I have no words to describe, as she suffered more 'birth pangs in the delivery of my soul' than of my body.

17. I see no way she could have been healed if my death in that state had stabbed to the core of her love for me. What then would be the issue of such prayers as she directed at you in a stream without interruption? They would be in your keeping, and could you, the God of pity, actually despise the heart of this pure and disciplined widow, so humbled before you, so crushed? She was constant in her charities, caring and supportive of your faithful ones, never missing a day in her offerings at your altar—twice each day, morn and night, coming to your church, not for idle gossip to be picked up from clucking old women, but that she might hear you through your word and you hear her through her prayers. Her tears begged for no gold or silver, for nothing mutable or volatile, but only for the rescue of her son's soul—could you, who made her what she was, discount and reject such tears? Surely not, Lord, since you were present to her, heeding, guiding things along the course you had laid out toward their completion. You are not one to be misleading her in the visions and responses you gave to her, those I have mentioned and others I have not, which she faithfully laid up in her bosom, praying always as if keeping you to your pledge. Since 'your mercy is for always,' for those 'whose debts you cancel' you stand in debt to your promise.

18. You brought me, the son of your maidservant, back from my illness, giving health to my body as a step toward a higher health and strength. I still lived with the [Manichaean] Holy Ones, misled themselves and misleading others, and dealt not only with Hearers (in one of whose house I stayed while ill and recovering) but also with those they call the Elect. I still held that it was not we who committed sin but some Other in us, since it flattered my pride to think I was not guilty. If I did some wrong, I would not testify that I had done so, 'that you might heal my soul' that had sinned against you. I was ready to exculpate myself and to inculpate some other force that was within me without being me. But there was only one me, and my own sin was the only thing pitting me against myself. That sin was incurable only because I would not own it as mine. With a damnable iniquity, I preferred to think you could not prevail against the wrong done in me rather than that you could prevail by the rescue wrought in me. You had not yet 'posted a sentry over what I said or a fence of correction at my lips, lest I blurt out false excuses for dealing with wrongdoers.' I continued dealing with the Elect, not for any further initiation into their false teachings but as muddling along with them, in a half-hearted and diffident way, till I might find something better.

VI
THE ACADEMICS

19. Around this time I began to suspect that the best philosophers were those men called Academics, who took a universally skeptical attitude and determined that the mind could not endorse the truth of any proposition. That, at least, was their obvious meaning, for me and for most folk, since I was not aware of any further teaching. I was not slow to caution the man in whose house I was staying against excessive credulity, which I thought he displayed toward Manichaean books crammed with grandiose fables. Yet I felt more comfortable with his kind than with other men. Though I was no longer active in supporting their views, I mixed with them daily, so numerous were they living secretly in Rome, and this dulled my interest in inquiring elsewhere. I had given up any notion of finding truth in your church, 'Lord of heaven and earth' and 'Creator of all things seen and unseen,' since the Manichaeans had made it look ridiculous to me, holding it shameful to think of you as having the form of human flesh, with all our limbs copied down to the last physical detail. Nonetheless, if I tried to imagine my God, I could think of nothing better than some vast material stuff, since it seemed to me that all reality had to be material—which was now my main and almost only source of imprisoning error.

20. From this I derived the complementary belief that evil was some physical stuff—foul, deformed, and thick in what they call earth, or a thin and diffusive physical stuff such as air, which they picture as an evil mentality infiltrating the earth. Since I still had enough reverence, of some sort, to make it impossible for me to believe that the good God created an evil nature, I posited two masses at odds with each other, both infinite, the bad with limited, the good with broader scope. From this pestiferous origin there followed other blasphemies. If my mind tried to recur to the Catholic faith, I was made to recoil, since the Catholic faith was not what I made it out to be. I thought it more reverent, my God, as your ministrations testify in me, to believe you infinite in all respects but one, where you were opposed by the mass of evil, making you finite in this one respect, rather than to think of your entirety as contracted into the shape of a human body. It seemed better to believe you could have created no evil—which I in my ignorance thought of not only as a separate entity but as a material one, since I could not conceive of mind as anything but a thin stuff diffused spatially—than to think of evil (so conceived) to have its origin in you. Even our rescuer, your only-begotten Son, I thought of as emanating from your vast stuff to come to our rescue, since what I could believe was limited to what my folly could conceive. Such an emanation could not, I held, be born of the Virgin Mary, since he would be carnally commingled, and I could not, within the limits of the image I had made for myself, think of a commingling that was not a contamination. I shied away from any carnal birth to avoid believing in carnal contamination. Your followers, familiar with spiritual reality, will laugh at me with a gracious indulgence, but just such a fool was I.

21. The Manichaeans had so misrepresented your Scripture that I thought it indefensible. But there were points in their own writings that I wished, at times, to examine with one of their scholars, to probe what he made of them. Even earlier, in Carthage, I had been upset by the lectures of one Elpidius, openly delivered in dispute with the Manichaeans, which made arguments from Scripture that were not easily refuted. In reality, the Manichaeans' response was feeble—they barely tried to answer in public, preferring to make their case to us in private, where they claimed that the text of the New Testament had been altered by unknown persons, who worked to bring Jewish law into the Christian faith, even though they could not produce any unaltered texts. Still, what held me in thrall, choking up my mind, was the thought of those vast material bodies, under whose weight I could not breathe the pure and limpid air of your truth.

22. I concentrated all the more on what I had come to Rome for, the teaching of rhetoric. Initially I brought together students in my residence, and I began to gain a reputation with and through them. But I realized I was subject to abuses quite different from the ones I had met with in Africa. Here there were no disruptions of the class by the fiendish young, but I was told that students would avoid paying their teacher by banding together and going as a group to another teacher, shirking their obligation and hoarding money in contempt of justice. I despised them, but not with a 'commendable despising,' since I despised what they could do to me more than the injustice itself, which could be inflicted on anyone. Of course these people are base and they 'commit an infidelity against you' by loving pleasant trifles that while away the time. They love the loathsome lucre that dirties any hands dealing in it, hugging a world that evanesces, avoiding you who abide, who call them back, canceling the infidelities of those who return. I still despise base and criminal students, but only as I love what they can become under instruction, that they may embrace the teaching they rejected for money—and, more than that teaching, they may embrace you, their God and truth, the font of undoubted good, their purest peace. But then I had no patience with the delinquents for what they did to me, instead of wishing to see them reformed for what they could become with you.

VII

MILAN

23. After an order came from Milan to the prefect at Rome, ordering that a court rhetorician be provided, with travel there provided by state carriage, I made an application through my Manichaean contacts, those still drunk with folly—from whom my departure would cause a break, though neither they nor I realized it at the time. The prefect, Symmachus, sent me because of a set piece I had delivered, and so I reached Milan and Ambrose, the bishop ranked among the best men in the world, your faithful servant, whose eloquence tirelessly provided your people with 'lavish food' and 'gladdening oil' and 'wine of sober intoxication.' You led me insensibly to him that he might lead me sensibly to you. He assumed a father's role toward me, to guide my wanderings with a bishop's loving care. I responded at first with an affection based not on his preaching of the truth, which I was sure could not be found in your church, but on his kindness to me as a person. I brought a technical interest to his discourses with the congregation, not for the motive I should have had, but to see if he lived up to his reputation. Was he more or less eloquent than report had registered? Weighing carefully his style, I treated the content with a lofty disregard. I approved his easy fluency, which was more learned than that of Faustus, but—in style at least—less witty and charming. As to content, of course, there could be no comparison. Faustus ambled about in Manichaean falsehoods, while Ambrose spoke to the point about our rescue—not that a 'sinner of my sort was close to such rescue.' But I was coming closer.

24. Though I did not care to learn what he was preaching, only to hear how he was preaching it—this silly interest being all I was capable of, since I had no expectation that he could lead me to you—yet some of his content, which I was not following, slipped into my thoughts along with the style I was following closely. I could not keep them apart. While I had an open mind for what he was saying deftly, what he was saying soundly reached me also, though only by degrees. At first he simply seemed not to be talking nonsense, so I could hold that the Catholic faith was not as helpless against the Manichaean critique as I had thought it, not when one passage, then another, then more passages of the ancient Scripture were expounded symbolically, where 'the letter had killed' in my previous readings of them. The more of his expositions I heard, the more I found fault with my own certitude that the law and the prophets had no answer to those who treated them with scorn and ridicule. I was not yet convinced that the Catholic faith should be embraced. It might have learned defenders, who could refute accusations with a number of serious arguments; but a good case made by either side was not enough to move me from the position I had reached. That the church was not defeated did not mean that it had won.

25. So I tried in a more strictly logical way to see if Manichaeism could be proved wrong, by definitive demonstration. All their constructs would have collapsed at a touch and been swept from my mind had I been able to conceive of some spiritual reality, but that was what I could not do. Rather, to deal with the material body of the world, and with everything observable by the senses, I was more and more inclined, on reflection and comparison, to find in the ranks of the philosophers more probable arguments. Adopting then what was supposed to be the skepticism of the Academics, I doubted everything and suspended judgment on everything. But this meant that I had to leave the Manichaeans, who seemed even less likely to have the truth than some of my philosophers—though I could not entirely trust the treatment

of my spiritual symptoms to them, since they did not acknowledge the rescuing name of Christ. So I resumed provisionally the learners' status in the Catholic church to which
my parents had in the past assigned me, there to stay until
some more certain light should be thrown on the path to follow.

BOOK SIX

MILAN

I
MONNICA FOLLOWS

1. Where were you then, you 'my hope from childhood,' whither 'had you withdrawn'? Were you not my maker, who 'set me apart in strength and intelligence from beasts and birds of the sky'? Yet here I was, 'moiling through darkness and slime,' looking for you outside myself, where I could not find 'the God my heart seeks.' I was 'walking at the bottom of a sea,' with no hope or prospect of finding truth.

My mother, strong in her devotion, now joined me, pursuing me across land and sea, protected from all perils by her trust in you. Tossed at sea, she comforted the sailors themselves, who ordinarily comfort the passengers who have no experience of the abyss. She assured them of a safe arrival, since you had assured her of this in a dream. I was the one she found in peril, where I had abandoned all hope of finding the truth. When I told her I was no longer a Manichaean, but neither was I a Catholic Christian, she was not overjoyed, since she had already suspected as much. Already taking for granted this stage of my travail, in which I still lay dead while her tears called for my resurrection, she placed me mentally on a bier, like the widow in the gospel, waiting for your words, 'Young man, I tell you to rise,' to make the son rise, speak, and be restored to his mother.

Her heart, therefore, was not shaken with a disordering joy, just because she heard that this much that she wept for daily was accomplished. I was loosened from error, but not fastened to truth. She was certain, nonetheless, that the rest would be fulfilled, since you had promised it all to her. With a calm confidence filling her whole soul, she told me that, as she trusted Christ entirely, before she ended her pilgrimage she would see me a believing Catholic. That was her assurance to me—but to you, font of pity, she multiplied her prayers and tears, that you would come sooner to my need, and 'scatter my darkness with your light.' For this purpose she hastened even more often to church, there to hang on every word of Ambrose, 'the fountain of arching water for eternal life.' She regarded him as God's angel, since she recognized that it was through him I had been brought at least to this wobbly state of balance, from which she expected me to advance, going from sickness to health, but only through a narrower passage of peril, like what the doctors call a crisis point.

AMBROSE

2. But when she took cakes and bread and wine to the martyrs' shrines, as was her custom in Africa, she was barred from entering. When she understood that this was by the bishop's order, she accepted it in reverent obedience. I was astonished that she became at once a critic of her own custom instead of a carper at the ban on it. It was not the drinking part of the rite that attracted her, since no fondness for wine stood between her and the truth—unlike those men and women who react when the praises of sobriety are chanted as drunks do if given watered wine. It had been her practice, after bringing her container of ritual food for tasting and passing around, to fill only one small glass of wine, watered to her temperate taste, and to take but a sip, out of deference. If a circuit of the shrines was to be made, she took the same cup around to them all, which was now not only watery but lukewarm as she passed it around, since she was more concerned with the commemoration than with her own enjoyment.

Thus did she comply readily when told that her famous preacher and reverend bishop had issued a directive against this being done, even by abstemious attendants, lest it tempt alcoholics to excess, or slide into a version of the pagans' cult of the dead. Taught thus, she took around to the shrines a heart full of prayers even purer than before instead of a basket full of the fruits of the earth. This made her better able to give what she had to the needy, and the only thing offered for partaking at the martyrs' shrines was the shared body of the Lord, whose passion the martyrs had imitated and been crowned for.

With my 'heart exposed to your scrutiny,' Lord my God, I doubt that my mother could so easily have uprooted a settled habit, if it had been banned by any she loved less than Ambrose. She was as fond of him for saving me as he was fond of her for her devout life, shown in her attendance at church with a spirit ardent for all good works. He would often, when he saw me, break into spontaneous praise of her, congratulating me on having such a mother, unaware what kind of son she had in me, a universal skeptic with no idea how to search for 'the path to life.'

3.   I was not yet ready to pray with a groaning humility for your help. My impulse was for intellectual challenge, I itched for argument. As for Ambrose, I thought him a prosperous man, as the world judges, respected by the successful, though I counted his celibacy against him. I had no way of knowing about, I was totally excluded from, whatever aspirations he might entertain—what struggles against the temptations of his high place, what solace found when he was baffled. His face gave no clue to what went on in his heart, to any interior joy he might savor while feeding on you, his bread. He, on his side, was no more aware of my own seethings, of the pit that was opening before me.

I could not ask him the questions I wanted, in the way I wanted, since I was sealed off from his hearing and responses by a crowd of those who had business with him, and whose needs he catered to. When he was free (but only for a time) from these importunities, he restored his body with victuals and his mind with books. When he read, his eyes scanned the page and his heart seized the meaning, while he formed no words with his lips. Often, when we were present—since he did not restrict access to himself, and the names of visitors were not announced—we watched him read, silently as he always did, and after we had been sitting there in a prolonged silence (with none so cheeky as to break his spell) we withdrew. We supposed that he had so little time he could call his own, for restocking his mental store, beset as he was by the problems of others, that he resisted involvement in more such affairs. He might have avoided reading a passage out loud before an alert listener since he could be asked to explicate it, leading to discussion of nice points. Time squandered that way would cut back on the number of books he wanted to peruse. He might also have found that silent reading helped preserve his voice, which tended to grow hoarse. Whatever his reasons, he clearly acted wisely.

4. But that meant, as well, that I had no opportunity to raise the points on which I wished to consult your holy oracle in his breast. I was limited to brief exchanges. Only if he were free for a long session could my seethings be fully explained to him, and that session never came. I heard him, of course, 'accurately expounding the word of truth' in public every Sunday. Increasingly it looked as if all those tricky knots of slander in which our deceivers had tied up the inspired books could be untied. I was finding out, too, that the creation of man 'to your own pattern' was not interpreted by your spiritual progeny—whom you gave a new life of grace in their Catholic mother church—as if they believed and held that you were yourself confined to a human shape. But I had no slightest notion, not even a symbolic hint of one, how pure spirit could exist. Still, I happily blushed at finding that my canine snarls had been directed, lo these many years, not at the actual Catholic faith, but at a simulacrum of it based on corporeal projections. I had been so rash and irreverent that what I should have learned by study I denounced by assertion. But you, as high above me as close beside me, as hidden from me as present to me, with no parts to be more or less, always everywhere and never not anywhere, have no corporeal shape, though you made man to your pattern, and he is from head to toe a spatial creature.

5. Ignorant as I was that a thing could be made 'to your pattern,' I should have knocked for entry into this belief, not mocked what I thought was being believed. The more I was inwardly eaten by an anxiety to know what I could hold as certain, the more I blushed over the many uncertain things I had called certain, babbling them when I was deluded by

false certainties offered to my childish ignorance and preju-
dice. That they were clearly false was only later made clear
to me. But that they were uncertain was, now, certain. I had
called them certain when I made blind accusations against
your Catholic church. I did not know yet that it taught the
truth, but I had come to know it was not teaching what I bla-
tantly claimed it did. 'I was in a state of confusion, I was
changing,' but I rejoiced, my God, that the sole church, the
body of your sole Son, in which the name of Christ had
marked me as a child, was not prey to childish nonsense, nor
did it claim as orthodox the view that you, the creator of all
that is, could be confined in one location, however ample and
extended, much less in the cramped limbs of a human shape.

6. I was relieved, too, that I no longer looked with a
jaundiced eye on the ancient law and the prophets. I had
treated them as nonsense when I attributed to your holy men
views they did not really hold. Now I frequently heard Ambrose in his sermons to the people say, as if laying down a
norm carefully formulated, that 'the letter kills, while the
Spirit gives life.' Where the literal sense seemed to present
absurd things, a symbolic reading opened new meanings 'behind the veil of mystery.' What he said was at least not unreasonable, but whether it was true I still had no way of
knowing. My heart shied from commitment, as if skirting
the peril of a cliff, leaving me stalled even closer to death. I
wanted a certainty about unseen things like my certainty that
three and seven make ten. I was not so simple as to think that
even such mathematical truths can be fully understood, but I
wanted at least that kind of assurance about material things
too subtle for our senses to apprehend, or about spiritual
things which I could not conceive as being entirely non-
material.

Belief could have healed me at this point, by giving me a
purer way of looking somehow toward your truth, eternal
and never-faltering. But it is the old story: I was leery of a
good physician after dealing with a bad one. So it was with
my soul's illness, which needed curing by belief, though I
fought off the cure for fear of believing again in falsehoods.

I rebuffed healing at your hands, who mixed the curative belief yourself and administered it to all the world's illness, giving it a miraculous healing power.

7.   I was already leaning toward the Catholic tenets, since I considered it more modest and less misleading to believe things without proof (either because the proof was there, but not grasped by all, or because it was beyond proof) than to be ordered [by Manichaeism] to ridicule belief, on the basis of premature claims to scientific knowledge, and afterward to believe in irrational fabulations that were themselves incapable of proof. Gradually and gently, Lord, from this point your healing touch was easing and restoring my heart, to see all the endless things I believed without having seen them, without being present when they occurred, such as events in the history of nations, events occurring in lands and cities I never knew, or the reports of friends, of doctors, of many sorts of men. Without believing such things we simply could not operate in this world. I could not even know with a firm conviction who my parents were unless I believed what was told me.

You convinced me then that I should reprehend those who rejected belief in your sacred writings, and praise those who accepted words whose authority you had vindicated among almost all peoples. Nor should I heed those asking how I know these books to have been given to the human race by the Spirit of the one true and all-truthful God, since this is just where belief comes in. No ferocity of forced denigrations, of the sort I found in the mutually contradictory reasonings of the philosophers I was reading, could ever take away my belief that you exist (though how you exist I still did not know) or that somehow or other you govern the world.

8.   While my belief could be stronger at times, weaker at times, those two points I clung to—that you exist, and that you have concern for us—though I was still in the dark about your nature and about the path that might turn (or return) me to you. Since 'we were still weak' at finding truth by mere lucidity of reasoning, and needed help from the

warrant of Scripture, I was more disposed to think you would not have made that warrant so compelling in every land unless you made it the ground for belief in you and the means for seeking you. As I heard persuasive explanations of the passages in Scripture that had put me off by their apparent nonsense, I more and more ascribed them to an exalted symbolism, and their authority seemed to me more venerable, and it earned more devoted belief, inasmuch as all could read in it an obvious sense, while hidden meanings were reserved in their higher dignity for deeper investigation. The Bible speaks to all in plain words and a humble style, but also tests the concentration of those 'not lightly caring.' It gathers all to its accepting heart, but also draws a few through a needle-eye toward you. There would be fewer to reach you did not Scripture tower so impressively on high, while it comes down so low in humility to gather the crowd in its ample embrace. I was coming to realize this, since you stood by me. I sighed and you heard. I lurched aside and you steered me. I was still going down the world's broad path and you were not giving up on me.

III

AMBITION

9. I panted after honors, wealth, marriage—and you just laughed. These ambitions gave me nothing but trouble, made more intense by your kindness in making them bitter since they were not you. Here is my heart, Lord, you who lead me to this account and testimony, let my soul adhere to you, who extricated me from the clinging muck of death. What a thing to be pitied was I. Yet you were probing to the quick my wound, so that leaving all else, I might turn and be healed by you 'who are above all' and without whom all would not exist. It became clear what a thing to be pitied I was, and how aware I was of that condition, on a day when I was preparing a panegyric to the emperor, in which the more I lied, the more would my lies be praised by those who knew they were lies. My heart pounded with anxiety over the event, I burned with a wasting fever of concentration, as I passed through a quarter of Milan and noticed a poor beggar, plainly drunk, who was merry and jesting. I groaned at the sight, and described to friends who were with me the multiple injuries we were inflicting on ourselves with our mad plans. In all toils of the sort I was engaged in at that moment, spurred by ambition, I dragged behind me a huge weight of worry, and was made more worried by the dragging, yet all we aspired to was some carefree worldly joy—the very thing this beggar had already gained and we might never gain at all.

What had cost him nothing but a few of the coins he begged, the enjoyment of a temporal joy, I was struggling toward through the baffling turns of a maze. His joys were not true ones, but they were not as false as the ones I strove

for with my career ambitions. At least he was jolly, while I
was harried. He was carefree, I was beset. Had I been asked
which were better, jollity or anxiety, I would have answered
that jollity is. But if I were asked whether I would rather be
in his shoes than in mine, I would have taken mine, whatever
cares and fears came with them. But why? I had no real
ground for putting myself above him. Was it because I was
better educated? My education gave me no joy. I was using it
to flatter others, not to instruct them, just to flatter. For this
reason 'the rod of your discipline' was 'battering at my
bones.'

10. I want none telling me that what counts is the
source of one's joy, that the beggar made merry over wine,
while I was aspiring to fame. What is fame worth, Lord,
apart from you? His joy was not a true one, but neither was
my fame true, and it dizzied my head more than wine dizzied
his—he would sleep off his drunkenness that night, while I
was sleeping and waking with my madness, and would be
sleeping and waking with my ambition for who knows how
long. I know that the source of one's joy matters, and if I had
enjoyed a believing hope it would have been far different
from my ambition. But as between the beggar and me, as
things stood, he was better off—not so much because he was
soaked in merriment, while I was desiccated by anxiety, as
because he bought his wine by begging coins with cheerful-
ness, while I fostered my swelling sickness by lying. I carried
on in this vein with my friends, and found that they, too,
were in my condition, which I knew to be a bad one. I
lamented it, and by lamenting doubled the pain. If any bright
prospect beckoned, I was too disillusioned to follow it, since
it would barely be in my hand before it slipped away.

IV
ALYPIUS

11. We often shared our despondency, my friends and I, with whom I lived. I spoke most often and intimately with Alypius and Nebridius. Alypius came from my hometown, where his parents were of high standing. He was my junior—in fact had been my student in the early days of my teaching, first in our town and then in Carthage. He was very fond of me for what seemed to him my good conduct and learning, and I loved him for his innate virtue, which was evident from an early age. Yet the moral maelstrom of Carthage had sucked him in, seething as it was with frivolous entertainments and especially with the craze for games in the Circus. While he was miserably entangled in that, and I was professing rhetoric in a public auditorium, he no longer attended my classes, because a dispute had arisen between his father and me. But I had formed some estimate of his deadly attachment to the games, and took it sorely, since he seemed about to destroy his bright prospects, if he had not already done so. But I had no standing, from a friend's good wishes or a teacher's authority, to admonish or put pressure on him to change his ways. I suspected that he held his father's view of me, though that was not the case. In defiance of his father he began to greet me again, coming into my classroom, staying awhile, then going out.

12. I had forgotten my earlier intention of telling him how his blind obsession with the folly of the games would fritter away his many talents. But you, Lord, who keep a guiding eye on what you have created, had not forgotten the man you meant to promote over his fellows to be a champion of your mysteries. His correction should be entirely attributed to you, though you acted through me as your unwitting instrument. For one day, as I was sitting as usual with my students, he came in, said hello, sat, and paid attention to what we were discussing. The text I happened to be expounding suggested a fitting comment on the games. To make my point clearer and fix it in the mind with laughter, I described satirically those held in thrall by that madness. You know, our God, that I had no intention at that moment of curing Alypius. But he seized on my comments, and took them as meant for him. What might have made another person angry at me, made this candid young man angry at himself and made him fonder of me. This was just as you said of old, imbedding it in your holy writ: 'If a man is wise, correcting him will make him love you.'

Yet I was not correcting him. You use men, whether they know it or not, on the schedule you alone know (and a just one). You 'blew on my heart and lips as burning coals,' by which you cauterized and cured a mind with good prospects from its self-inanition. Let them omit your praise who know nothing of your mercies, to which I testify 'out of my inner being.' After what I said, he wrenched himself from the deep pit into which he had eagerly plunged, blinded by his weird delights. With determination he took a grip on himself, the filth of the games was rinsed away, and he stopped going to them. Now he persuaded his resisting father to let him resume my classes. The father, yielding, concurred. Alypius took me again as his teacher, only to be smothered in my own heresy. What he loved in the Manichaeans was their pretended chastity, which he thought true and sincere. But that was a deranged and seductive virtue, 'a snare for precious souls' who had not yet sounded the depths of virtue but were misled by surface appearances, the mere mocking images of true virtue.

13. Not ready to abandon the earthly path into which his parents had cajoled him, he preceded me to Rome for the study of the law. There he was bewildered again by the be-

wildering lure of the games. Though he had showed a revulsion to such things, and denounced them, some of his friends
and fellow students, chancing to go from dinner to the open
circus, dragged him along with a joshing compulsion, despite
his strong refusals and resistance, to enter the amphitheater at
the time of its most savage and cruel displays. He protested
that even if they forced his body inside, and held it there, they
could not fix his eyes and attention on what was occurring.
He would be there as if he were not there, and would rise
above them and the show. This made them no less eager to
hurry him inside. In fact, it sharpened their curiosity to see if
he could stick to his determination. When they were inside
and had found what seats they could, everything was a frenzy
of extravagant excess. He shut tight his eyes to seal in his soul
against this evil—if only his ears had been closed as tight. For
when the fight took a dramatic turn, a huge roar from the
crowd crashed over him. Yielding to curiosity—though determined to scorn and reject what he saw, no matter its nature—
he opened his eyes.

The wound given to the gladiator he now wished to see
was nothing to the wound inflicted on his soul. His fall was
sadder than the fighter's, at which the crowd was cheering.
That shout, entering his ears, made his eyes fly open. The
mind thus buffeted and overthrown was more rash than
steady, and all the weaker for reliance on itself rather than
on you. The minute he saw blood, he was sipping animality,
and turned no more away. With eyes glued to the spectacle,
he absentmindedly gulped down frenzies. He took a com-
plicit joy in the fighting, and was drunk with delight at the
cruelty. No longer the person he was when he entered, he
was now entered into the crowd, at one with those who
forced him there. More—he stared, he shouted, he burned,
he took away the madness he had found there and followed it
back again, not only with those who had first drawn him,
but dragging them and others on his own. Yet your strong
and merciful hand drew him away, and taught him to 'set his
reliance on you,' not on himself—but not till long after.

14.   These matters were lodged in his memory for future curing. Another event for future use had taken place back in Carthage, when he was still my student. As he was going over his lessons (as students do) at noon in the forum, you let him be arrested by the forum guards as a thief, an event I am sure you intended to warn him, as a man of later consequence, against leaping to hasty verdicts when he sat in judgment on a man's guilt. For he had simply been walking alone beside the law court, with his tablet and stylus, when a fellow student, the actual thief, carrying a hidden axe, got access to the lead grilles that cover the silversmiths' shops. Alypius had not seen him, but when the man began to hack at the lead, the noise of his axe alerted the silversmiths, who raised a muffled outcry below, and they sent a party to catch anyone they found. Shouts of the approaching party made the thief run off in a panic, leaving his axe lest it be found on him. Alypius, who had not seen him go in, now saw him come out, and watched him immediately run off. Curious to know what this was all about, he went in himself, stood with the axe he found, and tried to make sense of the matter. That is how the party from below found him, all alone and holding the very axe whose noise had brought them there. They arrest him and start leading him away, while they boast to the forum residents that they caught him *in flagrante*. Then he was taken to be indicted before judges.

15. Since this was enough for him to learn his lesson, you affirmed his innocence, 'to which only you could testify.' For just as he was being led toward prison or punishment, a construction official met them, the one in charge of all the public works. The captors were especially happy to meet him, since they had been under suspicion of taking things stolen from the forum. Perhaps now he would see at last who were the guilty parties. But this man had often seen Alypius at the home of a senator whose hospitality he regularly enjoyed. The minute he recognized him, he drew him by the hand away from the crowd, and asked for an explanation of this disgrace. When he heard what had happened, he ordered the disorderly mob, frothing with threats, to follow him. As they approached the home of the young man who had committed the crime, there was a slave before the entry, one so young that he could tell the whole truth without fear of his master. He had in fact been with him in the forum. Alypius remembered this, and told the construction chief. Then he showed the axe to the boy, and asked who was its owner. We are, the boy instantly said. Further questioning revealed everything. The prosecution would proceed against this residence, and the crowd that had been crowing over Alypius was quieted. He went off, this future minister of your word and frequent judge in ecclesiastical court, with lesson learned and wisdom gained.

16.   This was the man I rejoined in Rome. Having formed firm bonds of attachment to me, he went on to Milan with me, not wanting to leave me and also hoping to pursue the law career for which he had been trained, more to suit his parents than himself. Three times he had already sat in as an assistant at court procedures, and was shocked at how men preferred bribes to their own probity. His own innate values had been tested not only by the lure of bribes but by the fear of violence. As assistant he kept records for the court of expenditures for all of Italy. A very powerful senator at that time swayed others with his promises of favor or threats of retaliation. He wanted to extract some favor or other by the usual force of his influence, though it was against the law. Alypius opposed. A bribe was offered. He laughed it off. Threats followed. He brushed them aside. People were astounded at this rare cheekiness, that he neither cultivated as a patron, nor feared as a foe, one famously equipped to advance or destroy careers in a multitude of ways. The very judge Alypius was assisting, though opposed to what the senator was doing, had not the nerve to oppose it openly. He said that Alypius had prevented him from granting it, shifting responsibility to his subordinate. In fact, if the judge had granted it, Alypius would have resigned.

Alypius almost succumbed to temptation on only one count, his passion for books. He could have obtained books copied at an official's rate. But as he weighed the rights involved, he inclined to the better course, preferring a severity that forbade over a laxity that allowed. Small as this matter is, 'a man honest in small things is honest in large ones.' Nothing spoken by your truth will ever be pointless: 'If you have not been honest in dealing with the world's goods, who will trade with you in more precious goods; and if you have cheated others, who will be honest with you?' But I was dealing with a man of integrity, my follower and the intimate of my planning, who considered with me what life we should lead.

V

THE QUANDARY

17. Nebridius, too, had left the area of Carthage and Carthage itself, his regular haunt, had left his ancestral estate, his home, and a mother who did not follow him to Milan, where he came for one reason only—to join with me in a burning pursuit of truth and wisdom. With me he sighed, with me wavered, fierce in the quest for a blessed life and acute in probing all difficulties. We were three hungry mouths, panting in our shared starvation, looking to you for 'sustenance arriving in time.' Our worldly ambitions left a sour taste in our mouth, by your merciful provision. When we tried to understand our bafflement, only darkness answered us, and we gave it up, wondering how much more we would put up with. This was our constant complaint— yet we did not give up our ambitions, since no other prospect shone with better promise if we abandoned them.

18. My own greatest shock came as I rummaged around remembering the long time wasted since my nineteenth year, when first I fell in love with philosophy and planned that, as soon as I mastered it, I should 'put aside all vain desire for the coarser forms of joy, all mindless play with falsehood.' Yet here was I in my thirtieth year, stalled still in the same mire of pleasurable pursuits, which skittered off and scattered me, while I kept telling myself that tomorrow will be different, everything will be clarified and I will be certain—Faustus will appear, a prodigy of learning, and sort it all out! Or, lo, the awesome Skeptics assure us nothing can really be known about the way to live. Or, that just means we should keep looking and never give up! Or, a new development, what seemed absurd in Scripture really is not, but can be given logical exposition! Or, it is enough to plod along in the path where my parents put me as a child, until truth turns up! But where will it turn up? When will I have time to turn it up? Ambrose is busy. Reading is slow. What books do we need? Where and when shall we find them? Who will supply them? Time is committed, hours are set aside for restoring one's energy.

New hopes arise. What we thought was Catholic teaching, was not. Our attacks on it were wasted, and educated Catholics abominate the idea that God is crammed into a human shape. Why do we linger, not knocking where things will open to us? Of course, pupils keep us busy in the morning, but what do we do with the rest of the day? Is that the time for our quest? But then how can we cultivate our patrons, from whom we hope for advancement? When can we prepare the lessons our students are paying for? When can we recruit our strength by an escape from the strain of business?

19.   To hell with this! Enough of these empty mad things! Only the quest for truth matters now. Life is misery, death unpredictable—it could sneak up in a moment, and how would we go off? Where can we learn things neglected here? Is there no price to pay for neglecting them? But what can be punished or learned if death cuts off thought by ending it? That, too, must be considered—but be it not so! Surely it is not an empty thing, a hoax, that the Christian faith is acknowledged throughout the world as the supreme authority. Why would so many and so wonderful things have been arranged for us if the body's death also blotted out the mind? Then what holds us back from leaving all earthly aspirations behind, to concentrate entirely on finding God and happiness?

But hold off a moment—worldly things, too, give pleasure, they have their own not inconsiderable sweetness. It is no light thing to toss all that aside—and it would be embarrassing to have to return to it. What a great thing is advancement to honorable office—who could ask for anything higher? It provides a circle of great patrons. If we give all our effort solely to this pursuit, a minor governorship at least should be attainable. Marriage to a woman of some wealth would be necessary, to provide expenses. That could be the extent of my ambition. Many men of eminence, models worth imitating, have combined philosophy with marriage.

VI

MARRIAGE

20. Such were the things I told myself, while such winds tossed my heart this-way-that-way and time went by. I kept putting off a turn to the Lord. Day after day I 'shunned a life in you,' while daily I refused to shun the death in me. I was in love with a happy life, but feared to go where I could find it. I sought it by fleeing it. I felt I would be wretched if deprived of a woman's embrace. You have a merciful medicine for such weakness, but I did not consider that—it was outside my experience. I thought chastity was a matter of one's own efforts, and knew I was incapable of it. I was such a fool that I had not even heard what Scripture tells us, that 'no one can be chaste without your gift,' a gift you would have imparted if 'with inner moaning' I had knocked at your hearing and 'thrown my cares' with resolute belief on you.

21. Alypius proved an obstacle to my marrying, with his regular refrain—that if I married we would not have the quiet life of total concentration on philosophy that we had long desired. Where sex was concerned, he was entirely chaste, wondrously so, considering that he had experimented with it when first he reached pubescence, but had not gone further. His disgust for it had grown, making him entirely renounce it and live thereafter entirely abstinent. I argued against him, citing cases of married men devoted to philosophy, who won God's favor without giving up friends. Not that I could be compared to such noble sorts, tied as I was to my own flesh's sickness, to its sweet deadliness. I dragged my own chains around with me, and feared any loosening of them. His words to advise me were like a hand fumbling at my chains—I struck it away as if a wound already bumped were being touched. Moreover the devil addressed Alypius using my tongue, trammeling, spreading delightful snares along his path, to trip up his forthright and free stride.

22.   Alypius thought so much of me that he did not understand how I could be so stuck in the mire of this pleasure as to say, in our frequent discussions of the matter, that I could not possibly lead a chaste life. When I saw how this puzzled him, I said in my defense that there was a great difference between us—his had been a hasty and furtive experience, barely remembered now and dismissed with an easy contempt, while my delights were of long habit, and if only the justifying name of marriage were added to them, he would have no reason to wonder at my not being able to give them up. He was now being drawn to take a sexual partner himself, not for pleasure's sake but for a transgressive knowledge—he said he wanted to see for himself why my life, which he generally admired, I would consider no life at all, but mere torture, if deprived of that pleasure. His very freedom from my bondage made that bondage mysterious to him, and lured him to sample the mystery. From that he might have fallen into the very bondage that had mystified him, for he was ready to make 'a contract with death,' and 'he who courts danger will have it.'

Neither of us was more than slightly aware of what gives marriage its dignity, the discipline of shared life and the bringing up of children. I was mainly held captive and tortured by the need to keep satisfying a customary appetite, while mere puzzlement was drawing him into captivity. That was our condition until you, Lord most high, who did not forsake our clay, should have mercy on us and succor us in your miraculously hidden manner.

23.   I was being urged by others into marriage. I had already made my suit and been accepted, largely through my mother's doing. She hoped that once married I would be cleansed in the saving waters of baptism. She was happy to see me more and more inclined to this, and thought that all her prayers and your promises would be fulfilled when I believed. At my request, and from her own impulse, she asked with a great inner cry that you would send her a vision of my future life in marriage. But you refused. All that appeared to her were the kinds of dreams, airy and delusive, that answer the human spirit when it is trying too hard. She recounted them to me, but made light of them, not exhibiting the trust that was normal when you revealed something to her. She used to say that she could tell the difference between your revelations and her own mere dreams by a certain odor indescribable in words. But the pressure was maintained, the girl was chosen, she pleased me, though she was two years below nubile age, and I was waiting for her.

24.   Many of my friends and I had been deeply mulling over a scheme, the subject of many of our discussions, for escaping with scorn from human life's onerous churnings. We had all but decided to withdraw from the mass of men and live a life of philosophical detachment. The detachment would be structured thus: we would pool all our belongings, creating a single household fund, so that in open fellowship no one would own this or that, but from the contributions of each there would be common property, the whole of it for each, and all of it shared by all of us. It seemed to us that ten or so people could live in such a community. Some of us were quite wealthy, above all Romanian from our hometown, whom serious financial difficulties had brought to court at the time. He was a close friend from my earliest years, and he was especially enthusiastic for this project, swaying others in discussion of it since his financial means far outstripped everyone else's.

We voted that two of our number, appointed for one-year terms like magistrates, should care for the community's management, leaving the others free of such concerns. But then we had to consider whether helpmates would consent to join the community, since some already had wives and others of us were planning to take them. This consideration made the whole carefully constructed scheme fall apart in our hands, utterly ruined and abandoned. There was nothing left but our old sighs and moans and travel farther on the worn broad ways of the world. 'Many are the thoughts in our hearts, but your design persists through eternity.' It was that design that made you laugh at our plans and prepare for us your own, 'with sustenance arriving in time' as you 'open your hand to fill our souls with your blessings.'

25. Through all this my sins were increasing. Since she was an obstacle to my marriage, the woman I had lived with for so long was torn out of my side. My heart, to which she had been grafted, was lacerated, wounded, shedding blood. She returned to Africa, with vows to you that she would know no other man. My natural son by her remained with me. To my sorrow that I could not equal this woman's resolve, I chafed at having to wait two years for the woman I was pledged to. Since I was not so much eager for marriage as enslaved by lust, I took another woman, not as a wife (of course), but that my soul-sickness should be maintained and prolonged, in the same or an advanced condition, ushering me under the protection of habit toward the state of matrimony. But this was no cure for the wound of losing the one cut away from me. Its inflammation and pain gave way to putrefaction, with a duller incurable ache.

26. Praise to you, glory to you, font of mercies—as I lamented wretchedly, you were coming nearer. Your right hand had almost reached me, 'to snatch me from the slime' and rinse me clean, though I did not suspect it. I would have been swirled even deeper into the maelstrom of carnal delight but for the fear of death and of your future judgment, which through all my shifts of opinion had never been entirely obliterated in my breast. I was at this time debating with Alypius and Nebridius the fate of the good and the evil. In my mind, I would have awarded the victory to Epicurus did I not believe that the soul lives on after death, to account for its acts—which Epicurus denied. If we could live forever, I asked, without interruption of sensual pleasures, and without even the fear of losing them, is that not all a man could ask in the way of happiness? I did not realize that it was the greatest misery to be so sunk, so blinded, as not to see the glow in uprightness, or in the free embrace of a beauty not seen by the physical eye. This required an inward seeing.

I did not consider the warm pulse flowing through this band of friends as we aired so sweetly such foul ideas. I did not consider that I could not be happy without these friends, even according to the concept of happiness I held then, no matter how many carnal indulgences swept over me. I loved my friends unselfishly and felt loved by them in the same way. How these paths twist about! Sad the lot of one rash enough to expect to find something better when he turns away from you. Let him turn and toss, on his back, on his side, on his belly, it is uncomfortable every way, and no rest to be found but in you. And you are at hand, you free us from our wretched errors and lead us out onto your path, you console, you bid us run to you, 'I will bear you up,' lead you home, and support you there.

BOOK SEVEN

NEOPLATONISM

I

MATERIALISM

1. Now that my youth lay buried, bad and unspeakable, I had arrived at young manhood, the older in years, the deeper in futility. I could not express a notion of any substance that would not be visible to the eye—not that I thought you could be expressed in the form of a human body. From the time when I began to have some grasp on wisdom, I continually shunned that view, and was glad to learn that the spiritual faith of our mother, the Catholic church, shunned it too. But I had no other way of expressing reality—I, as a mere man, and the kind of man I was, trying to find an expression for you, the high and 'sole and true God.' I believed 'in my bones' that you were a being not subject to decay, to harm, to change. Even though I did not know your origin or mode of being, it seemed plain to me—I held to it—that a thing capable of decay was inferior to the undecaying, and what could not be harmed I placed at once above what could be. 'My heart cried out in protest' against all my former materialist conceptions. I tried at one stroke to expel from my mind's view all flitting throngs of such unfitting things. But hardly had I brushed them away when, 'in the blink of an eye,' they were back, the whole crowd of them, assailing my vision, clouding it over.

I was compelled to express you, not indeed in the shape of a human person, but at least as something material located in space, either diffused throughout the world, or extended infinitely outside it. As a thing not capable of decaying or being harmed or undergoing change, I placed it above things that decay and are harmed or changed; yet it could not exist at all, I thought, except in some location. Outside it, it would be pure nothing—not simply a vacuum, such as occurs when a body is removed, leaving behind it a void unoccupied by any physical thing, of earth or air or water or fire. A place with nothing in it is still a place.

2. My 'heart was hardened.' I could not even keep myself visible to myself. I thought nothing could exist unless it were located in space, whether spread out or contracting, swelling or doing something else there. As my eyes traveled over the surface of things, my mind traveled over its images. It did not occur to me that this act of intellect, in forming such internal images, had no spatial being, though only a great power could form them. Yet even you, the life of my life, I gave expression to as a spatially immense reality pervasive through all the world's fabric and boundless through all the spaces in all directions beyond the world, so that you were in earth and sky and everything, and all kept their own limits within you, who have no limits at all. The physical air, the sky above the earth, does not block the sunlight from pervading it, passing through it without breaking into it or splitting it apart, just filling the entire sky. That is how I thought that you pervade not only the heavens and air and sea but the earth itself, all of whose parts, the largest and smallest, were penetrable by you, absorbent of your presence, so that by a hidden afflatus you directed from within and from without all things you have created.

This was my hypothesis, since I could find no better expression of you. But I was wrong. In that view of things, a greater portion of the earth would hold a greater portion of you, and a lesser a lesser, and if all things were full of you, an elephant would contain more of you than a sparrow, since it is larger and would provide a larger receptacle for you. You would be distributed in fragments throughout the world, bigger bits of you in bigger parts of it, smaller bits in smaller. That is not the case, but you had not yet 'pierced my darkness with your light.'

3. As for those deceived deceivers, who say nothing at great length because your truth is not speaking through

them, I was satisfied, Lord, with the refutation of them Nebridius had already made when we were back in Carthage,
confounding the rest of us. What, he asked, could the supposed forces of darkness, arrayed against you on the other
side, have done to you if you simply refused to fight? If it is
claimed that they would inflict some damage on you, then
you must be capable of being harmed and of decay. But if
they could not damage you, there was no reason for you to
fight them. Yet they imagine a fight in which some portion of
you, some limb, or some offspring from your substance, is
mixed with the adversary power not created by you, and to
that extent made capable of change or decay, devolving
down from bliss to misery, and needing assistance to be freed
and cleansed. This, they say, is the plight of the soul, which
your word is to assist, as something free coming to the rescue
of something enslaved, as something pure to the impure, and
whole to the fragmentary. But your word would be no more
beyond decay than what it was rescuing, since they both
come from the same substance!

So if they say that you, whatever your nature—whatever,
that is, can properly be said of you—are incapable of decay,
then everything that follows in their account is false and
shameful. If on the contrary they say you are capable of decay, that is false and on the face of it disgraceful. This argument should have been enough to make me retch them out as
something revolting to my system, since they could not
counter it without a frightful blasphemy, either of the heart
or of the lips, by which they could think or say such things
of you.

II
EVIL

4. Though I could now say and firmly believe that you are the true God, beyond taint, alteration, or change in any of your aspects, the creator not only of our souls but our bodies too, and of the entirety of each, I still had no way of unraveling and sorting out the reason for evil. Whatever that should turn out to be, I knew that it should be explained without my being forced to admit that the changeless God can change, lest I end up seeking to explain evil evilly. On this ground I could safely pursue this enquiry, certain that they were wrong whom I was now doggedly resisting, since in my own enquiry into the reason for evil I saw that they were 'filled with evil intent,' since they were readier to think that you could suffer wrong than that they could do wrong.

5. I bent my mind to understand what I had been told, that the reason for evil lay in the freedom of the will, that we could make evil choices and 'just would be your sentence' in punishing us, but I could not see clearly what this meant. I worked my mental vision up out of the depths, but was soon engulfed again. After each effort, I was again and again engulfed. What helped lift me up toward your light was a consciousness of myself in the act of choosing, as certain to me as the act of living. When I chose to do or not do something, I was sure that no one else was doing the choosing, and I came to a clearer and clearer realization that any sin I committed was my own act. But sometimes, I could see, I acted without choosing, more acted upon than acting, and this (I concluded) was not a sinful act but the punishment of sin, and I promptly expressed the conviction that this was the work of your justice responding to my injustice.

But this raised a further point. Who, after all, made me? Was it not my God, not only greatly good but goodness itself? Then why would he give me the power to choose evil as well as good? Was it so that his justice could be vindicated in punishing me? Who gave me this power, who sowed in me this 'seed so sour,' when sweet was God's making of me, all of me? If a devil is the instigator, where does the devil come from? If he was changed from an angel into the devil by a perverse will, where did this bad will of his come from when the angel in his entirety was made by the good God? These expressions of the matter sank me again into the suffocating mire, but I was not sucked so deep 'into that pit of error that I could not testify to you,' or would believe that you suffer evil rather than that men do evil.

6. I now made a great effort to find corollaries to my first conclusion, that the non-decaying is superior to the decaying, from which I testified that your nature, whatever it is, cannot decay. Nor is any mind, in the past or in the future, able to express something better than you, who are the highest and best good, since it is a sound and unshakeable truth that the non-decaying is higher than the decaying (as I had already concluded). I could have expressed something better than you if you could decay. And since I could see that the non-decaying is superior to the decaying, that is the point from which I should have pursued my enquiry, reasoning out from there the source of evil—that it is the source, outside you, of that decay that could not affect you. No principle of decay can taint our God, by deliberate act, by necessity, or by random occurrence—for as God he wills his own good and is that good. But decay is not itself good. Nor can you be compelled in any way, since what you want to do does not exceed what you have the power to do. If it did, you would be something exceeding yourself. But wanting to do and doing are, identically, what God is. What could spring up unexpected before you, who know all things? Nothing exists but by your knowing it. So why waste words explaining that God is non-decaying when, if that were not true, he were not God?

7.   So I was enquiring after evil and evilly doing it, and could not see the evil in my method. I 'called up before my mind' the whole range of creation, whatever is obvious in it to our senses—earth and sea and air and stars and trees and animals—and whatever is not taken in by our senses—the high spiritual canopy and all angels and all spiritual entities. But even the latter, like the former, I imagined as occupying some kind of place. I made out the whole of creation as one vast physical stuff, articulated into different sorts of material bodies—the real bodies or those I imagined as the spiritual realities. I made it out as vast, without giving it any specific magnitude (which I could not measure) but, be it ever so large, reaching a certain limit in any of its extensions. And you, Lord, I saw as embracing and pervading all parts of this mass, but stretching far outside it on all sides—as if there were a sea everywhere, and everywhere only this boundless sea throughout the endless reaches, and in the sea a huge but not infinite sponge, totally soaked with that sea in every particle of it. So I thought of your finite creation soaked in your own infinity, and I said: This, behold, is God, and this is his creation—benevolent, this God, and strongly, incomparably, prevailing; but good and making things good, surrounding—behold—and pervading all things.

Where in all this is evil to be found? How did it insinuate itself? 'What is its root,' what its seed? Or does it not exist? Then why do we fear and shun the non-existent? Even if it offers a phantom threat, the threat itself is an evil, by which the unthreatened heart is put on alert and put on the rack—the falser its terror, the more obvious is the evil of fearing what is not there to be feared. Do we fear a real evil, or is the fearing itself the evil? How can this occur, when 'God created all these good things' out of his own goodness? Even if the highest goodness made lower goods, everything involved is good, the maker and the things made. Then where is there room for evil? Is the matter from which he made things somehow evil, to which he gave form and rank but left some residue of it unchanged into good? How can this be? Was he so weak, he the all-powerful, that he had to leave some trace of evil behind when he shaped and transformed matter? If that were the case, why would he want to make things at all, instead of using all his power to prevent them?

Could matter have come to be against his wish? If it was eternal, why did God let it lie around for vast stretches of prior time and only much later decide to form something out of it? Or if he decided on the spur of the moment to do something with it, why did he not use all his powers to make it go away, so he alone would remain, entirely and truly the supreme and infinite good? Grant that it is not fitting for a good God to initiate and to shape anything that is not good, then why did he not cancel and erase all the bad matter, and begin with good matter for his shaping? He is not all-powerful if he cannot begin making something good without the help of matter not of his own making.

These things I was thrashing out in my mind, raddled as it was with a fear of dying before the explanation could be found. Yet I stubbornly held to belief in Christ, our Lord and rescuer, as that is sanctioned within the Catholic church. My faith was fuzzy still, was hazy about the standards of belief, yet my mind would not give it up—daily, in greater and greater degree, I was drinking it in.

III

ASTROLOGY

8. The scientific nonsense of the astrologers, their aberrant mental veerings, I had already renounced—let your many 'acts of pity to me testify' to that, from 'the inmost fibers of my being,' my God. It was your work alone. Who else can call us back from the death that every error inflicts but your life that cannot die, your light for minds that lack wisdom? Your wisdom never lacks the light to tend our world, right down to the least leaf trembling on a tree. It was your work to cope with my obduracy, my obstinate resistance to Vindicius, that wise old man, and to Nebridius, the brilliant young man, who both assured me—the former stoutly, the latter somewhat tentatively but very often—that there is not a way to predict the future, though human hunches often have the luck of the draw. If men say enough, some of what they say will happen, not because they foreknew it—they just chanced on it by not keeping silent.

You coped with my problem by sending me a friend. He was ready enough to consult astrologers, though he had not read deeply in their books—he was just, as I say, experimenting in transgressive knowledge, partly on the basis of what his father had told him about it (without his realizing how far what his father said went in undermining his view of the matter). Firminus was this friend's name, of good education and sound rhetorical training. As a close friend, he asked me for advice on some matters that had inflated his ambition for worldly success—what did I think of his astrological reading (as they call it). Though I had begun to incline toward Nebridius' doubts on this subject, I did not refuse to hazard a guess on his charts, offered in a dubious way, while I added that I had almost reached the view that this was a silly and useless exercise. That is when he told me what he had learned from his father, who had immersed himself in the volumes of transgressive knowledge, along with a friend of his, an equal adept of the school. With joint enthusiasm they collaborated in kindling each other's minds to this absurdity, so much indeed that if one of their domestic animals was pregnant, they timed the births and coordinated them with the planets' positions, as experiments in their putative science.

Firminus had learned from his father that when his mother was pregnant with him, the slave girl of his friend was also about to give birth—a fact that could not have been overlooked by a man who recorded with minutest precision even his dogs' whelpings. So one man watched his wife, the other his slave, and they kept exact account of the days and hours and minutes until both births took place simultaneously, and they had to make out the same reading of the charts, down to the same minute, for the freeborn infant and the slave. This could be done because the men had alerted each other, when delivery neared for the women, to events as they were progressing at either's home, and they prepared couriers to communicate, at the minute of its happening, that a birth had occurred, and to whom. Each set up his own end of this system for instantaneous transmission of the news, and those announcing the births met each other equidistantly from either house, so that neither man could distinguish one birth from the other by any slightest lapse of time or change in the position of the stars. Yet Firminus, from a family of high position, traveled the bright path of success, wealth growing as he went, one honor topping another, while the slave, never escaping his harsh yoke, toiled on for his owners, as Firminus confirmed for me from his own knowledge.

9. As soon as I heard this story—and I could not doubt it, seeing who told it—all my obduracy melted. I made it my first task to lure Firminus away from such transgressive knowledge. I told him that if I made a reading of his charts, the only way for it to be true would be for me to find there his parents' prominence in their own circle, their standing in a respected city, his prized education and advancement in the arts and sciences. And if I consulted the slave boy's charts, which were identical with his, I could be equally true only if I found there a family scorned, a state of slavery, and other factors far different from, and inconsistent with, his own. So, looking at identical charts, I could be true to the facts only if I found different results in them, while finding the same results would make me false to the facts. It was a certain conclusion, then, that anything that turns out true in such charts does so not by accurate knowledge but by a deceptively happy accident, and anything that turns out false does so not as a result of inaccurate reading but by a deceptively sad accident.

10. Given this opening, I pursued the matter further. One of those who peddle that nonsense for money might, if I tried to use this tale to undermine them with ridicule, respond that the story itself was just made up by Firminus, or else by his father. So I switched my approach to the subject of twins born at the same time. Normally one of these follows so closely on the other's emergence from the womb that only an inconsiderable time intervenes. Some will say that this interval makes all the difference in the nature of things. Yet it is impossible to register this with the necessary precision for it to be correlated with any difference in the position of the stars, at least one sufficient to let an astrologer make up different charts.

That a true reading cannot be reached this way is clear from the example of Jacob and Esau. One reading their charts would find them identical, though their later lives were not, so any reading would be false unless working from identical charts it gave non-identical results, and any truth hit on would be by accident, not by scientific accuracy. You, Lord, who guide the universe with justice, deal with the people who ask and give predictions this way—if one receives an appropriate answer, it is not because he or those responding to him know anything, but because of a 'judgment from your abyss' on the petitioner's 'unknown spiritual state.' So 'let no one ask what is happening, or why it should occur.' That is not for his asking, not for any asking by mere man.

11. Freed of these chains by 'you, who come to my assistance,' I turned back to the problem of evil. Though I found no solution for it, you did not let the tide of my inner expressions sweep me away from a belief that you exist, and you do so without change in your reality, which is the source of man's relief and your judgment in Christ, your son and our Lord. I now believed as well that your sacred books, sanctioned by your Catholic church, open the path to human safety in a life to come after our death. With these beliefs firm and unshakably buttressed in my mind, I was still thrashing out the problem of evil. In the strain of trying to give birth to a solution, how I moaned, my God, and your ears were attentive to each moan without my sensing it. While I was making my strenuous effort in silence, great outcries for your pity were made by the unvoiced repentances of my soul. You knew what was going on within me. No human did. My lips could disseminate little of it to even my closest friends. How could I find the time or the eloquence to report all the ravages of my soul?

Yet all of it was heard by you, 'the deep moans issuing from my heart, my yearning laid before you, my eyes without light to see.' The light was within me, but I was outside myself. This light had no physical place, and I was looking for a physical space to give me surcease. There was no such place where I could tell myself that it satisfied, that here all would be well—no place, even, that could send me on to a place where all would be well with me. I was a higher creature than any physical place, though a lower thing than you, and my joy is to be subordinate to you while subordinating to me the creatures lower than I am. That is the true balance, my middle state of rescue, where I live 'to your pattern,' making my body serve me while I serve you.

But when my own haughtiness lifted me up and I attacked you 'in the strong pride of my shield,' the things lower in creation moved above me, pressing me down, cramping me, suffocating. Before my eyes they attacked me in throngs, in thick droves. Before my mind even the mental images of physical things blocked my access to you, as if to ask where I, a negligible vile thing, thought I was going. My wound bred such things, since 'you have struck down the proud with a blow.' Pride bloated you out of my view, as a swollen face closes the eyes.

12. 'You, Lord, are everlasting' but 'your wrath lasts not forever.' You have pity on 'poor earth and ashes.' It was your will to untwist my distortions. With internal prods you were goading me, roiling me to win a clear sight of you. You reduced my swelling with the secret medications of your hand, as daily you brought back health to my inflamed and clouded eyes, cured me with the biting ointments of a healing sorrow.

IV

BOOKS OF THE PLATONISTS

13. As a preliminary way of showing me how 'the proud you rebuff, while favoring the lowly,' and how great is the pity you show to humans on the lowly Path of your 'Word made flesh in order to live with men,' you brought to me a man, himself inflated with raging winds of pride, to acquaint me with certain books of the Platonists, translated into Latin from the Greek. What I found in reading them, not precisely in these words, but saying the same thing in varied and very convincing ways, was this: 'At the origin was the Word, and the Word was in God's presence, and the Word was God. This was at the origin with God, and all things were made through it, and nothing was made without it. In it, life was made, and the life was men's light, and the light shone in the darkness, and darkness could not control it.' Further, that the human soul, however it may bear testimony to the light, is not itself the light. God's word is 'the true light that gives light to every man who arrives in this world.' Further, that 'he was in this world, and the world was made by him, and the world did not recognize him.'

But this I did not read there: 'He came among his own, and his own did not accept him, but to all who accepted him, who believed in his title, he gave the right to become God's sons.'

14. I did read there that the Word, God, 'is not born from flesh, or blood, or human desire, or of fleshly desire, but from God.'

But I did not read there: 'The word became flesh, to live with us.'

I did tease out from various expressions and modes of thought in those books that the Son, since 'he had the form of the Father, considered it no usurpation to be held God's equal,' since he was by nature his equal.

But those books do not contain: 'He emptied himself out into the nature of a slave, becoming like to man. And in man's shape he lowered himself, so obedient as to die, by a death on the cross. For this God has exalted him, favored his title over all other titles, that to the title of Jesus all knees shall bend, above the earth, upon the earth, and below the earth, and the lips of everyone shall testify that Jesus is Lord in the glory of the Father.'

They say: Your Son is before all time and above all time unchangeably present in eternity with you, and the bliss of all souls 'is derived from his overflow,' and the wise remain wise only in the wisdom that 'makes new by remaining itself.'

But those books do not say: 'At the time set he died for sinners,' or 'you spared not your Only-Begotten, but for all our sake offered him up,' or 'you have hidden this from the learned and revealed it to the simple, that they may come to him wearied from toil and he will restore them, because his heart is gentle and lowly,' or 'he guides the meek who are under judgment and opens new paths for the gentle,' when he 'sees how lowly and toil-worn we are and forgives all our sins.' Those who stride about in the high boots of esoteric teaching are too airborne to hear, 'Learn from me because my heart is meek and lowly, and you will find your souls' surcease.' Even when knowing God, they do not give him honor as God and thank him. 'Enclosed in what they express to themselves, their hearts have dimmed out. Claiming wisdom proves their folly.'

15. It was in those books, too, I read of your 'glory beyond change' by any decay attributed to idols and the simulacra of man's decaying form, or a bird's, a beast's, a serpent's—the very Egyptian pottage for which Esau forfeited his inheritance. Your primal people there adored in your place the head of an animal, 'giving their hearts over to Egypt' and subjecting their souls, your own image, to a calf's image, to a thing that eats hay—which was more sustenance than I could draw from those books. It was your decision, Lord, to 'remove from Isaac the slight of being the second-born,' so that 'the first-born, Esau, should serve him,' and you called the Gentiles yours as his progeny. Since I come to you as a Gentile, I studied the gold plunder your people took from Egypt according to your will. It was, whatever its source, your gold. And my plunder, the Neoplatonist books, was from Athens, where your Apostle told them, 'In you we live and move and take our being,' as some of them were able to acknowledge. So I was not interested in Egypt for its idols, which they made of gold properly yours when 'they melted truth into a lie, to worship as a creator what was a creature.'

16. The books of the Platonists did provoke in me a return into myself. You guiding, I entered my own recesses, though only you, helping me, made that possible. Entered there, I could see, so far as I could see anything with my poor soul's vision, something beyond my soul's vision, and beyond my mind, an always-unfailing light—not the light common to all our physical vision, nor simply like that but on a grander scale, as if it just got brighter and brighter, till nothing else could be seen. Nothing of that sort was it. No, of some other, some far different sort it was—not a thing layered above my mind, as oil floats above water, or heaven above earth, but something higher than I am because it made me, who am lower because made by it. To know truth is to know this light, and to know this light is to know eternity. It is the light love knows.

This is my God—eternal truth, and true love, and loved eternity, toward whom I aspire night and day. In my early stage of knowing you, you lifted me far enough to see there is something to be seen, but also to know I was not capable of seeing it. Your brilliance, striking my gaze, blinded its feebleness, and I shivered between affection and apprehension. I realized how far away I was, still, in the land of shadows. Yet 'from your far height I heard your call,' telling me you are the food of heroes, that when I grow I shall be nourished from you, not ingesting you as I do physical food, but being absorbed by you. I saw now how 'you educate man away from sin,' shriveling my soul 'as a spiderweb shrinks at a touch.' For I said within myself that truth cannot be non-existent just because it is not extended across space, whether finite or infinite! 'I am existence itself,' you responded from afar, but I heard it as a thing spoken inside my heart. I could no longer doubt truth's existence, known from what is created, any more than I could doubt that I was alive.

17.   All things that are less than you I ran through in my mind, as things that neither fail nor succeed in existing. They succeed insofar as you made them exist, they fail insofar as they do not exist as you exist. Only entire existence truly lasts forever. So 'my only good is to hold close to my God.' If I do not abide in him, I am powerless in myself. He, 'remaining in himself, makes all things new,' and 'you are my Lord, above all need for anything good from me.'

18.   Things that decay are good, I was assured. The highest good cannot decay at all, but other things cannot decay *unless* they are good. The highest good cannot decay because it cannot change. But if other things were not good, there would be nothing that could decay in them. Decay damages, and there can be no damage where there is no good to be lost. Since it is impossible to say that decay does not damage, it is certain that damage causes the loss of some good. A complete loss of good would be a loss of existence itself. If things were to continue in existence after that loss, they would be better for the loss, since they had proved beyond decay. But what could be more weird than to say that a total loss of good improves a thing? Loss of all good must therefore include loss of existence. Whatever stays in existence is, to that extent at least, good.

So the evil I was trying to explain was not itself a positive existent, which would as such be good, not evil. It would be a great good if it were beyond decay. But even if it were subject to decay, it would still be good in its measure. I saw now, and was assured of it, that 'all you made is good,' and there is nothing in nature that you did not make. Though

you did not make them all equally good, each is good insofar as it is made, and the entirety of them all is good, since
God made them all 'good eminently.'

19. There is not only no evil in you, there is no evil in
anything you made. There is no agent apart from you to
break into and break up the scheme of things you have
arranged. Some things, because they do not fit with others,
are thought to be evil, though they are good where they do
fit, and good in themselves. And those things that do not fit
with each other are all fitted into the lower part of creation
which we call earth. They fit under a fitting sky of wind and
cloud. I am far from saying that anything that exists should
not do so. Taken individually, I might prefer something different about them. But in the present argument I acknowledge the duty to praise each item individually. On earth,
everything shows that you should be praised—even 'monsters and abysses, as well as fire, hail, snow, sleet, hurricane.
All act on your command, as do mountains and every hill,
trees with their fruit, every cedar, wild animals and all cattle,
serpents, and flying things.' Let 'earth's rulers acknowledge
your title, with all peoples, princes and earthly judges, boys
and virgins, the elderly, the young.' And 'in heaven, let all
your creatures praise you, praise you on high,' our God—
'your angels, your hosts, sun and moon, all stars and every
light, heaven's heaven and the waters above heaven.' When I
look on all things taken together, I no longer wish that individual things were better. Obviously some things are better
than others, but the totality is better than would better
things be outside that totality.

20. 'There is no soundness' in the person who disapproves of anything you made—as I once disapproved of
many of them. Since I was not foolhardy enough to disapprove of God in my mind, I rejected the idea that what I disapproved of was yours. That is how my acceptance of two
substances arose. This, however, did not satisfy my mind,
which was voicing extravagant consequences. Recoiling
from those, I fashioned for myself a God diffused through
the infinite reaches of all physical space, and then lodged

that God in my heart, making of it a little 'temple of my idol-atry,' offensive to you. But after that you cooled my fever without my realizing it, you 'shut my eyes off from seeing empty things.' I gave up a bit on myself, my nonsense was lulled, and I woke up to you, and saw a new kind of infinity in you, one not connected with matter in any way.

21.   I looked around and saw that everything but you comes from you and is contained in you, not spatially, but as you hold everything in your hand, which is your truth. All things are true insofar as they exist, nor is there any false-hood but in what is thought to exist though it does not. I saw as well that all things fit in their place, and even in their time, and that you, who alone are everlasting, did not begin to create after vast stretches of time had passed, since times that have been and will be neither depart nor approach but as you ac-tivate them out of your eternity.

22.   Why should it be surprising, I now realized, that a food tasty to the healthy palate should be obnoxious to the sick? Or that a light soothing to the clear-sighted should hurt the diseased eye? Reprobates do not find your justice agree-able, but they also disapprove of snakes and worms, which you created good in themselves and fitted to the lower re-gions of your universe—just as the reprobates are fitted to such lower regions by the measure of their departure from you, though they can be fitted to the higher regions if they approach nearer to you. I had looked for evil and found that it was not a reality in itself but the twisting motion of a man who turns away from the highest reality—that is, from you—by 'emptying himself inwardly' and bloating himself outwardly.

23.   To my amazement, I could not maintain the love I genuinely felt for you (and not for some vain simulacrum of you), since I was alternately raised up to you by your beauty and rushed down from you by my weight. I moaned as I hit bottom. My weight was fleshly habit. But I still remembered you. I knew clearly whom I should hold fast to, but I was not yet one who *could* hold fast. 'The decaying body clogs the soul, the habitation of clay muddying the mind's many

thoughts.' I knew above all that 'your invisible attributes—
your everlasting power and godhead—can, from the creation
of the world, be known by inspection of the things you
made.' I asked, accordingly, on what grounds I judged the
physical beauty of things, in the heavens or on earth, what
norms were at hand for sure judgment as I pronounced that
this mutable thing was right, that thing wrong. Asking myself, as I decided, on what grounds I was deciding, I found
above my own mutable mind your immutable and true eternity of truth.

By gradual ascent, I moved up from bodies to the soul that
is aware of its body, and from that to the active principle in
the soul to which the senses' messages about the external
world are reported, which is an activity that even beasts
share. But I moved on beyond that to the power of reason
that evaluates the things reported to it by the body's senses.
My reason, while recognizing its own mutability, concentrated on its own activity, abstracting its expression from old
patterns, freeing itself from the blur of contradictory impres-
sions, to trace the ripple of light by which it promptly acknowledged that the immutable is above the mutable, and
that reason knows the immutable (how otherwise was it preferred to the mutable?)—and here reason, for one flicker of
an eye, reached the Is. I was seeing 'your invisible nature
through an understanding of what had been made.' But I
could not keep my gaze from wavering. My frailty recoiled
and I was plunged back into the everyday, retaining no more
than a loved memory, as I had caught the fragrance of a feast
I could not consume.

24. I sought a path toward acquiring the strength
needed to rejoice in you steadily, but no path could open to
me until I acknowledged the mediator between God and
men, the man Christ Jesus, the God blessed above all things
forever, who was calling, saying, 'I am life, and truth, and
path.' The food I was too weak to consume he mediated to
me through his flesh, since 'the Word was made flesh,' so our
infancy could take from you the milk of wisdom, in which
you created everything. I was not yet lowly enough to hold

the lowly Jesus, my God, nor to see what his vulnerability was meant to teach me. On high, higher than the heights of what you made, your Word, the eternal truth, lifts those humbled toward him to himself. But here below he built himself a lowly casement of our clay, so he could detach from themselves those to be humbled and draw them over to him, reducing their swollen state and coaxing love from them. He brings down reliance on themselves, makes them weak as they look directly at the divine weakness, wearing the same 'leather skin' we do. They collapse helpless into the weak arms where power now surges to lift them on high.

25.   But the only notion I had of Christ my Lord, my only conception at that point, was of a man wise beyond all others. I took special note of his miraculous birth from a virgin as a pattern for dismissing temporal pleasures in order to gain immortality. This divine concern for us gave special force to his teaching. But the mystery of the Word made flesh was still beyond my wildest guess. I knew only what I had read in Scripture—that he ate and drank, slept, walked about, was gladded, was saddened, and talked with others, and that his flesh could not have been united with your Word without a soul and a human mind. Everyone knows this who knows the immutability of your Word, and I, in my limited way, knew this and did not doubt it. To move one's limbs at will, or keep them still, sometimes to feel an emotion, sometimes not, to speak intelligible words or remain silent, all these are actions of the soul with a human mind. If what was written about these things were not true, then perhaps nothing might be true there, and Scripture held no promise of a rescue for mankind through faith.

But those things are true, and I recognized in Christ an entire human being, not simply a human body, or a body and soul without mind. But I saw in him only a man, not the walking truth, but a man above all others because of some higher quality in his manhood and a deeper entry into wisdom. Alypius, by contrast, thought Catholics believed that God took on flesh, but that is all there was in Christ, Godhead and flesh. He thought they did not teach that he had a soul with a human mind. Since he was sure that the things reported of Christ could not have been done but by a soul with reason, his advance toward the Christian faith was more lingering than mine. But when he learned that this was a heretical view taught by the Apollinarians, he came into a glad conformity with the Christian faith. For my part, I learned only later to distinguish Catholic orthodoxy from Photinian heresy in understanding how 'the Word was made flesh.' It is by the refutation of heretics that the church's meanings are identified, and sound teaching clarified. 'Divisions must occur to mark out those tested' from the weak.

26. The books of the Platonists that I had read prompted me to seek an immaterial truth. I looked at 'what you had made in order to understand your invisible nature.' Despite rebuffs, I had a glimmering of what my soul was too darkened to contemplate steadily—that you are infinite, that you are not diffused through space (whether infinite or finite), that you simply are and 'are always the same,' without any motion or other change in any part. 'All other things are from you,' a fact verified by their very existence. These things I was sure of, though I was too weak for continual enjoyment of you. I could, like an expert, glibly pontificate on these things, but if I did not keep seeking the path in Christ, our rescuer, I would be not expert but expiring. I wanted others to think me wise and my self-satisfaction was self-punishment, for which I could not even weep. I was 'puffed up with learning,' and nowhere to be seen was that basis of lowliness on which is built up the love that is Christ Jesus. That was not something I could learn from those books.

I believe you wished me to chance upon those books before I studied your Scripture, so I should remember their effect when your Scripture later softened me, made my wounds curable by your hand. Then I would know the difference between pretentiousness and testimony, between those who see where they are going but not how, and those who see a path to their blissful homeland, not simply as a thing to be glimpsed but to be arrived at. If I had first studied your Scripture, and you had made their sweetness a familiar thing before I encountered the other books, they might have torn me away from the lowly foundation of reverence. And even if I retained the healthy effect of Scripture, I might have thought that the same effect could be wrought on those who read nothing but them.

27. But as it was, I came to the revered writings of your Spirit, and especially to the apostle Paul, with a grasping eagerness. My previous doubts were dissolved, those that made me think he contradicted himself, that the points of his writing could not be reconciled with the evidence of the law and the prophets. All the holy words now presented a single countenance to me, and 'I took a cautious joy.' As I read I discovered that anything I had found in the Platonists was said here with the added assurance of your favor, so that a person seeing it should not 'preen himself as if he had not received' what he sees, but know that even the power of receiving was received—for 'who has anything but what he has received?' And such a one is not only taught to see 'you, who are always the same,' but is healed in order to hold you. Even if he is too far off to see where he is going, he can keep walking until, by arriving, he both sees and holds.

For what is to happen to the man who 'shares the joy of God's law internally,' but suffers 'another law in his limbs resisting the law of his mind, drawing him captive to the law of sin, which is in his limbs'? Since 'justice is with you,' Lord, and 'sin with us whose acts are evil,' and 'your heavy hand impends,' we are justly detained by the eldest evildoer, who rules the realm of death and who bent our will to the pattern of his will, 'which could not abide in your truth.'

What is left for 'wretched man'? 'Who will free him from his body which is death?'—only God's favor, in Jesus Christ our Lord, whom you begot from your eternity and made the origin of all paths to you, but whom a ruler of *this* world, 'finding no cause for death' in him, killed anyway. Thus was 'the sentence against us canceled.' None of this was in those books. The face of such reverence does not look up from any of their pages. Nor do any tears of testimony, nor 'the sacrifice of a repenting spirit, the bruised and lowly heart,' nor the rescue of the people, nor 'the spousal city,' nor the 'Spirit's assurance,' nor the chalice of our rescue. No one raises from those pages a chant, 'Will not God have my allegiance, from whom my rescue comes, my God, the rescuer who sustains me, who holds me steady always?' No one in those pages hears the call, 'Come to me who toil.' They cannot stoop to learn from one who 'is gentle and of lowly heart,' since you 'have hidden these things from the wise and cautious, and revealed them to the little children.' It is one thing to spot, from far off on a wooded promontory, the home of peace, not knowing the path there, to thrash helplessly through the snares and ambushes of deserting brigands led by 'the lion and dragon' as their chieftains. How different all that from the firm tread along a path leading there, past the sentries of the great ruler, where no bandits lurk, no deserters from the heavenly hosts, since they avoid this path like a torture. These thoughts strangely stirred me to my depths as I read 'the least of your apostles,' and 'wondered at your works, and trembled.'

BOOK EIGHT

VOCATION

I

ON THE BRINK

1. Gratefully, my God, may I 'call back to mind and testify to your pities lavished on me.' My very bones, suppled with infusion of your love, ask: 'Who, Lord, is your like?' 'You struck off my chains, a praise-offering I will sacrifice to you.' I will tell how you struck them off, so all who worship you may say on hearing it, 'Blessed be God, on earth as in heaven, great his honor, and to be wondered at.' With your words fixed in my inner bastion, you also fortified my outer works. I was sure, now, that you lived outside time, though I saw this 'as in a mirror's wavering image.' I no longer questioned the fact that there is one reality that cannot decay, from which all other realities are derived. Now I wanted more to rest in you than to reason about you, for my own life inside time was unstable, and my heart was 'unpurged of its old ferment.' Though drawn to the Path, who is my savior, I shied from its hard traveling.

You then prompted me—and I saw on consideration how wisely—to approach Simplician, who was your good servant in my eyes, glowing with your bounty. Beyond that, I had learned at second hand how true to you he had been from his childhood, and I considered him now, after his living long and deeply mulling the way your Path should be followed, to be a man great in experience and learning—as he proved to be. I determined to consult him about my seethings, that he might 'produce from his store' a rule for one in my condition to 'tread your Path.'

2. The church, I could see, was filled with people who had 'some this gift, some that.' As for me, the life I had led disgusted me. No longer on fire, as before, with ambition for glory or wealth, I could not bear the slave's grind of getting them. They could not be compared with your sweetness or 'my love for the orderliness of your house.' But woman still held me firmly in her grasp. The Apostle, it is true, did not forbid marriage, however much he urged a higher way, earnestly wanting others 'to be as he was.' Yet I in my frailty was opting for the softer course, and apart even from my general lassitude, debilitated as I was by flaccid anxieties, I returned always to one concern: whether I would be forced to put up with certain unwelcome aspects of married life, once bound to it. I have it from the voice of truth that 'There are eunuchs who have castrated themselves for the reign of the heavens.' But he [also] says, 'Claim it who can.'

Mine was no longer the emptiness of 'those men so empty that they see no God, unable to discover in the apparently good the one who is truly good.' From such vanity I was rising, I was recognizing the one to whom all created things give joint testimony, discovering you, the creator of us all; and, along with you, your Word, who is also God, one God with you, and the one 'through whom you created all things.' As for the other category of the irreligious, those who see that there is a God but do not honor him as God and give him their gratitude—I was slipping into that category until your right hand took and lifted me high to a healthy place, just as you told us: 'To be wise is to honor God.' And: 'Seek not to be known as wise.' And: 'Those proclaiming their own wisdom were stultified.' I was 'discovering the precious pearl, to buy which I should have sold all my possessions.' But I held back.

II

VICTORINUS

3. To Simplician, then, I proceeded. In administering the reception of your bounty, he had been a father to Ambrose, who was bishop at the time, and it was as a father that Ambrose loved him. I told him how I had wandered in a labyrinth of falsehoods. When I let him know that I had read certain writings of the Platonists, those translated into Latin by Victorinus—once an orator at Rome, who died (so I had heard) a Christian—he felt cheered at my prospects, since I had not chanced on other philosophers' writings, dense with sophistries and false leads inspired by worldly principles, but on writings haunted in all kinds of ways by God and his Word. Then, the better to prompt me toward Christ's lowliness, 'a thing hidden from the wise but revealed to the insignificant,' he called to mind this very Victorinus, who had been his friend while he was in Rome, and he told me his story—nor will I refrain from repeating what he said, since it deserves the testimony of praise to your bounty.

Here was a man who reached a learned old age, skilled in all the liberal arts, one who had read all the philosophers and could sift their worth, who had taught many of the most distinguished senators, had even earned and accepted the honor of having his statue raised in the Roman forum (a thing citizens of this world so highly prize) because of the great worth of his instruction, yet was also, deep into his years, a cultist of idols, the celebrant of evil rites, with which almost all the nobility had grown giddy—with a spawn misbegotten of mongrel deities, with latrant god Anubis, with the gods who chased Neptune, Venus, and Minerva off the field, as Rome bowed to the gods of their vanquished subjects—all this Victorinus, into old age, had defended with earthshaking eloquence, yet he did not, finally, blush to become a child of your Christ, an infant at your font, 'humbling his neck under your yoke' and branding his vanquished forehead with your cross.

4. Lord, O Lord, you who have bent the heavens to ride down on them, who struck to smoldering the mountains, how more subtly did you strike that man's heart? It was his practice, as Simplician told me, to read holy writ, to study other Christian writings constantly and carefully, until he said to Simplician, in the confidence of friendship, making no public statement: You can count me a Christian now. Simplician answered: I put no trust in that, nor rank you among Christians, till the day I see you in Christ's church. And he taunted back: Are Christians made by walls? So the one man kept claiming to be a Christian, the other made him the same answer, and the first repeated his taunt about walls. Victorinus did not want to lose the respect of his peers, those proud idolators, from the height of whose Babylonian pride, as from 'cedars of Lebanon not yet leveled by the Lord,' he feared a landslide of contempt. But by longer reading, by panting after truth, he drank in strength. He was now more afraid of being 'rejected by Christ in the presence of holy angels' than of 'testifying to Christ in the presence of men.' He himself counted it a great crime to blush at accepting the holy rites of your Word's lowliness, when he had not blushed at the evil rites of the devils' haughtiness, himself haughty as he mimicked them, shameless toward hollow things, ashamed of holy things.

But then he said out of the blue, when Simplician was least expecting it: Go we to the church, I would be a Christian. Simplician, barely containing his delight, set off with him. There Victorinus was steeped in the basic mysteries of the faith, and shortly after entered his name for the rebirth of baptism, to Rome's astonishment and the church's rejoicing. The haughty 'raged at the sight, grinding their teeth, pining away.' But your servant now placed all his hope in the Lord

God, no longer concerned with hollow things, with the illusions of deceit.

5. So when it came time for him to profess the creed—a thing that was done in Rome by a candidate for your bounty with words exactly formulated, memorized, and delivered from a high place before all the faithful—Simplician used to say that the elders offered him the option of making a secret profession, as they normally did to those who might falter from embarrassment. But he wished to proclaim his rescue before the holy congregation. He had, after all, publicly taught rhetoric, which rescued him from nothing. Why shy before your calm flock, when voicing your Word, if he did not shy from a wild mob of the bemused, when using words of his own? As he climbed to the place for reciting the creed, all those who recognized him—and who did not?—raised the glad outcry: Victorinus! Then the whole rejoicing crowd repeated in low whispers: Victorinus! The sudden shouts were from excitement at seeing him, and the sudden quieting was for concentration on hearing him. He recited the truths of the creed with an evident firmness, and they wished to clasp him to their breast, and the two arms clasping him were their love and their joy.

6. Good our God, what is going on within a man when he is happier to see the rescue of one there was no hope for, snatched from a terrible plight, than of one always hoped for or in no terrible plight? Well, even you, the father of pity, have greater joy 'for one returning than for ninety-nine who never strayed,' and we hear again with joy, no matter how many times it is repeated, of the 'stray sheep being returned on the shepherd's glad shoulders,' or how the small coin is returned to your coffers while 'neighbors of the woman who found it are happy with her.' Even while the mass is being celebrated in your house with joy, there are tears there when it is read how that younger son of yours 'was dead and is living, was lost and is found.' It is your joy we feel in us, and that of your angels, made holy by their holy love. For you, always the same, are unvarying in your knowledge of what is varying and never the same.

7. What, I ask again, is going on in a man that makes him happier with loved things found or returned than if he had possessed them always? Other examples [than the Scripture texts] confirm this, and life is full of evidence that fairly cries out that this is so. The conquering general prevails, but at the cost of having to fight a battle, and the greater the battle's damage, the greater joy conquest brings. A seastorm throws about those in a boat, and threatens to destroy the boat—all go pallid as their death impends. Then 'sea and sky grow calm,' and people are just as hysterical with joy as they had been with fear. A friend is stricken ill; his pulse portends the worst; all who hope for him are ill in spirit with him. Should he recover, though crippled, his friends are happier at this than they were when he walked with perfect health and vigor. Men even pamper their pleasures—not taking them as they come, spontaneously and unplanned, but arranging deprivations beforehand. Pleasure in food and drink is piqued by a designed hunger or thirst, as when drunkards eat salty things, to dry up their mouths and make the soothing draft more pleasurable. Society arranges that promised brides be not instantly handed over, lest the man, as husband, should hold lightly the prize delivered if not forced, as a groom, to sigh for the prize delayed.

8. It is just as true in vile and detestable joys, in innocent and licit loves, and in the example of one 'who was dead and is living, was lost and is found,' that joy is always greater after greater affliction. Why should this be the case, Lord my God, when your eternal joy is you yourself, and those near you have joy in you, while it is our part to be tossed between loss and gain, between disjoinings and rejoinings? Is this the natural bent of things, and did you ordain it so, you who order all that you created as good, all proper beings in their proper times and places, 'from the highest of the heavens' to the lowest of the earth, from time's beginning to its end, from angel to worm, from first stirring of existence to its completion? Yet you are highest of the high, and I, alas, am the lowest of the low, and barely we arrive at you who never depart from us.

III

SERGIUS PAUL

9. Come, Lord, shake us and carry us away, be a fire and a sweetness to us, since we would love, would run the race. Some men, sunk even deeper than Victorinus was in a pit of blinding darkness, turn back and 'come to you and are illuminated, receiving light.' Those who receive the light 'receive from you the power of being your sons.' But if they are not celebrities, even those who are aware of their conversion are less joyful over it, since individual affection is increased by being shared with others, by a kind of contagion or mutual conflagration. Celebrities reach more people by their good example, and where they go others will follow to their own rescue. They give joy therefore even to those who have preceded them on the way, since the joy is not just for the single person. This is far from saying that 'the rich are preferred in your holy place to the poor, or the highborn to the lowborn'— on the contrary, 'you have chosen the powerless of the world to confound the powerful, chosen the unknown and disregarded, and chosen the nobodies to be somebodies, making the somebodies of no account.'

Nonetheless, the very man through whom you voiced these words, 'the least of your apostles,' was glad to be no longer Saul but Paul because of a great victory—when, by his campaigning, the proconsul [Sergius] Paul 'submitted to your gentle yoke, all his pride warred down,' and became 'an officer of the great king.' Satan is more baffled when he loses one in his thrall through whom many others were in his thrall. He holds the proud by their claim to high title and he holds others by their reverence for that title. That is why Victorinus' submission was so prized—a submission not only of his heart, which the devil had claimed as a vessel not to be wrested from him, but of his tongue, which the devil had used as a great sharpened spear for destroying many. Your children, Lord, had reason for their greater celebration when our king 'bound the strong man and seized his vessels,' to clean them for your honor's service, as 'things useful for all the Lord's good work.'

10. No sooner had I heard Simplician's tale of Victorinus than I was on fire to do as he did—and no wonder: that is why he had told it to me. And he followed this up later with an account of how Victorinus, when Christians were forbidden by edict to teach literature and rhetoric in the time of the Emperor Julian, eagerly accepted the ban, preferring to leave the prattling schools for your Word, which makes even the tongues of wordless babes eloquent. I thought him more relieved than reluctant in recognizing this opportunity to be entirely free to serve you, since I was yearning for just that thing. But I was immobilized—less by another's static imposition than by my own static will. For the enemy had in thrall my power to choose, which he had used to make a chain for binding me. From bad choices an urge arises; and the urge, yielded to, becomes a compulsion; and the compulsion, unresisted, becomes a slavery—each link in this process connected with the others, which is why I call it a chain—and that chain had a tyrannical grip around me. The new will I felt stirring in me, a will to 'give you free worship' and enjoy what I yearned for, my God, my only reliable happiness, could not break away from the will made strong by long dominance. Two wills were mine, old and new, of the flesh, of the spirit, each warring on the other, and between their dissonances was my soul disintegrating.

11. So by experiment upon myself I was coming to realize what I had read of, how 'the desire of the flesh opposes the spirit, the desire of the spirit opposes the flesh,' for I was experiencing both—yet I felt more identified with that in me which I now wanted than with that in me that I found wanting. But, no, I was not more identified with it, since more of

me went along with 'what I did not will,' than went along
with what I willed.' Yet it was I myself who had made my
compulsion my punisher, since willed I to go where nilled I
to be—and what defense has a sinner if his punishment follows on his own acts? Nor could I plead at this point what
had served as my earlier excuse—that I could not renounce
the world to follow you while I was still undecided about
your truth. Now I knew. But I balked at following your en-
sign, since I was in service to earthly ties, and I feared more
their loss when I should have feared more their load.

12.   It was a sweet load pressing on me, light as a dream-
load, and the thoughts that I tried to direct toward you were
like the struggles of those trying to wake, only to fall back
into a depth of sleep. Though no one wants to sleep forever,
realizing that wakefulness is the higher state, yet a man puts
off waking when torpor, making heavy all his limbs, smoth-
ers him sweetly in slumber, against his better sense that 'it
was time to be rising.' In that very way, though I knew that
rising to your love were better than lapsing into my sloth, the
former act had my approval and wish, the latter my pleasure
and assent. No excuse was left me when you told me, 'Awake,
sleeper, rise from the dead, and Christ will give you light.' I
was defenseless when you urged your truth, since that truth I
had already accepted. All I could mumble, muzzily, was:
Later on. Or: Any moment now. Or: Wait a bit. But the any-
moment never came, and wait-a-bit stretched out to endless
bits. It mattered little that 'I took an inner comfort in your
law, since another law, that of my outer limbs, made war on
my mind's law, and took me captive to the law of sin in my
limbs.' Sin's law is the dominance of compulsion, which
leads and lords it over the unwilling soul, which was willing
to fall into such merited captivity. 'Who will deliver me, in
this pitiful state, from death's body, if not Jesus Christ, our
Lord, through his bounty?'

13.   I will tell what happened, and 'testify to your
honor,' Lord, 'my champion and rescuer,' how you liberated
me from the chains of carnal yearning tightly wrapped
around me, and from the drudgery of my secular career. My

now-ingrained panic was increasing daily, and I daily panted for you. I was spending in your church all the time I could spare from the clogging duties I resented. Alypius attended me, unemployed after his third term as assessor, waiting for clients to whom he could peddle legal service, as I was peddling glibness (presuming that is vendible). Nebridius, who gave in to our friendly urgings, was helping Verecundus, our dear fellow, with his classes. Verecundus, a teacher in his native city of Milan, urgently wanted and asked for his due of friendship from our company, the help he badly needed. Nebridius, gentle and accommodating as he was, lent a hand not from any desire for pay (he could have earned more, had he wanted, from teaching on his own) but from unwillingness to deny anything requested in the name of friendship. He did not advertise the help he gave, since he did not want to become known to people important by worldly standards, but tranquilly to devote as many hours as possible to the pursuit of wisdom by reading or conversing on the subject.

IV

PONTICIAN'S FRIENDS

14. One day while Nebridius was absent (I forget why), to our surprise a certain Pontician paid Alypius and me a visit at our dwelling place. He was our countryman, a fellow African, and an important official at the emperor's court. He had some request or other to make of us, and when we sat down to talk it over, he chanced to see the book that lay on our gaming table. He picked it up, opened it, and found, to his amazement, the letters of Saint Paul—he had expected it to be one of the books that had made my profession so wearisome to me. Smiling, looking intently at me, he was pleasantly surprised at finding, right off, this of all books, and only this, at hand for my reading. For he was a Christian and had been baptized, one who knelt long and often, Lord, in prayer to you at your church. After I told him that I was closely studying Scripture, we engaged in a conversation during which he told me about Anthony, the Egyptian monk whose name was treasured by your servants, though we had never heard of him. When he learned that, he told us all about the great man, making up for our ignorance even as he wondered at it. It stunned us to hear what marvels you had wrought, marvels so recent, so almost contemporary. All were astounded, astonished, we at hearing such wonders, he at our hearing them only now.

15. He expanded on the flocks of monasteries, the lives led there in your sweet service, the wild deserts made fertile—all of which was news to us. Even there at Milan, just outside the city walls, there was a monastery, populated with virtuous monks under Ambrose's care, that had escaped our attention.

He pursued the matter, speaking as we listened in silent absorption. He told us how, once upon a time in Trier, he and three of his fellow officers, while the emperor was attending afternoon games at the circus, took a walk in the gardens just outside the walls. They strolled in casual combinations, one ending up with Pontician, as it happened, and the other two drifting off together. Those two chanced in their walk on a house of some kind where your servants lived, 'poor in spirit, who belong to the heavenly reign.' They saw there a book containing the life of Anthony. As one of them began to read it, he was stunned and took fire, and even as he read began to consider taking up such a life himself, in service to you instead of the emperor (for they were both members of the Special Services). Suddenly filled with holy love and a correcting shame, angry at himself, he looked at his friend and said: Please tell me what, with all our busy striving, we are trying to reach? Where are we going? What keeps us in service? Is it the highest post at court, as the emperor's intimates? But what distinction is more risky or unstable? How many perils will we have to face to reach a post of even greater peril? And how long must we labor to get there? Yet God's intimate I can become on the spot, merely by wanting to be.

Those were his words as, racked by the birth pangs of a new self, he turned back to the book and, reading further, was changed in his depths where you were watching him, and—as was soon made evident—his mind sloughed off the world. Still reading, he rode his veering heart, castigating himself until, after sifting the choices, he chose the true course. Now safely yours, he told his friend: I have wrenched myself free from our career and set myself to serve God alone. Now, in this spot, in this house, I begin. If you cannot join me, do not hinder me. But the other said he would join him in such a campaign for such a return. Both of them, who now belonged to you, 'were building their tower at the estimated cost of abandoning all their goods to follow you.' At this point Pontician, strolling with his companion elsewhere in the garden, sought the other two and, when they met, urged them to hurry back since night was falling. But those two told what they had decided and intended, how they had reached their decision and been confirmed in it, and requested, if the other pair did not wish to join them, not to hinder them. Pontian told us that he and his friend, while not abandoning their own careers, nonetheless wept over it, and gave their friends loyal encouragement, commending themselves to their prayers—then, with hearts dragging in the dust, they returned to the emperor's quarters, while the other two, with hearts fixed on heaven, stayed at that dwelling. When the women to whom they were plighted heard what had happened, they dedicated their own virginity to you.

16. While Pontian was telling this story, you, Lord, used his words to wrench me around to front myself, dragging me out from behind my back, where I had cowered to avoid seeing myself, and 'planting me in front of my own face,' where I could see the foul me, how distorted and dirty, how spotted, how ulcerous. The sight revolted me, but there was no escaping it—each time I tried to turn my gaze away from me, he went on with his story; and you kept holding me there, thrusting me into my own face, so I might 'look on my sinfulness and learn to hate it.' I had known of it before, but I kept obscuring, giving in, not remembering.

17. At that point, however, the more I loved these men who, for spiritual health, surrendered themselves entirely into your healing hands, the more disgust I felt for myself, because of the contrast with them. Many years had drifted by me, a dozen or so, since that twenty-first year when I was inspired to seek wisdom by Cicero's *Hortensius*. I had delayed giving up worldly joys in order to seek wisdom alone, though even the seeking wisdom, not to say winning it, is far better than winning earthly pleasure, political power over others, or sensual pleasures swirling around one at will. But I was pitiable then, as a young man, at youth's outset, when I used to pray to you for chastity, saying, "Give me chastity and self-control, but not just yet." I was afraid you would hear me too soon, heal me too soon, from my sick urges, which I wanted intensified rather than terminated. I had

'gone down deviant paths' with the help of a false and blas-
pheming religion. I did not so much accept it as true—I simply preferred it to the one I was not virtuous enough to
pursue but was viciously resisting.

18.   When I 'put off, day after day,' the decision to spurn
worldly hope and seek you alone, the reason, I thought, was
that I was not certain about the right path to take. But the
day had now arrived when I was naked to myself and my
conscience rebuked me, saying: What have you to say now?
Till now you used to claim that you could not escape encum-
brance with hollow things because you were not sure of
the right course; but now you are sure, and yet are still
encumbered—while wings have long since lifted free men's
shoulders, who did not spend ten years and more considering
if they should fly.' In this way was I gnawed within, was I
stalled in a terrible regret, as Pontician was telling his story.
When he had finished, and concluded the errand he had
come on, he went away and I went in, in to myself, and what
complaints against myself did I not raise? With what verbal
reverberations I lashed my soul, trying to force it along with
me in my quest for you. But it balked, it would not move,
though it could not excuse itself—all its arguments had run
out, had been refuted. It could only tremble in silence, holding it death to escape the stream of habits that were draining
it to death.

V

THE GARDEN

19. In this great wracking of my inner habitation, which I had provoked against my soul in the intimate straits I shared with it, I went to Alypius with storm on my face and in my mind, and burst out: What is the matter with us? Has it come to this? Did you hear that story? Non-philosophers surge ahead of us and snatch heaven, while we, with our cold learning—we, just look at us—are still mired in flesh and blood. Just because they have got ahead, should we be ashamed to follow *at all*, rather than be shamed *at least* into following?

I said something or other of this sort, before my seethings tore me away from him, while he could only stare at me in a stunned silence, so little sense were my words making, as my frown, grimace, eyes, pallor, and tone of voice said more of what I was feeling than any words could. There was a garden where we were staying, which was at our disposal, like the entire house, since our host, the homeowner, was not in residence. Thither my inner turmoil carried me, where no one could interfere with my deep conflagration before its outcome was decided—in a way you foreknew but I did not; since I was now crazed to be sane, was dying to be alive, aware of how bad things were with me, unaware of how good they were shortly to become.

As I went into the garden, Alypius followed close on my heels, present but not admitted to what was occurring in me, though he could not leave me alone in such a state. We sat down as far away from the buildings as we could. I was 'deeply moved within myself,' outrage provoking deeper outrage, with sadness that I had not 'made my promised compact with you, my God,' though 'my very bones cried out' for making it, for honoring it in heaven. But where I was going no ship or carriage or walking could take me, though where I was going was not even as far as I had come from the house. Not only going but arriving there was simply a matter of willing it—but willing it with a strong and unified will, not a partial and wounded will, one jerking and lunging, part of it surging, part sinking.

20.   As I thrashed about, stalling, I made bodily motions some persons might be incapable of, even if they wanted to perform them, either because they lack a limb or the limb is tied, or they are weakened by malady or otherwise debilitated. Yet I, when tearing my hair, pounding my head, hugging tight my knee with laced fingers, was doing exactly what I willed with my body—the willing would not have been followed by this effect if my limbs' response had been blocked. Yet I could not do what I far more eagerly wanted to do, and which I should have been able to do at will, since what I wanted to do at will was—to will. Here the faculty to be affected by the will was itself. And what it had to do was to be itself. Yet it could not. My body's limbs were moved by the soul's lightest volition, receiving its direction, yet the soul did not respond to its own eager willing, when all it had to perform was to will.

21.   Why this enormity, whence arises it? May your pity shed light on the matter as I enquire if the answer does not lie in the secret penalties and shadowy remorses of descent from Adam. Is the enormity there? Thence does it arise? The mind commands, and the body is prompt to respond. The mind commands itself, and it is defied. The mind commands the hand to move, and is so much in charge that the command is hardly different from the response, though the mind is a mental reality, the hand a corporal one. Yet when the mind orders the mind, they are one and the same—and the command is not carried out. Why such enormity, whence arises it, I repeat, that the mind commands the will to respond, and would not order it if it did not will to do so, yet the command is not obeyed? Is it that the will is halfhearted, so the command is halfhearted? The intensity of the command comes from the intensity of the will to make it, and if the will fails to obey the command, that shows a lack of intensity in the will that gave the command. The will that commands is the same will that is commanded—no other is involved. The command must therefore be halfhearted if it is not obeyed. If it were wholehearted, it would not have to issue the command, it would already have willed it. There is no such enormity, then, as simultaneously willing and not willing. Rather there is a sickness of the soul, weighed down by compulsions that impede its response to the truth. In that sense there are two wills, each halfhearted, each lacking what the other has.

22. 'Let them fade away from your gaze,' God—as the 'empty talkers and mind's perverters' fade from it—who, assenting that there can be two wills hesitating over a decision, assert that there are two minds in a man, with two different natures. Men become evil holding such evil views, just as it will make them virtuous if they not only hold right views but hold close to their truth—as your apostle tells them, 'Once you were darkness, now in the Lord you are light.' Those who wish to be light in themselves, not in the Lord, become a deeper darkness, holding that the nature of their souls is itself God—which carries them off from you into a terrible pride, farther off from 'the true light that illumines each man as he arrives in this world.' Let them pay attention to your words, and blush, since 'you shall not blush if you come to him for light.'

But I, in my hesitation over whether to serve the Lord at last, as I had long been disposed to do, was the same man willing as was nilling, both were me. For my willing was as halfhearted as my nilling. I was at war within, was exiled from myself. My exile was unwelcome to me, caused not by a second nature in me but by the cost of sin. For it was 'no longer I that acted but the sin within me,' my lot as Adam's son, and the price of his freely sinning.

23. If different wills make for different natures in man, there will not be two such but many. If a person is trying to decide whether to go to a Manichaean gathering or to the theater, the Manichaeans will cry out: Here are two natures, a good one drawn in one direction, an evil in the other, producing this suspension of action between contending wills. If I say that both intentions—to attend their service and go to the theater—are evil, they answer that their meetings can only be good. But if one of our faith is of two minds about attending the theater or our own church, must the Manichaeans not be of two minds how to describe the situation? Either they must say, unwillingly, that our intention of going to church is a good one (as indeed it is for those who are baptized and hold to the sacramental life), or that the struggle within a single man is in this case a struggle between wills that are both bad—and that is enough to confute their claim that the two wills in man are always a good one and a bad one. Their only alternative is to be converted to the truth—that when one hesitates over a decision, he is tossed about by the conflict of various intentions.

24. Therefore, when they observe two intentions at odds with each other in a man, they have no grounds for saying that two substantially different natures are in conflict, reflecting opposed principles in the universe, the good against the bad. For you, the true God, can blame and out-argue and overwhelm them, since in deciding whether to commit murder with poison or a knife, both intentions are evil; as are the intentions to cheat this man or that man of his property, when one cannot do both; or the intentions to spend money in lust or hoard money in greed. Shall I spend my time going to the games or to a drama, when only one show can be chosen because they are playing simultaneously—or, to add a third option, shall I rather rob this house or that (given opportunity to do both); or, a fourth option, shall I commit adultery when that, too, becomes an opportunity on offer? Add them all up, as options simultaneously offered, all tempting though all cannot be indulged, and the will is scattered out among four or more different things it wants, yet they do not say there are as many different natures as desires in a single man.

The same variations can be found in good intentions. If I ask the Manichaeans if it is more virtuous to savor the words of the Apostle, or to savor a correcting psalm, or to analyze a gospel text, they will answer that they are all virtuous. But if all these seem equally attractive at any one time, will these contending possibilities not confuse the mind while it considers which we should prefer? All are good, but they compete with each other until one of them is chosen and the will can concentrate on it alone, no longer toying with the others. In this way, when the higher delights of heaven lift us, but the joys of temporal existence drag us back, the mind is not totally concentrated on one or the other, admiring the higher for its truth but mired by habit in the lower.

25. So sick was I, so tortured, as I reviled myself more bitterly than ever, churning and chafing in my chains, not broken free of them entirely, held more loosely now but still held, as you were working in my hidden places, with your fierce pity wielding the double whip of fear and shame to prevent my relapse, to prevent the loosening and lighter bond that still held me from strengthening its grip, to grapple me again more tightly than before. My inner self was urging me: Now is the time! Now! With those words I was moving to a resolution, I was almost there—but was not there. Still, I did not slide all the way back, but braced myself nearby, getting my wind back; then, renewing the effort, I was almost there—almost—and just I touched, just I grasped the prize. But, no, I was not there, I touched not, grasped not, not being ready to let death die in me so life might live in me, my ingrained evil thwarting my untrained good. The moment when I would become someone different, the closer it came, the more terror it struck in me—a terror, however, that no longer wrenched me back or fended me off; it just left me hanging.

26. The triflingest of things, the very hollowest things of the hollow-headed, had stalled me—my entrenched lusts, plucking me back by my fleshly clothing, whispering low: Can you cast us off? And: From this moment, never more to be with us! And: From this moment, never to do to this, not ever, or to do this! What they specified by *this* and *this*, keep far from me, God—what sordid, what disgraceful things they spelled out for me. Yet I less than half adverted to their words, since they no longer flaunted themselves before me on my way, but were tittering behind me, as if furtively picking at me while I pulled away from them, trying to make me look back. And held back in some measure I was, not willing to break off, to reject them finally, to cast myself forward to what was calling me. And harsh old compulsion was all the while asking, Can you live without them?

27.   Yet even its words were fading. Off in the direction I was turned toward, though I was afraid to advance into it, Lady Self-Control was revealed in all her chaste majesty, serene, quietly mirthful, smiling me on to her, lest I hold back. To welcome and to hug me she reached her holy arms out, and in them were throngs of persons setting me their example, innocent boys and girls, young men and women— all ages, including chaste widows and women still virgin in old age. In all of them, Self-Control was not sterile but 'fertile with children of happiness' by you, Lord, her husband. She teased me with a smiling insistence: Can you not do what all of these have? Or do you think they did it by themselves, without God their Lord? He it was who gave me to them. Why do you stand alone, which is no standing at all? Throw yourself on him! Do you think he will not stay your fall? Give up fear, and throw yourself—he will catch you, and will heal you.

I was profuse with blushings, since I still had an ear for the insinuations of the triflers, I was still hanging there in ir-resolution. But she went on, saying, as it were: Deafen yourself 'to your earthly limbs, let them be deadened'—they promise delights, but not the delights of the Lord your God's law.

This battle in my heart pitted me and no other against myself, while Alypius, loyal at my side, could only wait in silence for explanation of this weird behavior.

28.   By looking thus deep into myself I dragged from my inmost hiding places an entire store of pitiable memories and laid them out for my heart to see. A vast storm hit me at this point, and brought great sheets of showering tears. To retch this all completely out of me, I leaped away from Alypius— I needed to be alone for this labor of weeping—and I moved farther off, where not even his presence could inhibit me. He honored what was happening to me—perhaps it appeared from my voice, broken with sobs, as I said something or other. At any rate, I went away from him. He, in a state of shock, remained where we had been sitting, while I threw myself haphazardly down beneath a certain fig tree, loosing the reins on my sobbing, as tears tore themselves from my eyes, my condign offering to you, as I multiplied my laments, not exactly in these words but to this effect: How much more, Lord, how much more will this go on? Will you be forever angry, Lord, and never cease? Pay no further heed, I beg, to my entrenched vices. I felt still in the grip of those vices, and I blubbered pitiably: How long, how long—on the morrow is it, always tomorrow? Why never now? Why does this very hour not end all my vileness?

29. I was carrying on so, crying acrid tears of 'heart's contrition,' when I heard from a nearby house the voice of a boy—or perhaps a girl, I could not tell—chanting in repeated singsong: Lift! Look! My features relaxed immediately while I studied as hard as I could whether children use such a chant in any of their games. But I could not remember ever having heard it. No longer crying, I leaped up, not doubting that it was by divine prompting that I should open the book and read what first I hit on.

For I had heard how Anthony, though he merely chanced to be present when a certain passage of Scripture was read, nonetheless took it to heart as meant specifically for him when he heard: 'Go, sell all you own, give it to the poor, and you will have heavenly treasure—only come, and follow me.' At this divine signal he turned suddenly to you. I rushed back to where Alypius was sitting, since there I had left the book of the Apostle when I moved away from him. I grabbed, opened, read: 'Give up indulgence and drunkenness, give up lust and obscenity, give up strife and rivalries, and clothe yourself in Jesus Christ the Lord, leaving no further allowance for fleshly desires.' The very instant I finished that sentence, light was flooding my heart with assurance, and all my shadowy reluctance evanesced.

30.   I closed the book, marking the place with my finger or something, and spoke to Alypius with an altered countenance, after which he told me of what he had been undergoing, without my knowing it. He wanted to see what I had read. I showed him the passage, and went on to the next words which I had not read. I was unaware of what followed, but it was this: 'Welcome him whose belief is weak.' He found that the words expressed his situation, as he explained it to me. He was braced by this encouragement, and it took no turbulence of resistance for him to join me in the promised compact with you, since in the moral purity his decision involved he had long been my better.

From there we go to my mother; speak with her; she rejoices. We tell her all that happened. It is joy and glory to her, and she was thanking you, 'who can act beyond what we ask or think is possible,' since she saw you had granted her far more than she had requested with her pitiable long laments for me. You had so turned me to you that you freed me from seeking a wife or any other prospect in this world. I was standing at last on that ruler's edge of faith where you had shown me to her years ago. You 'changed her grieving into joy,' far beyond her intentions—with a chaster, sweeter joy than she had looked for from grandchildren born of me.

BOOK NINE

BAPTISM

I

NEW LIFE

1. 'I am your servant, Lord, your servant, son of your handmaid, you have ripped my chains away, to you I will offer praise in sacrifice.' May your praise rise from my heart and lips, 'my bones ask, Who, Lord, is your like?' Answer as I ask, 'tell my soul, I come to your rescue.' Who, what sort, am I—what if not evil, in what I do, or (if not in what I do) in what I say, or (if not in what I say) in what I want. Yet you are good and take pity, your right arm reaches the very depths of my dying and drains from the bottom of my heart all the store of my decay. This is all I wanted, to nill my own will, will yours. Yet where from the passing years could freedom of my will be retrieved, from what forgotten deep cranny could it suddenly emerge, so I should lower my neck to 'your gentle yoke,' and my shoulders to your 'light burden,' Christ Jesus, 'my champion and rescuer'? What sweeter now than the losing of sweet nothings? What less to be feared than the losing of joy? You were emptying them out of me, my true and highest sweetness, emptying and refilling me with you, sweeter than all delights of flesh or blood, brighter than all lights, deeper than all inwardness, nobler than any honor except to those who think honor can be bestowed on themselves. My mind had been released—from dreams that ate at it, dreams of pride, of greed, of filth, of lusts inflamed with scratching. I was giddy with addressing you, my purity, my riches, my rescue, my Lord God.

CASSICIACUM

2. I resolved 'under your gaze' not to break off teaching in a disorderly way, but gradually to give up my activities as a peddler of glibness in the marketplace, so no more boys could buy from my lips the weapons of their distraction, as they put their minds not to 'thinking of your law,' or of your peace, but to 'untruthful ravings' and verbal joustings. Luckily, only a few days were left before the harvest-time vacation. I could last them out and retire tidily, no longer, after you gave me release, to return to my racket. This plan I shared with you, but with none but a few of my associates, who agreed to keep it among ourselves. We were 'climbing from the valley of lamentation' and 'singing a song of gradual ascent,' while you directed 'stinging arrows' and 'cauterizing coals' against the tacit criticism of those who, feigning to help us, hinder, and love us only as they love a favorite food, to devour us.

3. Your arrow flew to our heart as well, to wound it with love, to transfix our inner self with your words. These arrows arriving thick in our thoughts were your saints, transformed by you from black to white, from dead to living, to be our models. They were a fire to wither up the sluggishness dragging us down. They kindled us, and 'all sly talk' opposing us just fanned the flames higher instead of putting them out. Admittedly, since 'you have made your title holy to the nations,' there would also be some to praise the decision we had promised you. But it would have looked like self-promotion for me to resign with the holiday so close. Given the prominence and visibility of my position, an abrupt

departure would have drawn everyone's attention, to wonder
why I decided not to wait the short time before the break.
Many would claim I was trying to make a stir—though what
would it avail to have my state of mind pried into for gossip,
making 'my blessing a thing to be reviled'?

4. Besides, the labor of teaching that summer had taken
its toll on my lungs. I was short of breath. Chest pains were
symptoms of trouble. I could speak only hoarsely or for
short times. This had worried me earlier as forcing me, almost of necessity, to give up my teaching schedule, or at
least to take time off for some cure and recovery. But now
things were different. A new plan had taken shape and become firm (as you, my God, are my witness), to 'retire and
behold that you are God.' I was glad to take this as a valid
response to parents whose concern for their sons' education
made them careless of my freedom. Comforted with this
reflection, I put up with the irksomeness of the time to be
served—I suppose it was about twenty days, and they were
made all the more irksome since I now lacked the desire for
money that had braced me to take on so much. It needed patience to stagger on under this load. I could well be faulted
by one of your saints, now my brothers, for letting myself
stay even one extra hour 'holding a chair of deception,' after
my heart was turned to service in your ranks. I have no defense against them. But, Lord most merciful, have you not
bathed away this sin, with other repulsive and deadly ones,
in your holy waters, and forgiven me?

5. What was a blessing to us racked Verecundus with
misgiving. He expected to lose our companionship because
of the ties that strictly bound him. He was not yet a Christian, and though his wife was, she more than any other im-
pediment held him back as we were faring toward our goal.
For he told us that he could not be a Christian in the only
[celibate] way he wanted to be. But he generously offered us
the use of his estate for as long as we wished to use it. May
you 'repay him when the just are resurrected,' since you
have already 'cast his lot with them'—for after we had left
him for Rome, he was struck ill and in his sickness left life

as a baptized believer. You thus showed mercy not only to him but to us, who would have been torn with unbearable sorrow if, after his shepherding kindness to us, we could not count him as one of your sheep—thanks to you, our God. We are all yours—you assure us so and console. Faithful to your pledge, you reward Verecundus with the comfort of your ever-verdant Paradise, in exchange for his country villa at Cassiciacum, where we enjoyed in you a shade from the scorching world. You forgave him his earthly sins on 'the mountain of flowing milk, your mountain, the mountain of plenty.'

6. But while Verecundus was still grieving, Nebridius shared our joy. He, too, was not yet a Christian, but he had emerged from a pit of deadly error—where he considered the flesh of your Son, the Truth, illusory—to become a fervent seeker after truth, though not yet receiving any of your sacraments. Shortly after our conversion and rebirth through baptism into you, he too became a believing Catholic, who served you in Africa with complete chastity. It was only after all his family had become Christians that you released him from the flesh, and he lives now in the bosom of Abraham. For whatever we discussed as meant by that bosom, surely he lives in it, that dear friend of mine, Lord, and your freedman promoted to be your son. Where else could such a one be? He lives in the place he used to ask me about so frequently, poor excuse as I was as an advisor on such things. His ears are no longer open to my lips, but his lips are open to your fountain, where he draws in as much wisdom as he can, with a happy eagerness never to end. I doubt it can intoxicate him so deeply as to forget me, since you, Lord, whom he drinks, forget me not.

So that was how it was with us—we were comforting Verecundus with an assurance that conversion did not end our friendship, recommending to him the faith proper to his state of marriage; and anticipating that Nebridius would soon follow our lead, as he was close to doing. In fact, he had at long last reached that point when my teaching days ran out. It had seemed a long time, as we measured its passing, since I was yearning to be free for contemplation, to 'sing to you from my entire frame: Your countenance is what I have longed for, what I seek, Lord, is your countenance.'

7. At last came the day when I left in fact what I had already left in wish, my rhetorical profession. No more. You freed my lips, as you had freed my heart. Blessing you and rejoicing, I went with my friends to the villa. My books record the discussions held there with the others and with myself in your presence. They were written to serve you, though they still panted with a proud air, as if I were merely pausing in my profession. Since Nebridius was not with us, letters record my exchanges with him. How could I find time to thank you for the many wonderful favors you did us, especially since I now rush on to even greater favors? Carried back to that time in thought, I savor, Lord, my testimony to the inner spurrings by which you tamed me—how you brought me down to lowliness, 'leveling the hills and mountains' of my mind, making my 'crooked ways straight and my rough ways smooth,' and how you brought Alypius, my heart's brother, into the service of your name, despite the fact that he had been fastidious about the use of that name in my dialogues. He wanted those works to breathe the refined air of the schools, more like high 'cedars the Lord stormed down' than the church's herbs for healing snakebite.

8. How I lifted my voice to you, my God, as I read the psalms of David, songs of belief, devotional sounds that drive out pomposity, sung by me, with a love not yet ingrained by use, by an initiate vacationing in a villa with my fellow initiate Alypius, and with my mother, our close associate. She had a man's faith in women's dress, an ancient's calm, a mother's love, a Christian's devotion. How I was lifting my voice to you in the psalms as they kindled me, kept me on fire to sing them, if I could, over all the world, to deflate all men's self-importance. Yet sung they are all over the world, and 'none can shelter from your beams.' The Manichaeans, it is true, roused me to harsh and stinging anger, but I soon relapsed into pity for them, as ignorant of your sacraments, your medications—the cure, had they not

raved senselessly against it, that would have made them well.

I wished they could somehow be near me, without my knowing they were there, to see my expression as I sang Psalm Number Four in that place of contemplation. They would have seen the effect on me of its words: 'When I called out, the God who judges me heard. You opened a way out of my troubles. Have pity on me, Lord, and answer my prayer.' They would have to overhear me without my being aware of them, or they would think I commented on the words with them in mind. But in truth I would not have had the words to say, or the right way of saying them, if I knew they could hear and see me. And if I could say the words, they would not recognize them as my mind's inmost and most feeling converse with and to myself about you.

9. With apprehensive trembling, but with hope glowing, 'I was lifted up by your pity,' Father. This was all expressed in my features and voice when your Spirit in his goodness turned to us and said, 'How long, human offspring, will your hearts be downcast? Why love things hollow and seek the false?' Such hollowness I had loved, such falsehood I had sought, though you, Lord, had already 'glorified your holy one, raising him from the dead and seating him at your right hand,' where, from on high, he sent down 'his pledge, the Supporter, the Spirit of Truth.' He had indeed sent the Spirit, though I knew it not. He had sent him because he was now glorified, rising from the dead and ascending into heaven. 'The Spirit was not given before, since Jesus had not then been glorified.' The prophecy proclaims: 'How long, human offspring, will your hearts be downcast? Why love hollow things and seek the false? Know this: the Lord has glorified his holy one.' It proclaims, 'How long?' It proclaims, 'Know this.' And I all the while was loving hollow things, was seeking false things, until I heard the prophecy with apprehension, recalling that I had been like those it addressed, for hollowness and falsehood were in the fantasies I had mistaken for truth. Loud and strong I wailed as I remembered them. I wish those who still 'love hollow things and see the false' could have heard me, it might have shaken them so

that they would retch it out of themselves. Then you would
have 'heard them as they cried out,' since 'he who pleads for
us died' a real death of the flesh.

10. I read on: 'Be angry against sinning more,' and the
words affected me, my God. I had indeed learned how to be
angry at my past, to sin not in the remaining time. I was
right to be angry, since it was not some shadowy force alien
to me that sinned in me, as those say who are not angry at
themselves but 'store up anger for the day of wrath when
your just sentence is brought to light.' But the goods I sought
were no longer outside me, to be seen in the light of our sun.
Those who look for joys outside themselves become empty,
they pour out their substance on 'things visible and transitory,' they lick shadows and their minds starve. If only they
would weary of their hunger and say, 'Who will show us
what is good?' Let us show them, let them hear, 'The light of
your countenance has marked us out.' We are not ourselves
'the light that gives light to all,' we take our light from you
so that 'having been darkness we are now light in you.'

If only they could find the eternity that is in them. I had
been given a taste of this, and chafed at not being able to
show it to them, even if they brought to me a heart that was
all outward gaze away from you, who are within, and asked
'Who will show us what is good?' I kept my anger within my
own inner chamber, where I had repented, slain and put off
my old self, and formed my hope in you out of the thought of
a new self, where you were becoming ever dearer to me, be-
stowing more joy in my heart. I cried a glad recognition
within to what I heard without, and no longer wished to be
rich in a multiplicity of outer goods, consuming what would
consume me, when I had, in the simplicity of eternal things,
an inner consuming of 'wheat and wine and oil.'

11. From my innermost self I greeted with a glad cry the
next verse: 'Oh, for the realm of peace, of the Self-in-Self!'
And the next words: 'I shall sleep, and mine shall be a
dream.' Who can be against us when the word shall be fulfilled that 'death is erased by victory'? For you are, entirely,
the Self-in-Self, who can never change. In you is surcease that

never knew labor, and 'none is like you,' nor is there anything worth seeking but you, for 'you settle me in a peace like no other.' I read the psalm, I was on fire, but I found no way to help men deaf and blind, as I had been when I was a pestilence, a blind canine snarler against your Scripture, which is 'honeyed with heaven's honey' and 'glowing with your light.' I 'shiver away from those' who oppose such writings.

12. How can I possibly do justice to all that happened in that vacation? But they are not forgotten, and I cannot omit the harsh whip you wielded and the wondrous swift mercy that followed. You tormented me with tooth pangs. When they became so severe I could not speak, 'my heart was prompted' to ask those around me to pray for me to you, who rescue in every way. I wrote on my tablet, gave it to them to read, and as soon as we fell on our knees in fervent supplication, the pain disappeared. What kind of pain could this be? And what kind of relief? I admit, my Lord and God, it frightened me. Nothing like this had happened to me in all my years. You were signaling to me in my depths, and I 'praised your name' in joyful faith—though that faith left me no comfort on the subject of my former sins, not yet forgiven me in baptism.

13. At the end of the harvest vacation, I notified my students that they must look for another phrase salesman, since I wished to dedicate myself to your service and I was not up to teaching with my shortness of breath and chest pains. I sent a letter to your spokesperson, the holy Ambrose, describing my past errors and present resolve, that he might recommend what readings would make me more ready and qualified to receive so great a grace. He prescribed the prophet Isaiah, I suppose as offering more obvious prophecies of the gospels and the calling of the Gentiles. But I did not understand what I read at first, and supposing the rest would be the same, I put off reading more until I should be better acquainted with the Lord's mode of expression.

14. Since the time had now come for me to enroll for baptism, we left the country and returned to Milan. Alypius had decided to be reborn to you with me. He had already humbled himself in a way fitting him for your sacraments and taken strong control of his body, to the bold extent of treading barefoot the icy soil of Italy. We made the boy Adeodatus one of our company, my natural son begotten in sin. He was finely made by you, about fifteen, but already more intelligent than many older and more learned men. I testify to the talents you gave him, my Lord God, who make everything and can reform what we deform, since there was nothing of me in my son but my sin. You and none other inspired us to bring him up in your teachings. I testify to these your doings.

One of my books is called *The Teacher*, in which he speaks with me. You know that all the ideas he expresses in this dialogue with me were his own, though he had only reached the age of sixteen at the time. I had observed even more astonishing things in him. His talent was intimidating, and who but you could frame such a wonder? You took his life away early, but I am content, having nothing to fear from his conduct as a child or a youth or (if he had become one) a man. We treated him as a peer in your favor as we underwent our education in your doctrines. Together we were baptized, and misgivings about our past were assuaged. I could not savor enough of your stunning sweetness in those days as I considered the vast scope of your purpose in rescuing mankind. How many tears I wept at your hymns and canticles, abruptly carried away by the sweetly tuned voices of your church. The voices flowed in at my ears, your truth distilled in my heart, a wash of emotion arose in me and overflowed in tears, and they were a comfort to me.

III

MIRACULOUS MARTYRS

15. The church at Milan had not long practiced this way of consoling and instructing each other by a fervent uniting of the brothers' hearts and voices in song. And for a year, or a little more, Justina, mother of the underage emperor Valentinian, had been persecuting your representative Ambrose, as a way of advancing the heresy that Arrians had lured her into. The community piously kept vigil in the church, ready to die with their bishop your servant, and my mother, who attended on you, was with the foremost in supporting him and keeping watch, her whole life turned over to prayer. We, more cool on the matter since your Spirit had not yet thawed us, were nonetheless shaken by the turbulence rocking the city. This is when hymns and songs modeled on the Eastern rites were introduced, to keep up the spirits of an anxious and weary people. The practice has been continued, following this example, by many of your communities—in fact, by most of them in other parts of the world.

16. At this point you sent a vision to the bishop I have mentioned, revealing where the bodies of the martyred Gervasius and Protasius lay hidden. For years you had preserved them incorrupt in your secret treasury, and now was the right 'time to bring them forth,' to check the ravings of a woman who was also a queen. Once uncovered and exhumed, the bodies were conveyed with all honor to the Ambrosian basilica, where those tormented by unclean spirits were healed, the devils themselves testifying to this. More than that, a citizen many years blind, a prominent man in the city, asked what was making people so rapturous with joy. Hearing the reason, he leaped up and asked his guide to lead him there. On arrival, he begged to enter, that he might touch with his handkerchief the bier of those saints 'whose death is precious in your view.' This done, he put the handkerchief to his eyes, which were instantly opened. At that, the story became famous, praise of you rang and shone out, and the woman's hostility, though not cured by sound belief, was narrowed in its persecuting range—'thanks be to you, my God.' How have you called and drawn me back in memory to these important events which I forgot to include earlier? Of course, at that time we did not 'run toward the wafting of your precious oils' fragrance.' I wept the more for that when I listened to the singing of your hymns. Once sighing sadly, now I sighed in gladness, as far as one can in this body of 'flesh that is grass.'

IV

MONNICA

17. You 'who unite people as one in a house' brought into our company Evodius, a young man from my town. He was converted and baptized before us, while he was serving in the government's Special Services. He left that regimen and buckled on yours. He joined in our holy resolve to live together. We discussed the best place for us to take up our attendance on you, and agreed we should return to Africa. When we had got as far as Ostia, at the Tiber's mouth, my mother died. I am omitting much as I hurry on—for those numberless things left in silence, my God, accept my testimony and thanks—but I will not leave out what my mind can express about her, your handmaid. Her flesh brought me forth to live in this daylight, as her heart brought me forth to live in eternal light. I shall not speak of her gifts, but of your gifts in her, since she did not create or teach herself, you created her, and neither her father nor her mother knew what she would become. She was disciplined by the rod of your Christ, the regimen of your Only-Begotten, in a believing family, an integral part of your church.

She claimed that her strict training came not so much from her mother as from an enfeebled womanservant, who used to carry my grandfather on her back when he was a boy, as older children carry younger ones. Because of this, along with her age and her good character, she was virtually pampered by her masters. She was trusted with the upbringing of the daughters of the family, a duty she discharged with diligence. She was firm, when need was, to correct them with holy severity and to educate them with measured prudence. Apart from mealtimes, when they ate modestly at their parents' table, they were not allowed to drink anything, even water—no matter how they burned with thirst—to prevent bad habits. She gave them the following advice: Now you drink water because you cannot have wine. But when you are married, you will control the storerooms and cellars, water will pall, but your restraint in drinking will continue. By such rational advice and strict rule she curbed the impetuosity of youth and brought the girls' thirst within sound limits, so what was not allowed would not allure them.

18. Nonetheless, as your handmaid confided to me as her son, slyly over time did the sly wine habit insinuate itself. Her parents, trusting her good behavior, used to send her to fetch wine from the cask. She put a dipper into the opening at the top and, before she poured the wine into a jug, she would take a little taste, just touching the tip of her tongue to it. She did not drink more because she did not like the taste. It was not a need for drink that motivated her, but the extra energies of youth, which overflow in playful antics, customarily repressed in young spirits by their elders. From one taste she gradually added more, sip by sip—since 'to neglect things is gradually to slide down'—until she had fallen into the habit of draining the cup when it was almost full.

Where now were the wise old woman's strenuous injunctions? Could she ever have conquered this sly sickness if you did not keep watch over us to cure us? Let father and mother and nannies all be gone, Lord, you still are there, the one who made us, calls us back, sets over us authorities to safeguard the health of our souls. How did you deal with her then, my God? What did you use to cure her, to make her whole? Was it not this way? By your hidden arranging of things, you cut out the rottenness with one sharp slash, using as your surgeon's knife the cutting remark you prompted in another person's tongue. A slave girl, who used to go with her young mistress to get the wine, had some quarrel with her. When they were by themselves, she used the harshest insult to accuse her, calling her a wino. This stabbed home. Recognizing her own foul conduct, she instantly condemned and repudiated it. As flattering friends mislead, quarreling foes can often correct. Not that you judge them for what you accomplished through them, but for what they thought they were doing. The slave girl, in her anger, tried to provoke her little mistress, not to cure her. She did it in private because the quarrel broke out then and there—or perhaps because telling others would be risky, after she had not reported the fault for so long. But you, the ruler of heavenly and earthly things, who deflect to your own purpose the unruly rush of events, bringing pattern to the tumble of the centuries, you also cured with another person's sickness the sick soul. Considering this, no one should boast of his own doing if a comment of his corrects one he thinks should be corrected.

19. Brought up strictly and temperately, my mother obeyed her parents at your bidding, instead of obeying you at theirs. She was married when she came of age, given to a husband she accepted as her lord while striving to make him your prize. Her actions spoke of you, and you made those acts so beautiful that her husband respected this admirable, this amiable wife. She put up with his marital infidelities, never quarreling over them, expecting him to become chaste when he became a believer by your mercy toward him. She also knew that, for all his great goodwill, he had a fiery temper, and opposing an angry husband, by deed or even by word, does no good. She waited, rather, for the moment when his storm had passed and he was calm, then quietly made her own case, as if he had just acted out of unconsidered irritation.

Other wives, though married to men less headstrong than hers, were bruised and disfigured by them, and complained of married life as they intimately confided in each other. But she chided them, with light tone but real intent, saying that the marriage contract they had read to them should be taken as a legal instrument, making them their husband's servants. Knowing their status, they should not try to get the upper hand of their lords. The others were amazed, since they knew what a fierce husband she had to put up with—but there were never any rumors or telltale marks of Patrick hitting his wife.

They had not, even for a day, engaged in domestic strife. When others asked her to confide her secret, she laid out the procedure I just described—some followed her advice, and were happy to see it worked; others did not, and were beaten as minions.

20.   Her mother-in-law had initially been irked with her, because of some slave-women's malevolent insinuations, but my mother wore her down with thoughtful attention, unfailingly patient and gentle. This made my grandmother report to her son the slaves' meddling words, which had caused dissension with her daughter-in-law, with a request that he punish them. After this, with respect for his mother's wishes, but also out of concern for household discipline and regard for family harmony, he gave the accused girls the beating their accuser considered condign. She furthermore promised that anyone seeking favor with her by bad-mouthing her daughter-in-law would get the same treatment. Since no one was so foolhardy after that, the two women lived together in a sweet reciprocation of kindnesses.

21.   You gave another great talent, 'my God who pities me,' to your servant in whose womb you made me. She had a gift for making peace, wherever possible, between people of all sorts, whether divided in mind or heart. When she heard the rancorous comments of different parties—all those bitter outbursts that unchecked enmity spews up, the present party expressing raw hatred in gossip about the absent one—she never repeated what one side said about the other unless it could lead to their reconciliation. I would count this no great achievement had I not learned from sad experience of the countless throngs, affected by sin's widespread contagion, who not only repeat what one angry person said about another, but add insults not actually spoken—whereas the least one can expect from a decent person is to say nothing that might cause or increase enmity, but to use only soothing words, in an effort to end the quarrel. All this she exemplified, intimately schooled as she was by you in the classroom of her heart.

22.   Toward the end of her husband's earthly life, she

won him as a prize for you. No longer need she bear in the
converted man what she had borne in the unconverted. For
everyone, indeed, she was 'a servant of servants,' and everyone acquainted with her gave her great praise, and loved you
whom they met in her heart, a heart revealed by the impact
of her 'holy behavior' on others. She was 'wife to one man
only.' She reciprocated her parents' care. She was devoted to
her household's activities. The 'good she did bore her witness.' She cared for her children, 'repeating her birth pangs'
for them whenever they strayed. Yet for our whole [bap-
tized] company she was as submissive as if we were her parents and she was everyone's daughter. You give me warrant
to speak for all, Lord, since before her death we all lived in
you as one community with her, having received the grace
of your baptism.

   23.   We did not know (but you did) that the day was approaching for her to leave this life. By what I believe was one
of your own secret disposings, we happened to be standing
alone together, leaning out of a window that looked upon a
garden. It was part of the establishment in which we were
staying at Ostia on the Tiber. We had withdrawn there, away
from human traffic, to recuperate from the effort of long
travel, readying ourselves to sail. We talked in the sweetest
intimacy, 'forgetful of what has been, yearning forward to
what will be.' The truth (which you are) was present with us
as we asked each other what kind of life the saints will live in
eternity, which 'eye has not seen, ear heard, nor heart conjectured.' Our hearts longed with open mouth for the waters
running down from your high fountain, 'the fountain of life'
in your midst, so that, bedewed with spray from it according
to our condition, we might ponder such a mystery.

   24.   Our talk led us to the conclusion that the sensual
delights of the body, considered in whatever earthly light,
when placed beside eternal life, are not worth comparing or
even commenting on. Reaching out more eagerly to the Self-
in-Self, we proceeded step by step through all material
things, even the heavens, from which sun, moon, and stars
brighten the earth. Ascending higher, within ourselves, to

speech and questioning and admiring such works, we en-counter our own minds, and go beyond them to the out-skirts of that region where 'you give eternal pasture to Israel,' feeding it on truth. There, living is the same as wisdom, through which all things were made, all in the past, all in the future, and which was not itself made but is as it always was and always will be, for eternity knows no past or fu-ture. And while we speak of this, and yearn toward it, we barely touch it in a quick shudder of the heart. Then we sighed our way back down from 'the Spirit's first harvest' into the sounds of our own words which proceed in time from their beginnings to their ends, by no means like to your word, Lord of us both, which is itself in itself, 'never aging but making all things new.'

25. Of our experience we asked this question: If fleshly importuning were to fall silent, silent all shapes of earth, sea, air; silent the celestial poles; silent the soul, moving (oblivi-ous of self) beyond the self; silent, as well, all dreams and in-ternal visions, all words and other signs, silent everything that passes away, all those things that say, if one listens, We did not make ourselves, he made us who never passes away; if, after saying this, they too were silent, leaving us alert to hear the One who made them; and if He should speak, no longer through them but by himself, for us to hear his word, not as that is relayed by human tongue or angel's voice, not in cloudy thunder or 'dim reflection,' but if we hearken to him we love in other things without those other things (as even now 'we strain upward,' and, in a mind's blink, touch the ageless wisdom that outlasts all things), and if this were to continue, all lesser vision falling away before it, so that this alone held the universe in its grip, in its enfoldment and its glad hidden depths, and eternal life resembled this mo-ment of wisdom that we sigh to be losing—would that not be what is meant by the words 'Enter the joy of your God'?— a joy that will be ours, when?—only when 'all rise (though not all are changed).'

26. Something like that is how I described our experi-ence to her, not in just that tone or those exact words. But you, Lord, know what she responded after our conversation on that day, in which the world and all its joys came to seem, in the process of our talk, utterly worthless—she said: As for myself, this world holds no more delight. What further I should do, or why I am still here, I know not. What I hoped for in this world is accomplished. One thing alone made me linger in this life a bit longer, to see you a Catholic Christian before I should die. My God has granted this and more, to see you serve him with contempt for temporal prosperity. What task is left me here?

27. I cannot be sure of my exact response to her—little more than five days after this she was struck with a fever. One day in the course of her illness she fell into a coma and was no longer aware of her surroundings. But soon she regained consciousness, and saw me and my brother at her bedside. She gave us a questioning look, as if to say, Where have I been? Noticing how stunned we were with grief, she told us: Bury your mother here. I, fighting back my tears, did not answer, but my brother said something to the effect that he held to the brighter prospect of her dying at home and not abroad. At the words she winced and directed a reproachful glance at him for such thoughts. Looking at me, she said: See what he can still be saying. A little later, she told us both: Bury me where you will, don't let it bother you. One thing only I ask, that wherever you are, you remember me at the Lord's altar. After expressing this wish, so far as her weakness let her, she fell silent, in agony as her illness worsened.

28. I reflected, my unseen God, on the favors you grant your faithful, producing results to marvel at, and I gave you joyous thanks when I remembered the fussy concern with which she had marked out and made ready her burial place next to her husband's, with whom she had been happy on earth. So little is the human mind suited to divine things that, in order to prolong that happiness and make it talked of in the future, she had hoped to be transported across the sea so that one earth would cover both spouses. When you began to empty such nonsense from her mind, by the richness of your goodwill, I know not; but I was pleased when she showed that you had—and even surprised, though she did not seem to be still desirous of burial in her homeland when she asked, in our conversation at the window: What task is left me here? I later learned that while we were in Ostia my mother confided one day to some of her friends, when I was not with her, how she had contemned life and accepted death. They were impressed by this courage in a woman (but you gave it her), and asked how she could be so calm about dying and being buried far from her native city. Nothing, she answered, is far from God—I have no fear that, when the time comes, he will not find where I am, to raise me up. So, in the ninth day of her illness and the fifty-sixth year of her life, when I was thirty-three, her devout and observant soul was separated from her body.

29. As I closed her eyes, a great sorrow flooded my chest, producing a flood of tears, but by ruthless mental effort on my part my eyes drew the tears back to where they were springing and dried them up, though I was racked with the struggle to contain them. When she had breathed her last, the young Adeodatus burst out sobbing, and grew quiet only after we had all restrained him. This helped me see that the child in me, which had been melting into tears, had to be restrained and silenced by the adult voice of my heart. We all agreed that it would be wrong to celebrate her funeral with tearful complaining or lament. These are the customary indications that one has died in a bad state, or else entirely ceased to be. But she was in no such condition, nor had she ceased entirely to be. Warrant for this was her conduct, her 'faith without pretense,' and the assurances we trusted.

30. Why, if this is so, was I inwardly shaken with grief? To be instantly torn away from accustomed joys of sweet and treasured concourse leaves a fresh wound. I took comfort in her assurances to me during her last illness that I was a devoted son. Responding with hugs to my continual attentions, she recalled with great emotion that she had never heard me criticize or belittle her. But how could that respect I paid her be compared, my God who made me, with the services she dedicated to me? To lose that solicitude wounded my soul, as if tearing my life in two, a life made up of us both.

31.   When we had stopped the tears of my son, Evodius caught up the psalms and began to sing one, and the household joined in with him, 'Your mercy, Lord, and your justice I will sing to you.' When news of her death spread, many of the brothers and pious women gathered. Funeral arrangements were made by those whom custom appointed to the task. But I politely withdrew—accompanied by those who did not think I should be left alone—to ruminate on the meaning of this event. I was using truth as a medication for the pain you knew me to be in, though they did not—they heard me speak calmly and thought I could not be suffering. But you heard me within, where they could not listen. I reproached myself for melting into sorrow; I dammed up the flow of grief, so it receded a little, then swept back, and carried things on almost to the sobbing point or the cracking up of my demeanor, which it never reached. But I knew inside what effort it was taking. It frustrated me to be powerless against my human limits, inescapable as they are in the natural order and our current lot, and I suffered a woe added to the first woe, woes doubling on me.

32.   When the body was taken out for burial, we accompanied it and returned tearless. Not even in the flow of prayers offered for her during the sacrifice of our redemption, with the body placed by the grave (according to local custom) before its burial—not even during those prayers did I weep. Instead, I spent the whole day in a concealed depression, while I made what pleas I could from my distracted mind for some cure to sorrow. You made no answer, if only by this one demonstration reminding me (I believe) how what we are accustomed to becomes a fetter to the mind, even when it no longer grazes on deceitful language.

I thought I might go to the baths, since I had heard the word *bath* comes from the Greek *balanion,* which means banish-ill. But in fact—as I testify before your pity, you father of us orphans—I entered and left the baths unchanged. The bitterness had not been soaked from my heart. But at last I slept, and awakened much relieved from sadness. Alone on my bed, I called to mind your servant Ambrose's truthful lines describing you:

> God, maker of all things,
> You rule the world with right,
> Change raiments of the sky
> From candid day to night,
>
> To knit up tired limbs
> Rebuilding them with rest,
> Restrengthening our minds,
> With anxious cares oppressed.

33. Gradually I could engage again with my feelings for your handmaid, for her conduct, reverent toward you, gentle and deferential toward us, and for the sudden loss of it all. Now I could weep freely over her and for her, over me and for me, and I loosed the tears I had held in, to flow as they would, letting my heart float out on them, resting softly on my sobs at ease, because only you heard them, no man to analyze my sorrow and feel superior to it. Now, Lord, as I testify to you in writing, whoever wishes can read me and, as he wishes, decide whether I mourned my mother excessively, by this or that part of an hour, but not deride me for it. She died in my eyesight after weeping for years that I might live in your eyesight. In your eyesight (as the father of all Christ's brothers) let any of generous disposition weep for my excess.

34. My heart is now healed of any wound whose infliction might be criticized for showing family affection. And I shed a different kind of tear for your handmaid, our God, flowing from my stricken heart at thought of the peril of anyone 'dying in Adam.' She, it is true, 'had a new life in Christ' and lived, even before her release from the flesh, as an honor to your name, in her faithfulness and conduct. But I am not so bold as to claim that never, since her rebirth in baptism, did a single word slip from her against a commandment of yours, since truth itself (your Son) has said, 'One

calling his brother a fool deserves hell fire.' Even those of
sterling conduct are in sad state if you scrutinize them without the screen of your mercy. But since you are not a fierce
detector of minor faults, we can hope for some place in your
company, though anyone counting up actual merits in his life
is just counting off your favors to him. When will men come
to 'know they are simply men,' and 'claim no doing but
the Lord's'?

35.   That is why I briefly set aside, my heart's God—
source of my life and of my praise—whatever good my
mother did, for which I render you happy thanks yet pray for
any sinful acts in her. 'Hear me' through the healer of our
wounds, who 'hung on the cross' and 'sits at your right
hand' to intercede for us. 'Cancel her debts,' if any were incurred in the many years she lived after baptism. Cancel
them, Lord, cancel I pray you, 'do not contest rights with
her.' Let your 'pity exceed your justice,' since 'your every
statement is binding,' and you have 'promised pity to those
who show it.' They could not have a pity you did not give
them, 'your pity is given to ones you pity—your pity extended to them, once pitied.'

36.   Already, I believe, you have accomplished what I request, but 'endorse what springs to my lips, Lord.' She did
not think, as the day of her release came near, how her body
would be richly wound about or preserved in precious oils or
given any marker. She no longer cared if she were buried in
her homeland—she left the matter to us, asking only that she
be remembered at your altar, from which she was never absent a day, and from which is distributed the sacred victim
she recognized as 'canceling the account against us.' Conquered is the foe who ran up our account and sought to
bring suit but 'found no grounds in him' who wins our case
for us. Who can buy back his innocent blood, or cancel what
was paid for us, or say he did not buy us? The chain of her
faith made her immovable from the mystery that purchased
her. May none break her away from your protection, 'neither
lion nor dragon' cutting her off by force or slyness. She will
not claim that she owes nothing, to be refuted and trapped

by the sly accuser—rather she will say that her debts are canceled by the one no one can repay, since he paid for us what he did not owe.

37. Peace, then, to her and to her husband, for she had none before him and none after, to whom she ministered, 'bringing about the result of patience' when she made him your prize. May you call others, 'my Lord, my God,' call others, your servants and my brothers, your sons and my lords, whom I serve with heart and voice and writings, that as many of them as read this may remember, at your altar, your servant Monnica and him who was her husband, Patrick. Through their flesh, in a way incomprehensible, you ushered my soul into this life. May they cherish in memory those who were my parents in the light of this passing world, and are my siblings under you, the Father, and our mother church, fellow citizens of the eternal Jerusalem, to which all your people on pilgrimage aspire. Thus may my mother's last request for prayers be more richly answered in the prayer of all those reading this testimony than from my prayers alone.

BOOK TEN

MEMORY

I

WHY SHOULD OTHERS OVERHEAR ME?

1. You, who know me, may I come 'to know, even as I am known.' Enter into my soul, you its invigorator, and make it capable of you, so that you can retain and maintain it 'without blemish or wrinkle.' This is my hope, my reason for speaking to you, 'glad in hope' when I am rightly glad. As for other things in life, apart from this, the only lamentable thing is lamenting their loss, or rather *not* to lament lamenting them. For 'truth is what you have loved,' and 'whoever enacts truth comes to the light.' I want to enact the truth—before you, by my testimony; and, by my writing, before those who bear witness to this testimony.

2. Were I not to offer this testimony to you, what would I be hiding from you, since 'the inmost depths' of human awareness lie exposed to your view? I would be sealing you off from me, not me from you. Instead of that, my sobs are a warrant against any satisfaction taken in myself, and you shine into me, soothe me, make yourself loved by me and longed for, so that I, an embarrassment to myself, abandon me and turn to you, finding no way to satisfy myself or you but in you. I, whatever I may be, 'am perspicuous to you.' My motive in testifying I have declared, and its means are not physical words the body utters, but words the spirit utters, for you hear the mind crying out to you. The testimony to my sin is simply my anguish at it, as my testimony to any good I do is simply not taking credit for it, since you, Lord, 'bless the just man,' but first you 'make him just.' Tacit, then, is the testimony I offer 'to your view'—yet not so. It is tacit in sound but clamorous in emotion. Nor can I say anything worthwhile to others that you did not hear from me first, any more than you can hear me say anything to you that you did not first say to me.

3. But why let others overhear my testimony, as if they could treat my symptoms? People want a transgressive knowledge of others' lives, but are blissfully ignorant of what might change their own. Why, anyway, should they care to hear from me about my own condition if they will not hear from you about theirs? If they hear me describing myself, how can they know whether I am telling the truth (since 'no man knows what is within but a man's own spirit, which is also within him'); but if they are listening to you about their own condition, what can they say—that the Lord is lying to them? Is there, in fact, any way they can learn about themselves *except* by listening to you? Whoever calls what he learns from you a lie is lying to himself. Yet since 'love is all-believing'—for those, at least, united to others by their 'union to love itself'—I shall risk testifying to you, Lord, in such a way that, even though I cannot be the one to make my own testimony credible to others, the love with which they listen will lend it credit.

4. Clarify for me, you who medicine my inmost self, my motive in continuing this testimony beyond my sinful past. Hearing or reading of what is past may give others heart when they see how you have forgiven that past, 'have hidden it away,' so I may find happiness in you, after your transformation of my soul by belief and baptism into you. From a slumbrous despair that says it can do nothing, they may wake again to a love of your pity, to the sweetness of your favor, which 'strengthens the frail' by first revealing to them their frailty. The virtuous are interested in the tale of sinners who have repented, not because the sins interest them but because, though they once occurred, they do so no longer.

But what is my motive in testifying not only to my past but to my present condition, writing here for others to read what I am aware of, day by day, as I rely not on any innocence of mine but on expectation of your pity? I have recognized and recorded what use was testimony to my past. Yet many have asked about my condition at this moment of my testifying—both those who know me and those who do not know me personally, but have read something written by me or of me. Though they cannot listen at my heart, which alone could tell them what I really am, still they would like to hear what testimony I can bear to my present interior state, which their own eye or ear or mind cannot reach. Why should they believe my report of what they cannot know directly?—because the love of virtuous people tells them I do not deceive them in my testimony. Their love goes warrant for my credibility.

5. But what is *their* motive? Would they share my joy when they hear how close, by your gift, I am lifted up to you, and share my prayer when they hear how far, by my own dead weight, I fall off from you? If so, to such I will open myself. For it is not a trivial help, God my Lord, to have 'many give thanks for me or for many to pray for me.' I hope that a brother in spirit will love in me what you show him is lovable, lament in me what you show is lamentable—a brother, not a stranger, not 'a race of strangers, the speech of whose mouth is void of meaning, the work of whose strong hand is baneful,' but one who feels joy at what he approves in me, sorrow at what he disapproves, but feels love in both his joy and his sorrow. To such I will open myself, to those who feel relief for the good, grief for the bad, to be found in me. Since any good lodged in me comes from you, is your boon, while any bad discovered in me is mine, and comes under your ban, their relief will be for the former, their grief for the latter, and their relief's singing or their grief's wailing will rise up to your presence, 'an incense from their heart's thurible, to please you, Lord, with this odor of holiness filling your temple,' so you will 'show pity to me commensurate with your great pity,' with your own honor, and you will 'not abandon what you have begun in me until it is completed.'

6. This, then, is what I hope for in testifying not only to my former but to my present condition—giving testimony, that is, not only in private, with my own 'fearful joy and

hopeful sorrow,' but giving it within the hearing of Christian people, companions of my joy as they are sharers of my mortality, members of the same city, on our pilgrim's way to it, all of them who have gone before, or will follow, or presently accompany me. These are your servants and my brothers, your sons whom you make my masters, for me to serve them if I would live with you and because of you. Yet your call to this duty would have little effect if you were just confining it to words and not confirming it by your deeds. To respond to it with my word and my deed I must be 'under your protecting wings,' all helpless before peril were my soul not nestled under those wings, my frailty not allowed for by you. I am nothing in myself, but you my father are at hand, taking special care of me—the one who created me and nurtured me. You, all-powerful, are my all, at one with me before I can be at one with you. To such men, then, as you have ordered me to serve I open myself, not as 'a judge in my own case' but only to be given a hearing by them.

7. You alone can be my judge. Though 'no one can know what is within but a man's own spirit, which is also within,' there are some inner depths not even the man's own spirit can know, while you, who made those depths, know them through and through. Yet I know certain things about you that I know not about me—though under your scrutiny, 'I am contemptuous of myself, accounting me mere earth and ashes.' Admittedly 'we see now only murkily, as in a reflection, not as facing you directly,' and in 'my exile' I am farther off from you than from me, yet I know that you can never be overcome, and do *not* know whether this test or that one will overcome me—though I have hope [not knowledge], since 'you are true to your word, and will not let us undergo a trial beyond our strength, but will provide an escape from every trial, to let us survive it.' Both what I know about myself and what I do not know will therefore be my testimony to you, since what I know I have seen by your light, and what I do not know is from my own darknesses, not yet scattered by your noonday gaze.

THE CURRENT SEARCH
FOR GOD

8. My awareness that I love you is now firm, not wavering—your word struck a blow to my heart, and I love. The very sky and earth, after all, bid me love you, as do all the things (all around me) they contain. They bid every one of us to love, 'lest there be any excuse' for those not loving you (and even then, at a deeper level, 'you will have mercy where your mercy wills, show pity where your pity wills'—why else do heaven and earth reiterate their call to those not hearing them?). But what, in loving you, do I find lovable? Not, surely, physical splendor, nor time's orderliness—not light's clarity (how kindly its aptness to the eye), nor sweet linkages of variable melody; not soft fragrances of flower, oil, or spice; not honey or heaven-bread; not limbs that intermingle in embrace—these are not what, in loving you, I love. And yet I do—*do* love a kind of light, a kind of song or fragrance, food or embrace—in loving you, who are my light and voice and fragrance and food and embrace, all of them deep within me, where is my soul's light that fades not, its song that ends not, a fragrance not dispersed in air, a taste never blunted with satiety, an embrace not ending in depletion. This is what, in loving my God, I love—yet what can I call this?

9. I interrogated the earth, which replied, I am not it— and all earth's contents gave the same testimony. 'I interrogated the sea, its depths' with their slithery inhabitants, which informed me: We are not your God, go higher. I interrogated the veering winds, and the entire atmosphere, with its winged breed, replied to me: Anaximenes was wrong, I am no God. I interrogated the cosmos—sun, moon, stars—which said: No more are we that God you are in quest of. So I addressed the entirety of things thronging at the portals of my senses: Tell me then of the God you are not, tell me *something* at least. And, clamorous together, they came back: He is what made us. My interrogation was nothing but my yearning, and their response was nothing but their beauty.

At that point, I steered me toward myself, asking me: Who then are you? And I answered myself: A man. Which brought to my mind two things belonging to me, body and soul, one external to me, one internal. Through which of these two should I search for God? I had already used my body to inquire after God from earth and sky, so far as my sight could venture out toward him. Better now to use the interior. It was this self, after all, to which all the body's messages had been reported back, for it to take charge of and evaluate the responses made by heaven and earth and all their denizens, reporting: We are not God, he made us. 'The inward humanity' gained intelligence from its exterior subalterns, but it was I within, the self, the mind acting through my body's sense, who directed the interrogation of the sun's physical stuff, and it was to me that it answered: I am not he, he made me.

10.   Is not their beauty evident to all who can perceive it with their senses? Then why does it not deliver to all the same message? I do not mean to beasts, of course, large or little, since they can see but not interrogate the beauty—they have no adjudicating rationality, to assess what their senses report to them. Men, however, can by interrogation 'see God's invisible things through the things he has made—unless attachment to the visible enslaves them, disqualifying them, as slaves, from sitting in judgment. For the visible things do not answer interrogation divorced from judgment—not because the physical creation changes its summons (that is, its beauty) according to whether a man merely sees it, or sees it and interrogates it, but because one and the same beauty is silent to the one while speaking to the other. Or, rather, it speaks to all, but only those hear who bring the outward report before the inner judge of truth—the very truth that tells me: Your God cannot be heaven, or earth, or anything material. Those things say this by their very nature. How so? By their mere bulk, less in its parts than in the whole, a point in which you excel them, my soul—if I may speak to you [instead of them]—since you activate the body's bulk, providing it with life, a service no body can perform for another body (though God animates you, the body's animator).

11. So what, in loving God, do I love? One who is higher than my own soul's highest point? Then from that part of the soul I must strive up toward him—not through the soul's adhesion to the body, giving life to all its assemblage of parts. Not through that connection will I find God—or then 'a horse, a mule, lacking intellect,' might find God, since they too animate their own bodies. What, then, of another power of the soul over the body that God has made for me—a power not only conferring life on the whole body but confining its senses to separate duties, assigning the eye not to hear, the ear not to see, but each of the several senses to perform its proper office with its proper instrument, while the single center of all these diverse actions is my mind? Even from that I must strive higher, since horses and mules have this power too, perceiving things by means of their body.

III

THE CONTENTS OF MEMORY

1. REPRESENTATIONS (*IMAGINES*)

12. So I must pass over that faculty in my makeup, striving up by degrees toward its maker—which brings me out onto the lawns and spacious structures of memory, where treasure is stored, all the representations conveyed there by any of my senses, along with the further expressions we derive from those representations by expanding, contracting, or otherwise manipulating them; everything ticketed here and stored for preservation (everything that has not been blotted out in the interval, everything not buried in oblivion). Some things, summoned, are instantly delivered up, though others require a longer search, to be drawn from recesses less penetrable. And all the while, jumbled memories flirt out on their own, interrupting the search for what I want, pestering: Wasn't it us you were seeking? My heart's hand strenuously waves these things away from my memory's gaze, until the dim thing sought arrives at last, fresh from depths. Yet other things are brought up easily, in proper sequence from beginning to end, and laid back in the same order, recallable at will—which happens whenever I recite a literary passage by heart.

13. Here all these things are stored, individually and by type, according to their means of accession—light, for instance, and all colors and physical shapes coming in by way of the eyes; but by the ears all varieties of sound; by the nostril all odors; by the mouth all tastes; and by the body's whole sensory apparatus the inner or outer feel of things, whether they be hard or soft, hot or cold, smooth or rough, heavy or light; all received for deposit in or withdrawal from memory's huge vault—with secret chambers deep beyond scrutiny or description—where each item is filed according to its entry point.

Not that the things come in themselves—sensible representations of them are vividly at hand for expression in the memory. Though it is obvious which sense seized each, and brought it in for storage, who can say how these images are formed—for when I sit in a darkness without sound, I can recall colors at will (singling out black or white or what else I prefer), without any sounds to cut across or jumble the visual image, since sounds, though they are stored in memory, are kept in different compartments. I can bring them up, on call whenever I want, to sing what song I like with my tongue not moving, my throat not sounding, and with no color images that might block or break up the return of some masterpiece from the stock my ears supplied. The variety of things, by my various senses selected and collected, are at my memory's disposal. I can, while smelling nothing, identify the wafture from a lily, contrast it with that from a violet. While tasting or touching nothing, I prefer in memory honey to wine, smooth things to rough.

14. All these things I transact within me, in memory's immense courtyard, where sky and earth and sea are present to me, and whatever I sensed in them (except those I have forgotten). And this is where I bump up against myself, when I call back what I did, and where, and when, and how I felt when I was doing it. Here are all the things I experienced myself or took on trust from others. From this store of things there are new and ever-newer representations of my experiences, or of things accepted in the past on the basis of trust. These I recombine with representations of the past to ponder future actions, their consequences and possibilities, all considered (once more) as present. Within that vast inner chamber of my mind, stocked with representations of so great number and so great variety, I say to myself: This I shall do, or that—and this will follow, or that will. I say to myself: If only this would happen, or that would! Or: God keep me from this, or from that. And the minute I say it, from that vast treasure store of memory the representations of what I am describing [as in the future] are supplied at once—I could not say any of those things if the representations were not available to me.

15. Vast, my God, is the power of memory, more than vast in its depths, immense and beyond sounding—who could plumb them to their bottom? Even though this is a power of my own mind, it is what I *am*, still I cannot take it all in. The mind is too limited to contain itself—yet where could the un-contained part of itself be? Outside itself, and not in itself? Then how is it itself? Over and over I wonder at this, dumb-founded by it. Men go out to wonder at mountain heights, at immense sea surges, the sweep of wide rivers, the ocean's range, 'the stars' revolvings'—and neglect [the spectacle of] themselves. They do not even wonder that when I spoke of all these things, my eyes were not seeing them, though I could not have spoken unless my memory was seeing them internally, and on the same huge scale on which they were seen exter-nally—not only the mountains and seas, the rivers and stars which I have seen myself, but also the ocean, whose existence I can take only on trust. I did not engorge the things I saw, the things themselves are not inside me, but their representations are—and I can tell through which sense each one came.

2. RULES (*PERCEPTA*)

16. Nor does this exhaust the memory's capacity, since any of the rules I have not forgotten, yet, from my liberal studies are also contained here. They are lodged, as it were, in a space more remote from my exterior (though it cannot really be a space), where I do not possess representations of a thing but the thing itself. The nature of grammar, the art of logical argument, the topics of rhetoric—I know these in such a way that they are immediately present in my memory, not by way of the representation of some sight outside me. That indeed, is how sounds [as well as sight] are represented, since they come and go, like a song that strikes the ear, leaving its pattern for me to remember as if it were still being sung when it is not. An odor, in the same way, drifts by and is dispersed in air, but has so acted on the nostrils that it left in memory its representation—to be, by remembering, re-experienced. Food can no longer be tasted when it is being digested, though the memory in some way tastes it still. And anything felt by the body on contact with it can be remembered after that contact is broken. All these things do not themselves go into the memory. Their representations are absorbed—with wondrous celerity, and filed in wondrous receptacles, and wondrously rendered back in the act of remembering.

17. But when, by contrast, I hear that there are three topics posed in rhetoric—whether a thing exists, what is its essence, and what are its accidents—I do indeed keep representations of the words in which these subjects were sounded out, and realize that the words reverberated in my ear during their passage, then faded away. But what was described in those words I never absorbed through my senses, never beheld except in my mind; so my memory retains not any representations of these things, only the things themselves— and let them tell me, if they can, how they came to be inside me. I patrol all the gateways of my body, and find no entry point for these things. My eyes say: Had they been colored shapes, we would have ushered them in. My ears say: If they had made a noise, we would have conveyed it to you. My nostrils say: If they had wafted an odor, we would have passed it along. My taste sense says: Unless they can be savored, make no inquiry of me. Touch says: Unless it had bodily shape, I could not feel it; and if I cannot feel it, I cannot report on it. Whence, then, and through what channel came these subjects into my memory? It stumps me. For when I learned them, I was not taking them on trust from some other person's convictions, but accepting them on my own, establishing their truth, then filing them in my mind where I could withdraw them when I want to. Were they already in my mind—but not in my memory—before I learned them?

Where, then? And why, when these matters were simply stated, did I instantly assent, and say: Of course, it must be so? Or were they in memory after all, but stored there deep, behind other things, in secret crevices, so I might not ever have expressed these truths to myself had not someone provided an occasion for their being brought up from below?

18.   We can conclude, then, that to learn these things— those, namely, whose representations are not pulled into us through the senses, but directly perceived, in and for themselves inside us, with no aid at all from the senses—is to express in a connected way what was latent in the memory (but scattered about in disorder), and to make provision for their manageable arrangement (so that the scattered and disordered elements are reduced to a state readily accessed for the mind's use). What a quantity of such items my memory is stocked with, things discovered and (as I said) kept ready for use, the kind of things we say we have learned already and continue to know. Yet if I forgo their retrieval, even for brief intervals, they sink out of sight again, sliding deep into some inner windings, and they must be pressed up out of that place (for where else could they have gone?) and pressed again into knowable form. We must, that is, reconnect them after their dispersion. This is what we mean by *expression,* which comes from pressing, as *exaction* comes from acting, or *extension* comes from tending. In fact, this is a concept so commandeered mentally that *an expression* no longer means anything pressed-out in a general way, but common usage reserves it for what is expressed *in thought.*

3. AXIOMS (*RATIONES*)

19.   The memory also contains the endlessly extensible rules and axioms of mathematics and geometry, none of which is borne in upon memory through the senses, since none of them is colored, audible, scented, flavored, or tangible. Admittedly, when these sciences were being discussed, I heard words describing their axioms, but the words were not the same thing as the axioms, since the Greek language uses different words from the Latin for what are themselves neither Greek nor Latin concepts, or those of any other language. If I look at an architect's depiction of dimensions, even if they are drawn in lines as tenuous as a spider's thread, these sensible images are not geometric lines, which no sensible images can convey through the eye. These one knows from within, without the need for giving them any physical expression. In the same way I count with the senses of my body the number of external things, but the numbers of mathematics, by which we number, are not the same as numbered things, nor are they the representation of such things. They exist apart from them. One who cannot see such bodiless numbers may mock me for speaking thus, but I condole with him for mocking thus.

20. All these things I not only remember but remember learning them. And many arguments against them I remember hearing; and however false the arguments may be, my memories of hearing them are not false. And I remember distinguishing between what was true and what was said against the truth—an act of distinguishing I remember one way now, which is different from the way I remember often going over the distinction while I was expressing it. I remember these frequent acts from the past, and what I distinguish and conclude now I am laying away in memory, so I can remember in the future what I conclude at this moment. So, just as I have a memory of past remembering, so in the future, if I recall what I conclude now, I shall be recalling it by the power of memory.

4. REACTIONS (*AFFECTIONES*)

21. The mental reactions I experienced are also in my memory, but not with the relation the mind had to those reactions while undergoing them—in a different way, rather, according to the relation memory has with itself. For I can remember being happy, without being happy as I remember; or remember being sad, without being sad; or fearlessly recall being afraid, or sinlessly recall sinful desire. As a matter of fact, remembered sorrows can comfort, remembered joys distress me. There is nothing odd about this if I am remembering bodily sensations, for the mind is not the same thing as the body, and why should it be odd for the body's pain to be remembered to the mind's comfort? But this is a case of the mind remembering itself—why else would we commit something to memory by saying: *Be sure to keep this in mind*? Or, when forgetting, say: *That does not come to mind*? Or: *It has slipped my mind*—equating memory and mind? But if this is so, why is it that, when I take joy in remembered sorrow, the mind is happy at the memory's sorrow? How can the mind rejoice because it contains joy, but the memory not be sad because it contains sorrow? Is memory separable from mind after all? How could we claim that? The memory must, instead, be a kind of mental belly, where happiness and sorrow are like sweet and sour food, which—once they are digested— are retained but no longer tasted. The analogy is admittedly undignified, but not without a partial basis.

22.   It will be clear that I am drawing on my memory when I say that the mind has four categories of excitement— desire, joy, fear, and sorrow. And it is in memory that I find and produce whatever reasonings I can make about them, distinguishing them by genus and species, and defining each. Yet I am not excited by these excitements when I recur to them by remembering them. Before they were identified in memory, and called up from it, they had to be laid away there, otherwise I could not have decanted them by the act of memory. Could they be recalled from memory as food is belched from the stomach? But why, in that case, does the expressive mind's mouth not do what the body's does—experience again the sweetness or the bitterness of recalled joy or sorrow in the act of renewing the memory? Does the analogy fail because they are unlike in this respect? If they *were* alike in this way, too, who would want to discuss sorrow or fear, when every time we mentioned one we had to be sad or frightened? Yet we could not discuss them at all without having in memory the meaning of those excitements registered formerly by our senses—we do not recall merely the names for them, but the meaning as well. This meaning does not come from outside the mind through any bodily aperture—rather, the mind conceives the meaning while it is undergoing the impact made on the body's senses, and lodges that meaning in memory.

23.   Unless memory performs the act on its own—for who can be certain that the representations of the passions do not themselves cause the memory? When I use the word for, say, a stone, or the sun, even though the things themselves are not present to my senses, their representations are on call in my memory. Similarly, when I use the word for pain, it is not present to my senses if I am not hurting at the moment. Still, I could not know what is meant by the name for pain unless a representation of it were in my memory; nor, in conversation with others, could I distinguish it from pleasure. And even if I pronounce the word for health when I am healthy, thus experiencing the thing itself, I would not be remembering unless the representation of health were in my memory, any more than the sick could recognize what the word health signifies unless what is not in their body were supplied from what is in their memory. But when I pronounce the word for numbers, for what we use in counting things, it is not their representation that is in my memory. Number itself is there. If I refer to a representation of the sun, and I am remembering it, it is not the representation of the representation I recall, but the representation of the thing. That is what I have on call in my memory. And if I pronounce the name for memory, and recognize what I am pronouncing, where does that recognition take place but in the memory? So memory must have an immediate access to itself, not intermediated through a representation of itself.

5. FORGETTING (*OBLIVIO*)

24.   But if I say the word for forgetting, I recognize what is referred to, and how would I recognize it if I were not remembering it? It is not merely the sound of the word I recognize, but what it signifies. Unless I were remembering that, the sound of the word would have no effect on me, and I could not effect any understanding to it. So, though memory is in my memory when I remember remembering, both forgetting and remembering are in my memory when I remember forgetting—remembering *that* I forget, and forgetting *what* I once remembered. What can forgetting be but a lack of memory? And then how can forgetting be present, for me to remember it, when its very presence makes me lack it? All things we remember are in our memory—and since we must remember forgetting, or we would not know what the word means when we hear it, then forgetting must be in our memory. It is there for us to remember, but its being there means we forget. Or should we say that forgetting is not there itself when we remember it, but only some representation of it, since its being present itself would make us lack memory? Who can fathom such a thing, or make any sense of it?

25.   Here I labor at hard material, Lord, and I *am* that material. I am 'a terrain of trouble,' worked with much 'sweat of my brow.' What we are doing here is not, after all, 'studying heaven's distances,' not measuring interstellar spaces, not 'poising earth on balance,' I am what I am remembering, my own mind. It is no surprise for some non-me to be distant from me, but what is nearer to me than I myself? I cannot understand myself when I am remembering, yet I cannot say anything about myself without remembering myself. And what am I to make of the fact that I am positive that I remember having forgotten? Shall I say that what I remember is not in my memory? Or that forgetting is in my memory, to remind me to forget? Both are the purest nonsense.

Is there a third way to pose the matter? How about claiming that I do not remember forgetting but only the representation of forgetting? Yet how can I say that, when a representation of forgetting could be present in memory only if there had been, in the first place, a forgetting to be represented? That is how I remember Carthage or other places I have been, the faces I have seen, the external things I have been alerted to by my senses, or my body's own health or sickness. When these things were presented to me, memory took representations of them for my present consideration, or for later recollection if I remembered them in their absence. So if I remember not forgetting itself, but forgetting's representation, then forgetting must have been present when the representation was formed from it. Yet if forgetting is made present to the mind, how can its representation be taken into the memory when its very presence means the cancellation of what is memorized? Yet wild and inexplicable as all this may be, how can I deny that forgetting, which wipes out memory, is something I do remember?

26. The scope of memory is vast, my God, in some way scary, with its depths, its endless adaptabilities—yet what are they but my own mind, my self? Then what can that self be, my God? What is my makeup? A divided one, shifting, fierce in scale. In memory alone there are uncountable expanses, hollows, caverns uncountably filled with uncountable things of all types—some of them representations, like those of sensible objects; some present without need for representation, like the tenets of the liberal arts; while others are there by some mysterious registration process, like the mind's reactions, which the memory retains though the mind is no longer experiencing those reactions—still, if in the memory, how not in the mind? I rummage through all these things, darting this way and that, plunging down as far as I can go, and reaching no bottom. Such, then, is memory's force, this life force in the living man who dies.

My God, you who are my real life, what course is left me [reaching no bottom of memory]? I will pass over even this force in me called memory, pass over it while venturing toward you, 'my sweet illumination.' Are you telling me this? Striving up through my own faculties to you who are above them, in an effort to reach you where you are reachable, to 'embrace you where embraceable,' I will pass beyond the scope of what is called my memory—for even birds and beasts have memory (or how could they find again their nests or dens, or whatever other places they haunt, which could only become their haunts because remembered by them?). So I will pass beyond my memory in quest of him 'who sundered me from quadrupeds and made me wiser than the flighty birds.' I will pass beyond memory to find you— where? Where, my sure and loving stay, shall I find you? If I find you beyond memory, is that not to forget you—would I be finding by forgetting you?

27. The woman [of the gospel] who lost her coin and went looking for it with a lamp could not have found it unless she remembered what she was looking for. Even if found, how could it be recognized as the one she lost if she no longer remembers what she lost? I remember having lost many things myself, which I found again; and while I was looking, if anyone asked me whether this or that was it, I kept answering no until what I was looking for turned up. If I had not remembered what was lost, I would not have recognized it when it turned up. That is always the case when one searches for lost things and finds them. If we happen to lose sight of a thing, but not the memory of it, its representation is preserved within, and it is searched for till restored to sight. Then it is recognized by matching it with its internal representation. We could not say we had found what was lost if we did not recognize it, and we could not recognize it without the memory of it, since it was lost to sight but not to memory.

28. But what if the memory should itself lose something—as happens when we forget something and try to remember it? Where should we go looking for it but in the memory [that lost it]? And if something else than what we look for turns up, we reject it until the right thing comes along—upon which we say: Here it is. That is a thing we could not say without recognizing it, nor recognize without remembering it—despite the fact that we *had* forgotten it. Or had all of it not slipped the mind, but a part of it remained to make us seek what was lost, as if the memory had some feeling that it was not moving with something it had moved with before, but was limping, as it were, from the lack of what it was used to, and trying to recover what was missing. If, for instance, we see or express in the mind someone we know, but try in vain to remember his name, any other name that comes to mind does not click. Since it did not express the man in the past, it is rejected—unless, of course, the right one comes to mind, and its exact fit is acknowledged. What could establish that but memory? Even if another affords us the occasion to remember [by supplying the name], that occasion is provided for the memory's activity. We would not accept it on trust, as if new to us, but acknowledge only what tallies with our memory. If the name had been entirely expunged from memory, we would not remember it even when given the occasion to—so even things we remember we forget are not entirely forgotten. If they were, we could not still be looking for them.

6. HAPPINESS (*BEATA VITA*)

29. But how, Lord, do I look for you? In looking for you, I seek the happy life. It is 'life for my soul I look for,' since you vivify the soul as the soul vivifies the body. How shall I look for this life of happiness? I do not yet have it, or I could say: This is all I need. Whereas now I can only say that I am still looking for it—do I have some memory of it, at least as a thing forgotten but which I remember having forgotten? Or is it an unknown thing some instinct for knowledge prompts me to discover—a thing unknown entirely, or unknown in the sense that I no longer remember having forgotten it? What is a life of happiness but what all men want, what none can *not* want? Where caught they some report of what they should want, where some glimpse of what they should love? Somehow, I know not how, we do want it. People may at times experience a certain degree of happiness, or a sense of withheld happiness. This is not the held happiness of those in heaven, yet it is better than having no happiness, either withheld or held. And some kind of happiness even the unhappy have, enough to know what they want (as indeed they do continue wanting).

Somehow or other they have caught a glimpse of happiness, provided them by some or other way of knowing, which puzzles me—was it by remembering happiness? If so, we must have known some prior happiness. It is not my present inquiry whether we knew it separately, or all together in the man who committed original sin, 'in whom we all have died,' and from whom we are all descended in sorrow. No, I ask simply if happiness is a thing remembered—for how could we love it if we could not recognize it? As soon as we hear the word for happiness, we admit that is what we all crave. It is not the word that draws us—when a person speaking Greek hears the name for it in Latin, he is not drawn to it, not recognizing what is meant; but we who speak Latin are drawn by it, as the Greek speaker would be to his own word for the same thing; since joy itself is not Greek or Latin, but the thing all Greeks and Romans pant to acquire, as do the speakers of every other language. All have the concept of happiness, and all would answer yes if asked whether they want it—which could not happen if happiness, and not merely the word for it, were not remembered.

30.   But is it remembered as one remembers having seen Carthage? Hardly. For happiness is not seen by the eye, like a physical object. Do we remember happiness, then, as we remember mathematical truths? Not that either, for those who know those truths are not still trying to acquire them, while we who know enough about happiness to love it, are still trying to acquire it, to *be* happy. Well, then, is this like remembering persuasiveness? Not really. Some who understand the word when they hear it are not themselves persuasive; and many would like to be persuasive, which shows they have some understanding of what it is—but they have observed with their senses the persuasiveness of other people, which pleased them and made them want to acquire it, a pleasure that shows some inner grasp of its meaning, and a desire to acquire based on that pleasure, while we have not grasped the meaning of happiness from observing others with our physical senses.

Can it be that we have an idea of happiness from memories of our own joyful experiences? Perhaps. For I can, though sorrowing, remember joy, looking back on the happy life in a state of desolation, and the joy was not being experienced by my eyes or ears or nostrils or tongue or fingers. Rather, it was something the mind experienced during a past period of happiness, some record of which was lodged in memory, enabling me to recall it, sometimes with revulsion, sometimes with longing, according to the different sources of my memories. Shameful things that once filled me with joy I now remember with disgust and reviling. At other times, joy in virtuous and upright things I recall with longing, if they are gone, and my former joys sadden me.

31.   But happiness [not mere joy]—where or when did I experience that, so that remembering it, I should love it; and loving it I should long for it? And not I alone want this, or some elite I belong to, but everyone without exception wants it. We could not want it with so determined a will had we no equally determined knowledge of it. But how is this knowledge determined? Offer two men a choice—between, say, becoming a soldier or not—and one person will take that course, another refuse it, though both instantly say yes if asked if they hope to be happy. In fact, the one who becomes a soldier hopes that will make him happy, and the man refusing hopes the same. Is this just a matter of individual preference? Even so, they are at one in wanting happiness, just as they would agree in saying that they want delight, which they equate with the happy life. Though they pursue it in different courses of life, yet they are striving toward the same object, that which delights them. And no one can deny he has experienced happiness, since something fixed in his memory responds when the word for it is pronounced.

32.   Let me not, Lord, in this my heartfelt testimony to you, accept as happiness every joy that I encounter. There is a 'joy not given sinners,' one given those who freely seek you, who find you are their joy. This is true happiness in life, to take joy in you, for you, because of you—this, nothing else, is happiness. Those who do not know this pursue their joy elsewhere, and though it is no true one, yet they cannot wrench their desire entirely free from some representation of that joy.

33. Or do all men not want happiness after all, since those unwilling to find joy in you, who alone are true happiness, must to that extent *not* be wanting it? Or do all want happiness, but because 'flesh's urges oppose the spirit, and the spirit's oppose the flesh,' they cannot accomplish what they desire, and they settle for what they can accomplish? Incapable of what they desire, they do not desire enough to become capable of it. Yet when I ask anyone if he prefers to find true joy or false, he is as quick to say he wants the true one as he is to say he wants happiness—yet happiness is itself a joy in the truth, and that is a joy in you, God, who are the truth, 'my enlightenment, the rescue of my honor, my God.' You are the happiness that everyone desires, the only happiness. All desire to take joy in the truth. I have met many who enjoy lying to others, but none who enjoy being lied to themselves. How did they learn that there is a happy life but in the way they learned that there is truth? They prove they have a love of truth by not wanting to be lied to—when they show a love for the happy life, which is nothing but a joy in truth, they show to that extent that they love truth as well, and they could not do that if they did not have some sense of it in memory. Then why does not truth itself give them joy? For the same reason that they are not happy? The memory of true happiness is dimmed by their engagement with things making for unhappiness. 'As yet the light they have is attenuated—let them travel on, keep traveling lest darkness overtake them.'

34. How can 'truth itself breed enmity,' or 'a man become their foe by preaching the truth,' when happiness is what is desired, and happiness is joy in truth? Is it because, though truth is loved, other things are also loved, and those loves pass for love of truth? Since they do not want to be deceived, they persist in thinking their falsehoods are not deceits. By staying true to what they love they become enemies to the true. They love a supporting but not 'a rebuking truth.' Because they hate to be lied to, but like to lie, they love to find things with the help of truth, but hate to be found out by it. But this is the revenge truth takes on those men unwilling to be found out by it: It not only finds out the truth about them but prevents them from finding it out. To this, even this, is the human mind reduced, to this blind, weak state, that it wants to hide its foul vileness from others, but wants nothing hidden from it. But truth turns this upside down—so that the mind does not hide the truth, but the truth is hidden from it. Yet even so, the miserable thing would still prefer truth to falsehood, and it could be happy if it did not place obstacles in its own way, but rejoiced instead in that truth that makes all things true.

7. GOD (*DEUS*)

35.   See what a long ramble I have made through my own memory in quest of you, Lord, and I have not found you anywhere but inside it. Nothing about you have I found but what I remember from the time I began learning about you. Nor have I forgotten what I early learned of you, for in each truth I learned I was learning about my God, who is truth itself, nor did I forget that. In my memory, then, you have been lodged from the time I first learned of you, and there I find you when I remember you and 'take delight in you,' take the holy delights your pity grants me as you consider my deprivation.

36.   But where in memory can you be lodged, Lord, where lodge you there? What hallowed place have you made for yourself in me? You honor me with your presence as a lodger in my memory, but where you may be lodging I am still to know. While calling you to mind, I went beyond the precincts of memory that even animals manifest, where I did not find you among the representations of physical objects. I moved on, to the precincts where I store my mental reactions, and did not find you there. I entered my mind's chamber, for it too is seated in memory (how else could the mind remember itself?). But you were not there, either. Just as you are not a representation of objects, or the reaction of the soul (whether we are happy, sad, desirous, fearful, remembering, forgetful, or whatever), neither are you the mind, for you are the mind's lord, God, though you deigned to lodge in me from the time of my early memories of you. Why, in fact, am I inquiring where in memory you lodge, as if there were physical precincts there? All I can know is that you must be there, since I do have a memory of you from my early days, and there is where I find you when remembering.

37.   Where, however, did I find you, to know about you? You could not have been already in my memory, before that first learning of you. Where could I have found you, for learning about you, but outside of me, and within you? And that could not have been in a place, a place I might enter or leave—surely, there is no such place—for as truth you hold audience anywhere and with anyone who approaches, responding at once to all their different concerns. Clear is your counsel, not always clearly accepted. Your best suppliant is not the one who asks to hear what he wants but to want what he hears.

38.   Slow was I, Lord, too slow in loving you. To you, earliest and latest beauty, I was slow in love. You were waiting within me while I went outside me, looking for you there, misshaping myself as I flung myself upon the shapely things you made. You were with me all the while I was not with you, kept from you by things that could not be except by being in you. You were calling to me, shouting, drumming on deaf ears. You thundered and lightninged, piercing my blindness. You shed a perfume—inhaling it, I pant for you. For your taste, I hunger and thirst. At your caress, I am feverish for satiation.

IV

THE FLESH'S URGES

39. When 'all of me clings to you,' there will be no more 'sorrow or toil' for me, but you will bring my life to life, filling it with you. For I am not yet filled with you, since you draw up what you fill while I weigh myself down with delights I should regret and regrets that should delight me, confused about which will prevail. Pity, oh, take pity on me, as sorrow for past wrong contends with happiness over present good, and which will prevail confuses me. Pity, O Lord, take pity on me—you see I am exposing my wounds, the patient before the doctor. Pity the pitiable me. 'What is man's life on earth but a testing'—and who would have chosen its burdens and hindrances? You tell us to bear but not to love them. No one who merely bears a thing is loving it, even if he loves the bearing of it. He may be glad that he can bear it, while preferring that he did not have to. So in affliction I want ease, but when eased I fear affliction. Is there anywhere between the two states, where life might no longer be a testing? Not, surely, in worldly ease, which is twice dangerous, from fear of its reversal or from disintegration by its indulgence. Nor, even more surely, in worldly trial, which is twice and thrice dangerous, making us hope for ease, undergo its own harshness, and lose heart to bear it. Without any remission, therefore, is 'man's life on this earth a testing.'

40. I have no hope at all, then, but in your pity for me. Granting what you require, require whatever you will. You impose on us self-discipline. Well, as the writer has it, 'Since I realized that no one can be self-disciplined unless God grants it, knowing who grants it is a mark of wisdom.' Self-discipline is a gathering inward, toward oneness, from our dispersal out into severalness. For no one loves you well who loves anything else except because of you. You, my love, who burn forever without consuming, set me on fire, for the charity of God. You impose self-discipline? Require anything, granting what you require. **41.** You unmistakably demand that I check 'the flesh's urges, the eyes' urges [to know], and worldly designs.'

1. THE FIVE SENSES: TOUCH

You ordered me to give up my sexual partner—and even marriage, though allowed me, you advised me to forgo. I complied, since you granted me the power, even before I became a priest of your mysteries. Yet there are representations of things formed by preceding habit, and they linger in the very memory I have been delineating—representations that throng on me, though weakly, while I am awake, but with enjoyment in my dreams, where I yield to the imagined act. So strong in my flesh is this fictive representation that sleeping falsehood prevails where waking truth could not. Am I not my real self then, Lord? Is there some border between two different selves which I cross and re-cross in sleeping or waking? What happens in this process to the self-rule that stays strong against such promptings, unbending under buffetings, even in the presence of real women? Does it go to sleep because the body's external senses do? In that case, how could we stay strong at times even in sleep, remembering wakeful resolves to stay chaste, not yielding to these sensual solicitings? Yet the border between the two selves remains clear enough that, when we do fail in dreams, we can awake to a clear conscience. Because of the distinction between the two states, we did not do willingly what we regret was done passively in us.

42. Clearly you could, if you would, 'remove with your healing hand the symptoms of sin' in my soul, to blot out in 'an overflow of bounty' all lustful stirrings, even in my sleep. Gradually, by degrees, you will give me strength, that my soul, still mired in lust, will detach itself and obey myself as I obey you. Then it will put down its own rebellions against itself, not greeting the sensual representations with shameful action of uncleanness, even to seminal emission, but will not want such a thing, even in sleep. It would not be hard for you, 'able with overflowing bounty to grant more than we ask or could think of asking,' to free me, not merely at some stage of my life but at this one, from finding pleasure in these things, or from finding more than it would be easy for one chastely disposed to resist, even in his sleep. Meanwhile I have testified to you, God, who favor me, that that is not my condition so far with regard to this flaw. 'Cautiously joyful' for what you have granted, mournful for what I still lack, I look forward to the completion of your pitying acts in a final peace, one that will fill my inner as well as outer self, at the time when 'death is by victory obliterated.'

2. THE FIVE SENSES: TASTE

43. Another 'trouble of the day' I have, and would it were 'fitted to each one.' For daily our body deteriorates, and we build it back up by eating and drinking—till the time when you 'blot out both food and the stomach,' canceling hunger with a wondrous plenitude and 'clothing disintegration with integrity eternal.' But at present hunger is a sweet compulsion, which I must wrestle into control, lest it overcome me. I treat it as a foe by fasting, 'treating my body as my slave,' yet hunger's pain is only stayed with pleasure—for hunger and thirst are a kind of pain, they burn us like a fever till they be medicined by eating, so we call this crisis of our body a delight, since your soothing gifts, the products of earth and water and sky, accommodate our weakness.

44. As medicine, then, you teach me to use food. But while I pass from hunger's exigence to a soothing plenitude, that very passage takes me into a snare of urges, since the process is so pleasing, and there is no other way of passing from need but what the need itself demands. We eat and drink to maintain our health; but a seductive satisfaction tags along with the act, and sometimes tries to slip ahead of it, so that the pleasure I claim or wish to be using for my health I am actually using for its own sake. It is hard to find the proper match between them, since what is enough for health is too little for pleasure, and it is often hard to distinguish my health needing nourishment from my gluttony demanding submission. My soul in its weakness takes advantage of this ambiguity, making a cover of it, happy not to know what health truly demands, making health a mere excuse for stealthy dealings with delight. Try as I may to resist such daily troubles, I call on your intervening arm and turn over the problem to you, since I have not been able to settle it myself.

45. I acknowledge what you have decreed, 'Clog not your hearts with dissolute or drunken ways.' Alcoholism is not my problem (may your pity keep me far from it), but gluttony subtly steals over me, even in your service. May your pity also keep me far from that, as 'No one gains self-discipline but by your grant.' What we ask in prayer you often bestow—but a thing bestowed before we ask is equally your gift. And 'by your gift' we come to see it as your gift. Though not an alcoholic myself, I have known many of them whom you made sober. So you keep some from ever having the addiction, and keep others from forever having it, and keep both groups from thinking that freedom from the addiction is anything but your gift.

I have heard another of your injunctions: 'Follow not your urges, but shun indulgence.' Still another thing I have heard in your Spirit, which gives me great comfort: 'What we eat will not make us better off, nor what we refrain from make us deficient'—which means that I will not be happy for what I eat, nor sad for what I do not. I also know this saying: 'I have learned to cope with what comes, familiar with plenty or privation, able to do all things in him who strengthens me.' There spoke a soldier of the celestial militia, not the kind of dust that we are—though remember, Lord, 'we are but dust,' it was from dust that you shaped man, 'who was lost and has been found.' So Paul, too, made of dust, could not of himself say he was 'able to do all things in the one who makes me content' unless you breathed strength into him, the act that has made me love him. Strengthen me to be content in that way. Granting what you require, require whatever you will. Paul gives testimony to what he received from you, and 'what pride he takes is pride taken in the Lord.' A quite different voice it was, one requesting aid, that said, 'Relieve me of the belly's urges,' making it clear, God sacrosanct, that what you say *should* be done, *can* be done only by your aid.

46. It is your teaching, good Father, that 'For persons who are clean all things are clean.' Thus 'it is the person eating [not the thing eaten] who does wrong if his diet hurts another,' since 'all things are good that you have made, and nothing is to be rejected so long as it is taken with gratitude.' Nor does 'diet ingratiate us with God.' Neither should anyone 'categorize us by our food or drink.' Moreover, 'he who eats [certain foods] should not shun one who does not eat them, and he who refrains from them should not condemn the one who eats them.'

This is what you have taught about food, for which I am grateful, God my teacher, and praise you, when these words 'knock on the door' of my ears to shine light in on my heart. 'Rescue me from each of my testings.' I have no qualms about ritual uncleanness in the food, but about unclean urges toward it. I realize that Noah was allowed to eat of any food at hand, that Elijah was strengthened by meat, that [the Baptizing] John, while supernaturally strong in his abstinence from other animals, was not ritually tainted by the locusts that were permitted him. I know as well that lentil pottage was used as a lure for Esau. David regretted his untimely thirst, and our Prince was tempted [by the devil] not with meat but bread. Thus those who made the exodus through the desert incurred blame not for wanting meat but for criticizing the Lord when he did not provide it.

47. In the midst of such tests, then, I surely have 'trouble of the day' from my urges toward food and drink, since I cannot resolve to abstain from food once for all, never indulging in it again, as I gave up sexual intercourse. The bridle on my appetite for food must be adjusted with calibrated tightenings or loosenings of the rein, and who, my Lord, can maintain the exact degree of required tension? That is the mark of a hero, 'whose soul expands to your honor'—and I, a sinful man, am not such a person: Yet my soul, too, expands to your honor, and 'this world's conquerer' will 'interpose himself' between you and my sins, accepting me as one of 'the weaker members of his body,' one of 'all those written in your book, though you see his imperfection.'

3. THE FIVE SENSES: SMELL

48. To allurements from the sense of smell I am, for the most part, indifferent. Sweet smells I neither long for when absent nor reject when present; but I could do without them entirely, so far as I am aware. I could be wrong—knowledge of my own capacity is hidden in a murkiness I lament, and the mind, trying to estimate what it is able to do, cannot rely on itself. My inner resources are hidden from me until exposed by trial. No one should count himself safe, in a life known as 'a continual testing,' as if immune to relapse just because he has once reformed. There is only one hope, one thing to rely on, one steady commitment to us—your pity.

4. THE FIVE SENSES: HEARING

49. I was more entangled and submissive where the pleasures of hearing are concerned until you cut me loose and gave me back my freedom. Now when I hear music vibrant with your Scripture, sung with skill in a sweet voice, I yield to some degree, I must admit, but am not hypnotized by it, since I can break off at any point. Nonetheless, when the music carries a meaning that enters into me, it makes something in my heart honor it, I know not how properly—do I prize it higher than I should? When music is added to the sacred words, I find that our souls are kindled to more ardent piety than when they stand alone, as if each emotion of our spirit were being touched by its own special tone or tune, intimately responsive to it by some secret tie. A delicious physical sound should not melt our reason, but should attend it as its subordinate partner—but once admitted on these terms, it tends to skip ahead of reason and take the lead from it. When this occurs, I go wrong without realizing it, and only recognize what has happened later on.

50. Yet at other times, suspicious of being misled, I adopt too great a caution, harshly willing to ban all melodic sweetening of David's words sung in the psalms, not only from my own hearing but from that of the entire church—though I think it safer to follow a rule often reported to me as being that of Athanasius, Alexandria's bishop. He had the cantor so flatten out the tune that he seemed rather to be speaking the psalm than singing it. But in the last analysis, when I recall the tears I shed at the church music when I first returned to the faith, and how moved I am even now by the meaning of the music rather than the music itself—so long as the words are sung in a clear voice appropriately fitted to the tune—I see just how useful music can be.

So, though my mind hovers between pleasure's danger and the custom's benefits, and I would not want to adhere blindly to one view of the matter, I increasingly favor the practice of singing in church, which can strengthen the wavering soul's feeling for religion. Yet I must testify for myself that when I am moved more by the music than by its meaning, I feel this offense should be punished, and wish I had not listened to the cantor. That is my plight. Weep for it, all you whose concern for virtue issues in good works—those without that concern will not care enough to weep for me. But you, Lord my God, hear me, heed, look on with pity, and heal me, before whom I am made a riddle to myself, which is the symptom of my sins.

5. THE FIVE SENSES: SIGHT

51. The last sense I must include in this my testimony is the sensual pleasure I derive from the body's eyes. Let the ears of 'that temple which is your people' be brotherly and devout to me as I end this account of my testing by the flesh's urges, under whose pummelings 'I groan and yearn to be covered round with my heavenly shelter.' Shapes beautiful or striking, colors bright or soft, delight my eye. I would not have them fill my soul—let God alone do that, who 'made them firmly good,' since he is my good in ways that they are not. My every waking moment, sights brush across my eyes, not intermitted as sounds are when the cantor falls silent, or the choir does. For light, the empress of all colors, floods all things visible everywhere—wherever I am in the day, wooing me with its variable coloring even when I, at my tasks, am not adverting to it. But so powerfully pervasive is this light that our impulse is to call it back if it is suddenly removed, and to be depressed if it is gone for long.

52. O Light!—that Light Tobias saw within him when, eyes blighted, he showed his son the path to life, a path he was treading beforehand, with love's feet that never strayed! O Light that Isaac beheld, with aged eyes too wearied, too outworn, to identify his sons for blessing, yet whom his blessing identified! O Light that Jacob beheld when bowed and blinded by the years! The rays from his heart shone down the generations of that people prefigured in his descendents. When his son Joseph tried to uncross the hands he laid with mystic power on his grandsons, he did not heed the outer view of Joseph, but the inner light haloing his grandsons. All those lights are one Light, and 'one are all those' who look on it with love. The physical light earlier described sweetens with a lure of danger the life of the world for lovers of the world. But those who know how to praise light properly, 'You All-Creating God,' lay claim to the light by singing of you, and are not claimed by the dark in dreams of their own. Let me be in that choir of singers, resisting the eyes' enticements lest my feet be enmeshed as I tread your path. I lift inner eyes to you, so you may 'disentangle my feet from the snare.' You continually disentangle my feet, no matter how often I am thrashing in the snares laid about me. 'You sleep not, nor slumber, standing guard over Israel.'

53. How many snares for the eye men contrive by ingenuity and art—dresses, shoes, vessels and other craftwork, pictures and other images, things going far beyond the norms of utility, economy, or religious symbolism. Outwardly they make idols of their own handiwork, while inwardly they unmake the handiwork they are, effacing what God fashioned in them. But these very things lead me, my God, my source of pride, to sing a hymn to you, making of praise a sacrifice to my Sacrificed One, since the work of an artist's skilled hand, made under the direction of his soul, just passes on a beauty that was shed on that soul from a source above. Toward that source my soul aspires night and day, while the creators and appreciators of art learn from above how to admire beauty rightly but not how to use it rightly. The right use is there for them to see, but they stray beyond it, not 'preserving their power for you,' but dissipating their work in pleasant trivialities. Yet even I, proclaiming and accepting these things, become at times enmeshed in beauties that I see, and you disentangle me, Lord—you do so since I see your pity for me, yet remain pitifully enmeshed, and you in pity disentangle me, sometimes without my realizing it because though I have sometimes stumbled only slightly, I fell painfully at other times, and was thrashing in the net [when rescued].

V

TRANSGRESSIVE
KNOWLEDGE
(*CURIOSITAS*)

54. There is another way we can be tested, one more insidiously perilous. Beyond the cravings of the flesh, of all that delights or lures the senses, luring men far off from you to their perdition, the soul takes in through those senses an empty and transgressive urge, not to indulge the flesh but to use it in experiments rationalized in the name of mental expression or science. Since this is a craving to know, and the eyes lead the other senses in quest of knowledge, it is called in Scripture 'the eyes' urges.' Though only the eye sees in a literal sense, we apply the word to the other senses when we employ them to know a thing. We do not do that with the other senses—do not say: Hear that red, or Smell that white, or Taste that glow, or Feel that brightness. We do say, however: See how it shines (which only the eyes can do). More than that, we say: See how it sounds. See how it smells. See how it tastes. See how hard it is. So all sensible knowledge is called an urge (as Scripture puts it) of the eyes, since seeing, which is the prerogative of the eye, is taken as a loan word by the other senses when they, by a kind of seeing, are deployed to know.

55. This should make it easier to tell the difference between use of the senses for sensual pleasure and use of them for transgression. The former turns toward beautiful sights, resonant sounds, sweet aromas, flavorful tastes, and soft touches. The latter experiments with their opposites, not submitting to the gross for its own sake, but from the drive to experience and know. Pleasure is not exactly what one takes in the sight of a mutilated corpse, which makes men shudder—yet if one is encountered, people flock to be repelled by it and stricken pale. This is something they do not want to see [in terms of sensual pleasure] even in dreams, or if forced to look at it while awake, or if lured to the sight expecting something pretty. (The same [contrariety] can be found in the use of the other senses, though it would take time to run through them.) It is for this perverse craving that unnatural things are put on in the theater. This also leads men to pry into the arcane elements of nature, which are beyond our scope—knowing them would serve no purpose, yet men make of that knowing its own purpose. And even in real [non-magic] religion, this makes men 'put God to the test,' badgering him for 'signs and miracles' with no saving purpose, just providing excitement.

56. In this vast forest, full of snares and perils, see how much I may have cleared and cleansed my heart of, as you gave me strength to do, 'God of my rescue.' But will I ever be confident, while so many things buzz around me in my daily life, be confident enough to claim that nothing of the sort will compel me to go view it, that I am no longer addicted to such nonsense? Admittedly, the theater no longer enchants me, nor do I indulge astrology, and I never trafficked with spirits for their knowledge—superstitious occultism I detest. Yet how many devious modes of insinuation does the Enemy use to make me seek a sign from you, whose service should be simple and unassuming. I beg you for the sake of our true king and our holy Jerusalem, the home of the humble, that, as I am far from consenting to such things now, I may become far and farther from it in the future. For when I pray for the recovery of some sick person, my aim is not at all for a magic cure, but that I may submit willingly to whatever you will.

57. Who, indeed, can list all the minute and unnoticed ways by which this transgressive urge tests us daily, tripping us up? How often do we put up with empty gossip, to humor its silly bearers, only to be drawn in by the gossip as we listen? I no longer go to the arena to see a hound course a hare.

But if by chance I catch sight of that in a field, the hunt attracts me, distracts my concentration on the most important matters. It reins aside not my horse's pace, but my heart's regard. I would stay stupidly rooted to the spot did you not jog me with memories of my former weakness, urging me either to use the sight as a sign of something higher leading me to you, or to brush it dismissively aside and ride on. Even sitting at home I can be hypnotized as a fly is snatched from the air by a lizard or as it blunders into a spider's web. Is the hunt any the less for the hunters' trifling size? I can, indeed, admire in them your marvelous way of ordering even slightest things—but that is not what fascinated me at first sight. And a quick recovery from that first stumble is not the same as freedom from stumbling at all. Yet I am constantly succumbing in this way, and I have no hope but your deep and deeper pity for me. My heart is a dumpster for such things, stuffed with superfluous trash, which often intrudes on and muddies my prayer. Even as my heart's words strain up toward your ears, my serious effort is baffled by a flood of silly thoughts flowing in from somewhere or other.

58. Should I just discount these petty things? Should they not rather drive me back to the hope I have of your pity, since you have changed so much in me already? You know what stage I am at in the changes you have worked in me. For a start, you cured me from my drive toward self-justification, as a first step toward dealing with my other sins, so you strengthen what is enfeebled, restore what is decayed, bringing pity and compassion as a crowning work, to satisfy with good things all my longings. It is for this you broke with your menaces my pride, and gentled my neck into your yoke, the yoke I bear, 'a mild thing' to me, just as you promised and as you made it (it was light all along, though I knew it not, since I shied from submitting to it).

VI

WORLDLY DESIGNS

59. Tell me, you whose rule is not overweening—for yours is real lordship, under no other lord—has a third kind of testing slacked off in me, or can it ever slacken? I mean my desire to be an object of others' awe and affection, for no purpose at all but to take joy in that which gives no joy. Pitiable, is it not, this filth of self-promotion? It diverts real love and untainted awe from you, who 'rebuff the proud and shed favor on the lowly,' you whose thunder strikes worldly schemes, 'makes mountains tremble to their roots.' The enemy of our true happiness uses the fact that society requires love and awe for its officers—he makes '*Bravos* heaped on us' his snares. Eagerly amassing such praise we become insensibly addicted, detaching our gratification from truth and attaching it to human flattery. It now delights us to elicit love and awe not because of you but in place of you, as the Enemy fits us to his own company, not convened with him in love but convicted with him in punishment. He has 'set up his throne in the North,' where in the dark his ice-cramped followers may bow to his crooked and misshapen aping of you. But we, Lord, are 'your little flock,' keep us yours, spread over us your wings, for us to take refuge there. Be you all our boast, all affection for us be directed at you, all awe be for your word preached by us. The man who seeks human praise while you are indicting him cannot rely on those who praise for exoneration while you are judging him, nor for pardon when you are condemning him. This applies not only when 'the sinner is praised for pleasing himself or blessed for doing evil.' Even the man who is praised for some talent you bestowed on him—if he delights more in being praised for having the gift than in having the gift that is praised—he wins human praise but your indictment. And the one praising him is better than he is in being praised, since the former takes delight in a talent bestowed on a man by God, while the latter treasures being given the praise by men more than in being given the talent by you.

60.   Such testings are we put to daily, Lord, incessantly are we tested, tried day after day by 'oven of the tongue.' Here, too, when you impose self-discipline, grant what you require, require whatever you will. You are familiar with my heart's moaning and my eyes' flooding over this concern. I cannot judge rightly how far I am purged of this infection, since I fear that the sin has just gone into hiding, where it is visible to you but not to me. For my other ways of being tested I have found some method of self-evaluation, but not for this one. With carnal activity or a transgressive occultism, I can measure my progress in relinquishing them by the degree of anguish, greater or less, that I feel if deprived of them, whether by choice or by chance. With riches, again, which can supply means for any or all three of the sinful urges, if a man who has them cannot tell whether he is too attached to them, he can measure his detachment from them by giving them away. But how are we to test whether we could live without praise? Clearly not by leading lives so wicked, so damned and grotesque, that anyone who knows us must revile us. What crazier ploy could be devised or adopted? If praise is customarily and rightly a concomitant of virtuous activity, it cannot be removed from what it accompanies. But if it cannot be removed, how can I test my willingness, great or little, to do without it?

61.   What testimony, then, can I offer you, Lord, on this part of my testing? I can only admit that I like being praised, though I like more whatever truth there may be in the praise than the praise itself. Given the choice between being universally praised for mad and exotic behavior, or being universally denigrated for consistent and proper behavior, I am confident which I would choose. Still, I wish I were not elated by praise for good behavior—but elated I am by the tribute to good behavior, and just as dejected, I must confess, by denigration of it. And when this failing nags at me, excuses suggest themselves, how validly only you can tell, since I cannot be objective.

You have imposed on us not only self-discipline (whereby we withhold our love from certain things) but justice (whereby we confer love on proper objects), and have given as one object of such love, our fellow men. Well, I often think that I am pleased at another's progress or promise when he has shown the good sense to praise me—or that I am displeased because another denigrates in me what he does not understand or what is actually laudable. Moreover, I am annoyed when another praises in me what I am not proud of, or praises inordinately what I do not consider one of my strong points. Now how am I to know whether I react this way because I insist that anyone who praises me do it on my own terms, not out of any regard for his enlightenment, or because what I like in me becomes more satisfying when others endorse that liking? In some way, then, I can accept no praise if the praiser does not share my self-image, since he is either praising what I am not proud of at all, or praising too much what I take little pride in. How can I ever be objective about myself?

62. In you, who are my truth, I acknowledge that praise should be welcomed not because it is my praise offered me for my actions, but because it edifies my neighbor. But whether I meet that standard I cannot tell, where even to know you were simpler than knowing myself. I beg you, God of mine, show me *me*, that I may testify to what I find mangled in me, and my brothers can then pray for me. Let me honestly ask myself, why, if I welcome praise only if it edifies the praiser, am I less concerned when others are falsely accused than when I am? Why do I feel more hurt if insulted myself than if I see another insulted, even if the insult is equally unjustified in either case? Is this, too, beyond my knowing? Must I conclude that I 'lure myself into my own trap' and am not 'enacting truth'? 'Keep me far from such crazed action,' Lord, let not my own self-description be 'a sinner's oil to make heavy the head.'

63. 'Poor and beggarly am I,' but better at least when recognizing this with inner sobs and seeking your pity, till you complete what is depleted in me and confirm the completion in a peace no haughty eye beholds. But every word pronounced, every act performed, before others incurs the dangerous test of wooing praise, wheedling a coaxed endorsement of one's self-estimate. Overcoming this test becomes a new form of test—to glory vainly in rejection of vainglory, for one is not rejecting the glory if one glories in the rejection.

64. Inward, deeper in, there lies a variant on this temptation, whereby people are vain of nothing but their own approval, whether others approve of them or no, not even trying to win their approval. But you profoundly disapprove of self-approvers—they count as a distinction what disfavors them; or count real distinctions as their own, not as coming from you; or count them as coming from you, but by their own desert; or count them as your gift, yet not as something to be enjoyed with others, but to be withheld from them. You observe how my heart trembles at all three prospects, and all similar perils and toils. And I realize that I have not so much stopped wounding myself as you have not stopped healing me over again.

VII

CONCLUSION

65. Where, my God, my Truth, have I ever wandered without your being there with me, to teach me what I should shun, what seek—whenever, at least, I took my own faulty perceptions to you for correction? I have surveyed what my senses could of the outer world. Those senses themselves, and the body that feels them, and the life that moves the body, I have observed in myself. After that, I proceeded down receding depths of memory, their complicated vastness, mysteriously crammed with riches beyond counting—'I pondered it, and trembled'—and nothing could I have known of this without you, though nothing of it was you. Nor could I, who did the searching, be you. I ran through it all, trying to inventory each item and assign it its proper worth. I assessed the reports brought in from my senses (though some things were mingled with matter from my internal inventory) and I distinguished and numbered which sense was bringing what report. Making a survey of this rich store, some things I deposited there, and some withdrew. In all this activity, I—or, rather, the faculty by which I did it—was not you, for you are the light everlasting which I turned to for seeing whether and what each thing was, and what it was worth. You were what I heard teaching and guiding, as I often do—it is my comfort, and to it I resort, whenever I can, from the press of affairs. Nor in all these things that I look at (in your light) do I find secure refuge but in you. In you my 'scattered selves are reunited,' not to be 'parted in exile' from you. At times you admit me into feelings of deep sweetness, honeyed I know not how, which, were they made complete, would make this life something beyond this life. But then I am toppled back to earth, weighted with heavy burdens, plunged into compelled ways, netted, wailing strongly but strongly netted still. So great is compulsion's heavy baggage. Here, I can abide but do not wish to; there, I wish to abide but cannot—miserable either way.

66. I have performed an examination of the symptoms left in me by sin, conducting it under the heading of the three urges, and I have called your right arm to my rescue; for even with a wounded heart I recognized your splendor. Stricken down, I asked: Can anyone strive upward? 'I am hurled off from the gaze of your eyes.' You are the truth ruling all things, yet I, while greedy not to lose you, wanted to have you and keep my own lies too—much as the liar does not want to lie so well as not to recognize the truth himself. That is why I lost you, who will not share your habitation with a lie.

67. Who will help me to rejoin you? Should I employ angelic agencies? If so, by what approach? What forms should I submit? Many, of whom I have heard reports, have tried this, who wanted to return to you but felt unable to do it themselves. Addicted to the lure of occult visions, they met only with delusion. Lifted up by pride in their learning, with swelled chest rather than humbly beaten breast, they fell in with comrades of a similar disposition, fellow conspirators in pride—'the masters of this lower air'—who befuddled them with black arts in their quest for a purifying mediator, who was not to be found there. Their mediator was the devil, that 'changeling into an angel of light,' whose incorporeal state had a potent charm over their proud corporality. They were mortal and sinning, where you, Lord, to whom they were haughtily seeking reunion, are immortal and sinless. A mediator between God and men should be in some way like God, in some way like men, lest in these two respects he should be similar to men but far from God, or similar to God and far from men, and fail to be their meeting point. That false mediator, whose pride was rightly misled by your hidden judgment, does have one thing in common with men—sin—and would like to be seen as having one thing, too, in common with God: he pretends to immortality because he is not clothed in mortal flesh. But since 'the wage paid for sinning is death,' he is like men in this as well, and is condemned to death.

68. The true mediator, revealed to us only by the secret of your pity, and sent to teach us lowliness by example, is 'Christ Jesus, mediating between God and men'—placed between mortal sinners and the immortal innocent, mortal with men, innocent with God. By the justice linking him to God, he can give to sinners, linked to him by redemption, a reprieve from the death that he willingly shared with them, since the wage paid to innocence is life and peace. He was revealed to the holy men of antiquity, so they could be saved by faith in his suffering to come, as we are redeemed by faith in his sufferings undergone. He is our mediator in terms of likeness as a man, but not as the Word of God, who is equal (not like) to God—he is 'God in company with God,' though there is only one God.

69. What love you bore us, best of fathers, in 'not sparing your only son, but giving him over for us,' the sinful! What love you bore us, since for our sake, though 'he did not think equality with you a usurpation, he became obedient even to the point of dying on a cross.' As the only 'free man among mortals,' who had 'power to lay down his life and to lift it up again,' he became both victor and victim for us, victor because victim, both priest and sacrifice for us, priest because sacrifice, making your 'servants become sons,' because he is both son to you and servant to us. My hope in him is not empty, since you will 'heal all symptoms left by my sins,' through him 'who sits at your right hand' and interposes himself for us—without whom I had despaired, since sin's symptoms in me are many, many and severe, but stronger is your medicine than they. We might have taken the word of God to be too far above us for any traffic with men, and been without hope for ourselves, had he not 'become flesh and taken up his dwelling with us.'

70. Ground down by my sins and by the weight of my

sorrow, I troubled my heart with thought of escape into the desert, but you forbade it and strengthened me by saying: 'This is the reason Christ died for all, that those who live should no longer live in themselves but in him who died for them.' So now, Lord, see how 'I throw all my worry over to you,' to 'live in wonder at your scripture.' My 'ignorance and sins you are familiar with,' but teach me and heal. It was your Only-Begotten Son who 'bought me with his blood,' and 'in him are secreted all riches of wisdom and knowledge.' Let no haughty ones crow over me, since I know 'at what cost I was purchased'—I eat it, drink it, give it out, and want in my neediness to be filled with it, among those who 'eat and are filled,' since 'those in quest of the Lord shall praise him.'

BOOK ELEVEN

FATHER (ORIGIN)

I

PRAYER BEFORE
STUDYING SCRIPTURE

1. Surely, Lord, you cannot be ignorant of anything I tell you, nor in your eternity do you see time simply as it develops. Then why do I arrange in sequence what I narrate for you? I do it, not as informing you, but as stirring up my own reaction to you, and so that people reading this may say 'vast is the Lord, and as vast should be his praise.' As I have maintained, and still maintain, this is done out of love for your love. We continue to pray, even though Truth itself tells us 'Your father knows what you need before you ask him for it.' We lay open to you our reaction to you, testifying to our pitiable state and your pity for it, so you may free us entirely as you have already partly done, making us no longer pitiful in ourselves but happy in you, since you have called us to be 'poor in spirit, gentle, mournful, hungry and thirsty for justice, merciful, pure in heart, and bringers of peace.'

That is why I have offered you this long account, to the best of my ability and desire, since 'your goodness shows in your endless pity.' **2.** And now I have the opportunity for 'my pen to articulate' the whole of your encouragements, your warnings and consolings and guidings, by which you brought me to preach your word and share your mysteries with your people. Even if I have the opportunity, still, to continue my narrative, the water drops of time are too precious for me to do so—I have for too long been 'burning with a need to study your law,' to testify about what it is I understand and what I have no sense of—through the dawning of your light and the lingering shades of my own night—and how far my frailty has been taken up into your strength. I would not have any hours diverted from this, apart from those I must spend on the restoration of the body, the drawing together of the mind's resources, and the services I owe, or pay without owing, to others.

3. 'Hear my prayer,' Lord my God, let your pity assist my desire, aflame not only for my own enlightenment but for service to my brothers in love. You know this of me, since you see my heart. For me to offer up my thought and voice to your service, grant me what I may offer. Of myself 'I am without resource and poor,' but you prove 'wealthy for all who call on you.' Free of care, you care for us. 'Circumcise my lips' from every rash or deceptive utterance, outward or within me. Purify my delight in your Scriptures, so I am not misled in them myself nor misleading others. Lord, draw near, Lord my God, and pity, you light of the blind and strength for the frail—and light, as well, for the seeing, strength for the vigorous. Draw near my soul and hear me 'crying from the abyss.' If you do not hear in the abyss, what resource have we? To whom shall we cry?

Yours are the days, the nights, the moments that flit by as you decree. Lengthen my days for the study of your law's inner meanings. Open the door to them when I knock on it. You had a purpose in causing the Scripture to contain so many pages dark with obscure meaning. This dense wood shelters deer who have taken refuge in it, restoring their strength, pacing its lanes and grazing there, resting and ruminating. Lord, make me complete for the receiving of these matters. I take my joy in what you say, richer than piled-up pleasures. Grant what I love, for the fact that I love was itself your grant. Leave me not, keep what you planted from withering. May I testify to whatever I find in your books, and hear 'the voice of your praise,' and drink from you, and 'ponder the marvels of your law' all the way back to the origin of what you made, heaven and earth, all the way forward to the perpetual reign to be shared with you in the city you make holy.

4. Let your pity, Lord, assist my desire—it is not, I believe, a desire for worldly things, for gold or silver or gems or

fine vestures, honors or power or sensual pleasures. Nor is it
for the requirements of the body as we pass through this pilgrimage of life—all these will be 'supplied to those in quest
of your reign and justice.' You behold, my God, the source of
my yearning. 'The wicked have described their delights, but
they are nothing to your law, O Lord.' Behold the source of
my yearning. Behold it, Father, and seeing it, prosper it. Favoring me with your pitying gaze, open as I knock the way to
your words' inmost meaning. I ask this of you through our
Lord Jesus Christ, 'the man of your right arm, the son of
man, whom you have appointed as your mediator with us.'
Through him you sought us out who were not seeking you,
and sought us in order that we might seek you. He is your
word, through whom you created all things, and me among
them. He is your Only-Begotten, through whom you have
called the company of believers, and among them me, into
your sonship. I ask you through him 'who sits at your right
hand and interposes himself on our behalf.' 'In him are all
the hidden treasures of wisdom and of knowledge.' These
are what I seek in your books. Moses wrote of him, who
speaks here himself—the truth speaks to us.

II

GENESIS ON CREATION

5. May I listen so as to grasp how 'in the origin you made heaven and earth.' Moses wrote these words, wrote them and departed from us, passing from us to you, and he is not here in my sight. If he were, I would clasp him to me and would request, would beg through you, for him to explain these words to me, I would bring my ears up close to every word flowing from his mouth—not that I could understand him if he spoke Hebrew, which would knock at my ears without reaching inward to my intellect. But if he could speak Latin, I would know what he was saying. Yet even then how could I know that what he was saying was true? If I did know that, it would not be on his word that I relied. Within me, where my thoughts are at home, truth itself would speak, not in Hebrew or Greek or Latin, or any uncouth tongue, it would speak without the body's organs, without mouth or tongue, without the sounding out of syllables. It would tell me that Moses spoke true, and I would confidently assent to your emissary, admitting that he spoke true. Since, in any event, I cannot cross-examine him, you are the one I beg, you who inspired him to speak true, you the truth itself, you I ask for forgiveness of my sins, and ask that you make me understand the truths that you made him utter.

6. Look at heaven and earth. They proclaim that they were created by the fact that they change and do not remain the same. A thing that exists without being created has nothing missing from it that it ever was. That would be evidence of change—it is not all that it once was. They proclaim, as well, that they did not create themselves—that they had to be created, and that they could not pre-exist themselves to create themselves. They proclaim this by the very way they exist. For they are beautiful (since you are beautiful who made them), and good (because you are good), and existing (because you do)—but they do not have the beauty or goodness or being of you, their creator. Their beauty and goodness and being are as nothing compared with yours—as our knowledge of this fact (which is from you) is as nothing compared with your knowledge.

7. How did you make heaven and earth? What apparatus of construction had you for so huge a project? You did not work like a human artisan reshaping physical materials to give them the form seen within by the directing mind. Where could that directing mind come from but you? But for all the soul's directing power, it gives form only to things already in existence and having some prior form, whether as clay or stone or wood or gold or whatever. And these would not have existence already if you had not contrived it. You are the creator of the artist's body, of the soul that works its limbs, of the material he reshapes, of the talent that masters his art and devises internally what he will fashion externally, of the body's perceptual system that transmits his design from the mind into the stuff he works, and then reports back to the mind what was made, so it can compare it with the inner model to see if it corresponds with it. All these things praise all things' creator.

How did you bring all these things about? In the way you created heaven and earth—because you did not make heaven or earth out of their own materials, not out of air or water (for they are just elements of heaven and earth). The whole cosmos could not be made out of the whole cosmos, since no place existed for making it until it was made to exist. You had no manual tool for manufacturing heaven and earth. For where would you get a tool for creation that you had not already created? What exists but from your existence? You used your Word to make them, and in your Word they were made.

8. How was that Word spoken? Not as the voice came

from a cloud to say 'This is the son I love.' That voice sounded and ceased, it had a beginning and end. The syllables were enunciated and passed by, the second after the first, third after the second, each succeeding in its time, and silence succeeded the last. It is evident from this that the voice was caused by changes in the physical surroundings—serving your timeless purpose, it is true, but temporal in themselves. These words sounding in time passed through the ear to the judicious mind, whose interior ear is alert to your timeless word. The mind compared the words sounding in time against the timeless word heard in silence, and concluded that they were entirely different things. The sounding words are a lesser thing than man, in fact are nothing at all, since they flew by and are gone. The Word of God, however, is a greater thing than man, since it changes never.

If, in order to make heaven and earth, you had said 'Let there be heaven and earth' in sounding and passing words, there would have been a physical medium before the creation of heaven and earth, a medium in which the words could make changes in time in order to run though their temporal sequence. But no physical stuff existed before heaven and earth. And even if it had, you would not have made it with a passing voice, since what was being made would be the medium for the passing voice in which it would be said, 'Let there be heaven and earth.' And whatever was the stuff of which that voice should be fashioned, it would not have existed unless you made it. So what word did you use to make the physical stuff of which the words could be made?

9.   You summon us, then, to understand 'the Word that is God in company with God,' which is eternally uttered and in which all things are eternally uttered. In it one thing is not said so that another may succeed it, with others to follow to the end, but all is said at once and for all time. Were this not so, time and change would already exist, not eternity and immortality. This much at least I know, my God, I thank you for the knowledge and testify to my knowledge before you, anyone knows it along with me who blesses you, who resists not your unshakable truth. We know this, Lord, know it for

a certainty: Insofar as anything is not now what it was before, or was before what it is not now, it is a thing that dies or comes into being. But your Word does not fade out or follow in sequence, it is immortal and eternal. Therefore it is with a Word that is eternal that you utter, all at once and for all time, all things you utter, and whatever you utter comes to be. And it comes to be by nothing *but* your utterance. But what you utter is not, like the utterance itself, all at once and for all time.

10.   Why should this be so, I ask you, Lord my God? I have some grasp of it, but how to explain it is beyond me, unless I can put it this way: All things that begin to be or cease being do so when your eternal reason, which neither begins nor ceases, knows that it ought to begin or cease. That reason is your Word, 'the origin, since he speaks to us' as such—for so in the gospel [of John] he spoke in his incarnate self, and these words sounded externally in men's ears, that it might be believed and internally examined, and understood in the eternal truth where all learn from him who is the true and 'only teacher.'

There I listen to your voice speaking to me—for all teachers must speak to us, and those not teaching might speak without speaking to us—and who can teach but the immutable truth? Even when we are pointed toward the truth by a mutable human, we are being guided toward the immutable truth where we truly learn by waiting for and listening to him and, overjoyed with 'joy at the Bridegroom's voice,' we return ourselves to our own origin. He is our origin, since we would have no place to return after wandering unless he were continuously there. And whenever we return from wandering, it is by understanding that we are returning, and he teaches us to understand this because he is 'the origin insofar as he speaks to us.'

11.   It was at the origin that you made heaven and earth, God, in your Word, your Son, your power and wisdom and truth, by wondrous utterance and wondrous creation. Who can take it in? Who can give an account of it? What is this light that shines through me and transfixes my heart without a wound? I shudder off from it and burn toward it, shuddering off because I am so deeply unlike it, burning toward because I am so deeply like it. It is Wisdom, personified Wisdom that shines through me, piercing the shades that so obnubilate me that I faint under the light, from my own darkness and the burden of my punishments. 'My energy is drained by my own neediness,' and I cannot sustain my own well-being until you 'look kindly on all my evil inclinations and treat all their symptoms.' For you will buy my life back from its decay, and honor me with your compassion and pity, and so fulfill my yearnings with good things that 'my youth will come back to me as an eagle's.' It is 'hope that rescues us,' and we await with confidence what you have promised. Let anyone who can do so, heed you speaking inwardly, but I will outwardly speak with confidence from your own revealed words: 'How wondrous are your works, Lord, all that you have in your wisdom created!' That wisdom is the origin in which he created heaven and earth.

12. What but 'old nature, unredeemed' makes people ask what God was doing before he made heaven and earth? If, they say, he was at leisure and did not busy himself, why did he not stay that way indefinitely, continuing to refrain from labor as he had in the past? If something new occurred to God as the result of a new decision on his part, to create something he had never done before, how could there be a genuine eternity where a decision not formerly made was eventually made? That decision is not itself a creature, but has to be made before the creation, since nothing would be made if no decision to make it had been formed. So the decision had to be part of God's very being—and if part of his very being occurs that was not there before, his being cannot be called eternal. If, on the other hand, the decision to create was eternal, then why is not the resulting creation eternal?

13. Those who argue that way have not even begun—no, God of wisdom, Light of minds, they have not begun—to see how things are made in you and by you. They try to savor everlasting things, but their heart flits back and forth between things that have passed and are still to come, and

remain sterile. Who will catch and calm the heart, so a gradual stillness will come over it, and a gradual gaining on eternal quiet, to be compared with the unquietness of time, and
to be found incompatible with it? Then it can see that a time
is made long only by a succession of many things moving
past. If they all occurred at the same time, it would not be a
long time. In eternity there is no such succession of things,
the entirety is present, and that cannot be a time. In time, the
past is shoved away by the arriving future, and the future
trails behind the past, and both past and future are constituted by the present they flow through. Who will catch and
calm the heart, to see in stillness how it is the stillness of
eternity that controls past and future, without itself being either past or future? Is my hand up to this great work, can
the words from my mouth catch and calm like a hand?

14.   How do I respond to those who ask what God was
doing before he made heaven and earth? Not as one is said to
have responded by way of jest, to avoid the brunt of the
question, claiming God spent the time getting hell ready for
those who pry into serious matters. Since mocking is not
solving, I would not say that. Rather than have one person
mocked for asking a serious question and another person
flattered for answering with a smart lie, I would, if I did not
know the true answer, simply say I do not know. But I say
that you, our God, are the creator of all creatures; and since
all creation is included in the term heaven and earth, I can
answer boldly that at the *time before* he made heaven and
earth he was *not,* in fact, doing anything—if he had been, it
would have been making heaven and earth; and I wish I were
as sure of other things it would profit me to know as I am
that no created thing was created before creation.

15.   But if someone of unsteady mind, shuffling representations of times past, is astonished that you, the omnipo-
tent, the omni-creant, the omni-tenant, should have waited
through numberless ages before making such an imposing
world, he will see that his astonishment is misplaced if he just
rouses himself and pays heed. How could there have been
numberless ages before you made them, you who make and

begin all things? What times could have been before you began them? How could times pass before they were there for the passing? Since you set all times in motion, if there were any times before you made heaven and earth, how could anyone say you were doing nothing *at the time*? You would have been creating time, and there could be no time past until you made time first. If there was no time before heaven and earth, you could not have been doing anything then—since there was no time, there was no *then*.

16. There is with you no time before time—if so, you would not be before that time; yet you are before all times. In your transcendent present state of eternity, you are before all past time and after all future time, since the future is still to come and when it comes it will be the past, but you are ever the same, and 'your years wither not.' Your years neither come nor go; but ours do come and go, so that all may file by. Your years stand all together, since they move not, and departing years cannot be driven out by arriving ones, since none recede. Our years will not be entire until they are entirely gone, but your years are one day, not one in a series but a today that yields to no tomorrow and follows on no yesterday. Eternity is your today, so you eternally beget the Son to whom you said, 'Today I have begotten you.' All times are made by you, who are before them. There was never a *time* when time was not.

III

THE NATURE OF TIME

17. There was, therefore, no time before you made any-thing, since time itself is something you made. No time could be eternal along with you, since you are always there; and if time were always, it would not be time. Then what is time? Who can give that a brief or easy answer? Who can even form a conception of it to be put in words? Yet what do we mention more often or familiarly in our conversation than time? We must therefore know what we are talking about when we refer to it, or when we hear someone else doing so. But what, exactly, is that? I know what it is if no one asks; but if anyone does, then I cannot explain it. But this at least I can venture: If nothing were passing away, there would be no past time; and if nothing were still coming, there would be no future time; and if nothing were passing, there would be no present time. But what mode of existence can those first two times have, since the past is no longer and the future is not yet? And the third time, the present, if it were not pass-ing away, would not be the present but the eternal. But if the present is only a time because it is passing away, how we can say that it exists, since the reason for its existing *as time* is that it will soon not be, which means we can only say it ex-ists because it is on its way to non-existence?

18. Yet we speak of time as being long or short, though it is only about the past or future that we say this. We say a long time from now, in the past, when we mean a century or so ago, or in the future when we mean a century or so hence. A short time means, say, ten days ago (for the past) or ten days hence (for the future). But how can something that has no being be long or short? The past no longer is, the future is not yet. So perhaps we should not say a time is long but that it was long, or will be long. Lord, my illumination, is your truth just having fun with man? Does a long time past become long when it has passed away, or was it long while it was passing in the present? It could only be long when what was being long *was*. When it had passed away it no longer *was,* so it could not *be* long. So we should not say that something was a long time ago, since we cannot establish what was long if we try to find it in a past that is no more. Should we, rather, say that it *was* a long *present* time, since its passing through the present was long? Before it had passed away, there was some being that could be long; but as soon as it passed away, it ceased to be long because it ceased to be.

19.   I ask you, my human mind, since you experience the lapses of time and their measurement, whether present time can be long. Come, what is your answer? The current century, is that a long time? First we must ask how a whole century could be in the present. Take year one of the century. If we are in it, then we still have ninety-nine years to go, and we are not yet in those, since they are still in the future. If we are in the second year, then one year is in the past and the rest are in the future. And so with any year down the line, whenever it is present, the rest will be either in the past or in the future. So the century as a whole cannot be in the present. What about the year we are in, can that at least be present to us? But here, too, if we are in the first month, the rest are to come. If in the second, the first is gone and the rest are still coming. So the present year is not present as a whole, and if not present as a whole then not present as a year. There are, after all, twelve months in a year, and if any of the twelve is present, the other eleven are either in the future or in the past. But not even one of these months is actually present, but only one day at a time—if the first, then the rest are to come; if the last, then the rest are already gone; and if any day between, the rest are divided between past and future.

20.   See, now, how the present time, which we saw as the only one that can be called long, has been reduced to barely a day—no, we have to amend that, since not even a day can be present. A day is nighttime and daytime, twenty-four hours, and the first hour leaves the rest still to come, the last leaves the rest behind it, and any other stands between past and future. And each hour is itself articulated into fleeting minutes. Those that have already flown off are in the past, and the rest are still in the future. If we suppose some particle of time which could not be divided into a smaller particle, that alone deserves to be called the present. Yet it flies in so headlong a way out of the future and into the past that no bit of it can be fixed in pause. If it paused, its earlier part could be divided from its later. Thus the present itself has no length.

Then is there any time we can call long? How about future time? Well, we cannot say that *is* a long time since there is not yet anything to be long—we have to say it *will be* a long time. When? Not while it is still in the future, since it must first be in order to be long. But when it moves out of the future, which is not yet, into the present, where it can *be,* and therefore be *long,* the present vociferates what we have already heard, that the present cannot be long, either.

21. For all that, Lord, we observe the different ways times lapse, and compare them, and call some longer and some shorter. In fact, we measure how much longer or shorter one time is than another, and we conclude that one is twice or thrice as long as another, or perhaps of the same length. It is passing time we measure, as we experience it. For who can measure past time, which is no more, or future time, which is not yet, unless he is bold enough to claim that he can measure non-being. So time can only be measured as it passes. Once past, it is no longer there to be measured.

22. These are queries, Father, not conclusions. Control and guide me, my God. Will anyone claim that what we learned as children and teach our children is not true after all, that there are *not* three tenses, past, present, and future, but only the present, and that the other two do not exist? Or that the other two exist, but only as emerging out of mystery, when the future turns into the present, and submerging into mystery, when the present turns into the past? If, after all, the future did not exist, how could prophets foretell it? There would be nothing there to foretell. And if the past does not exist, how could historians use their minds to put together a true account of it? There would be nothing to put together.

23. Help me, you ground of my hope, to deepen my queries. Steady my searching mind. If the future and the past are, I wish to know where they are. If I cannot learn that, I can at least be sure that wherever they are, they are not there as the future or the present, but both are the present. For if the future is there as the future, it is not there yet. And if the past is there as the past, it is no longer there. So whatever they are, and wherever there, they must be there in the present. When a history of the past is truly related, the memory does not bring back the events themselves, which have gone out of existence, but the words describing them—and these words were taken from the senses as the events left on them a print of their passage. My boyhood, for example, which no longer exists, is in the past, which also no longer exists. Then what does? A representation of it does—that is what I see in the present, stored in my memory, whenever I remember or recount my boyhood. Does something similar happen in prophecy, representations of what does not yet exist being somehow made present in the mind of the prophet? I cannot tell that, my God, but at least I know this, that we often make provisions for our future actions, and the provisions exist, because they are in the present, but the actions do not exist, because they are still in the future. But when we come to perform the actions for which we made provisions, then the actions will exist, since they are no longer future, but present.

24. Whatever occurs when secrets of the future are foreseen, they could not be foreseen if they did not exist. And what exists is in the present, not the future. So when some are said to foretell the future, they are not seeing the future, which does not yet exist because it is still to come—perhaps they see some preconditions or indications of the future, which exist already. So to them the objects of their prediction are not future but present; they are materials from which the mind can form estimates of what will be. These estimates, too, are in the present, and those predicting the future are actually seeing their own present estimates.

From many possible examples of this, I cite one. Looking at the morning twilight, I predict the sun will rise. What I see is present, what I foresee is future—not that the sun will exist (it already does), but that its rise will exist. That has not yet occurred, so I could not predict its rise without having an image of that event in my mind (as I do even now when I mention it). Two things I see—the twilight preceding sunrise, which yet is not sunrise, and the image of sunrise in my mind, which is also not sunrise. Both these things must be seen in the present for the future to be predicted—the sun's rising. Future things are not yet. And if not yet, then not at all. And if they are not at all, they cannot be seen. But they can be predicted from things which already are, and are already seen.

25. What means do you employ, you ruler of the universe, for showing select souls the future—as you did the prophets? By what means do you, for whom there is no future, reveal the future? Or do you, rather, reveal present things that indicate the future? For what does not exist cannot be shown. Whatever means you use of showing the future is far, far beyond my range of vision. 'It unstrings me, I have no power.' But power I would have, sweet Light of my inmost eyes, if it were your gift.

26. What should be clear and obvious by now is that we cannot properly say that the future or the past exist, or that there are three times, past, present, and future. Perhaps we can say that there are three tenses, but that they are the present of the past, the present of the present, and the present of the future. This would correspond, in some sense, with a triad I find in the soul and nowhere else, where the past is present to memory, the present is present to observation, and the future is present to anticipation. With this proviso, I can see and grant that there are three times after all;

and the customary way of talking about three different times—past, present, and future—may be accepted, despite its imprecision. I do not worry, oppose, or criticize it, so long as one understands, beneath the language, that what is future is not yet, and that what is past is no longer. We rarely speak with real precision, but often use words loosely while understanding what is intended.

27.   Earlier I said that we measure time as it passes, making us able to say that one time is twice as long as some other, or equal to it—and so of all other segments of time we can measure and describe. That is how we measure time as it passes. If someone should ask me how I know this, I answer that we are measuring something, that we cannot be measuring what does not exist, and that the past and future do not exist. But how can we measure the present, when it has no extent of its own? We must measure time as it passes, since it cannot be measured once it has passed, when it is no longer. Where does the time we are measuring come from, pass by, and pass to? Where from but the future? Where passing by but in the present? And where going but to the past? But that must mean that it comes from what does not exist yet, passes by what has no extent of its own, and goes to what exists no longer. Time must be measured in something with extent, or we could not say that things extend longer by double or triple or whatever amount. But in what extended thing do we measure time as it passes? In the future, from which time proceeds? We cannot measure what is not yet. In the present, by which it proceeds? We cannot measure what has no extent. In the past, to which it proceeds? We cannot measure a thing that is no longer.

28.   My mind has burned to understand this knotty problem. Do not seal, Lord my God and good Father, do not seal off from me things so esoteric yet so everyday, but open them to my longing and bathe them in the light of your pity for me. Is there anyone else I could learn from but you? What good would it do me to testify to my own ignorance before anyone but you? You are not annoyed by the importunacy of my burning need to know your Scripture. Grant

this thing I love, since my loving it was your grant. Grant it, Father, since you know how to make your gifts a boon to your children. Grant it, since I have set out on the path to understanding, and 'the task is beyond me' until you open a way for me. By Christ I beg you, for the honor of him who is the holy one of holies, let no one forbid my journey. 'I too have faith, from which I speak.' This is my ground of hope, for which I live, 'to contemplate the Lord's delights.' It is you who 'prolong my days into age,' yet their mode of passing is what I do not understand. We talk of this time and that, these times or those—of how long ago it was when this one spoke or that one acted. We say it has been a long time since we saw something, or that these syllables have twice the length of a single short one. That is how we talk, or hear others talk, and we are understood by others and understand them. It is the stuff of our everyday converse, yet it is all masked in darkness, and an understanding of it is still to be found.

IV
TIME AS THE MOVEMENT OF BODIES

29. A scholar once told me that time is nothing but the motion of the sun and moon and stars, without my agreeing. If that were true, why should not time be motion in any or all physical objects? If the lights of heaven should go out, but a potter's wheel were still turning, would there be no time by which we could measure its rotation, saying that each takes as long as the others? Or if some rotations are slower, others faster, can we not say that the former takes more time, the latter less? And in the act of saying this, do we not speak in time? Could we call syllables long or short unless some took a longer time, some a shorter time to pronounce? Grant to man, my God, to see in small matters principles that are common to small things and great. The stars and luminaries of the sky are there 'to serve as indications and times, as days and years.' I grant that, and would not maintain that a turn of the potter's wheel marks a day. But that scholar could not claim, either, that it does not mark a time.

30. I long to understand what time does and what it is, how we measure motion by it, and say, for example, that this motion takes twice the time of that one. This is my query: In the complete circuit of the sun around the earth, does the sun's motion itself constitute a day, or does the amount of time it takes, or both? We do not call a day simply the time when the sun is above the earth, marking day as distinct from night, but the whole time from one sunrise to the next, according to which we say so many days have passed, counting day and night together, with no separate status for night, but the entire circuit of the sun must be completed to make a day. If it is the mere circuit that makes a day, then if the sun should speed around the earth in an hour, would that be a day? But if the amount of time consumed makes a day, then making the circuit in an hour would not constitute a day, but only the consumption of the full twenty-four hours. If it is *both* the circuit of the sun and the amount of time it takes that make a day, it could not be called a day if either of two things happened—if the sun made its circuit in an hour, or if it stopped in place for the twenty-four hours it normally takes to complete its circuit from sunrise to sunrise.

My query is not at this point about what we should call a day, but about the time we use for measuring the sun's motion—by which we might say that, if the sun made its circuit in twelve hours, it was taking only half the time it usually does. I am interested in the time we use when we compare the two and say that one is two times what the other is, no matter whether the sun goes from one sunrise to the next in the longer time or the shorter one. No one can tell me that time is the motion of celestial bodies, since there was a man at whose prayer the sun stood still, to carry a battle through to victory, and time kept going, though the sun did not. All the length of time that was needed to carry on and finish the battle was run through to completion. So I think that some kind of reach in opposite directions [toward future and past] is at issue here. I think that—or do I merely think I think it? You must settle the matter, my Light, my Truth.

31. Do you require that I acquiesce when told that time is the motion of physical bodies? You do not. I hear that no body moves except in time—you say it. I do not hear that the body's movement constitutes time—you do not say that. Time is what I use in order to measure the movement of a body, marking it from the beginning of the motion to its end—unless I fail to see the beginning and it continues on after I have stopped looking at it, and then I can only measure from the time I began looking to the point where I stopped. If I am watching for a long time, I can call that time long but I cannot tell *how* long the whole motion was, since we measure things by comparison, saying things like: This took the same time as that. Or: It was twice as long. And so on. But if we can pinpoint the expanses covered by the bodies, where the motion began and ended (or a turning began and ended, as on a lathe), we can say how long it took for the body to cover the distance marked out (or to make a complete turn). So the body's motion is one thing, and the way we measure how long that motion lasts is another—and who can doubt which of these should be called time? If a thing is sometimes moving and sometimes still, we can measure not only the motion but the still time, saying that it was still as long as it was moving, or it was still for twice or triple the time that it was moving, or whatever our estimate concludes or approximates (more or less, as we say). So time is not itself the motion of physical objects.

32.   I testify to you, Lord, that I still do not know what time is; and testify as well, Lord, that I realize it takes time for me to say this—in fact, I have been speaking a long time about time, which could not have happened but by a lapse, precisely, of time. If I know that, how can I not know what time is? Do I know it, but do not know how to put it into words? 'Nor am I deceptive in this before you,' as you know, my God. I speak straight from my heart. It is you who 'will bring light to my lamp,' Lord my God, who 'will bring bright light into my darkness.'

33.   Does my soul not bring true testimony to you, testifying that I measure time in fact—even if that means, Lord my God, that I measure without knowing what I measure? I measure the motion of physical objects. Can that be measuring time? Could I measure the motion of an object, its duration in passage from one point to another, except by measuring the time in which the motion occurs? But how do I measure the time itself? Do I measure longer times by shorter ones, as we measure a beam by a foot ruler? That is apparently how we measure the expanse of a long syllable, by the expanse of a short one, saying that it is, say, double the short one's length. And so we measure the length of a poem by the number of its verses, of its verses by its feet, its feet by its syllables, and its syllables (as short or long) by their length. This is not counting pages, which allows you to find places in a text. But when a text is being spoken, we say that this is a long poem because it has so many verses, with long verses because they have so many feet, and long feet because they have so many syllables, and each syllable counted long if it lasts twice what a short one does.

But this cannot be the only way to measure passing time, since a short verse can fill out a greater length of time if it is pronounced slowly, as a long one can be pronounced rapidly—and so with a poem, a foot, a syllable. This leads me to think that time is nothing but a reaching out in opposite directions. A reaching out of what I am not sure, but I suspect it may be of the mind. What precisely am I measuring, I ask of you, Lord, when I say vaguely that a thing is long or more specifically that it is twice as long as something else? I am measuring time, that I recognize, but I am not measuring the future, which is not yet; nor the present, which is spread across no length; nor the past, which no longer is. What am I measuring, then—present time, not the past? That was my preliminary position.

34.   Do not, my mind, waver here, but keep stoutly at it. God will help—he made us, not we him. Keep at it, there is a hint of some truth dawning. Put it this way: Somebody emits a sound, the sound continues—continues—and then stops. Now there is silence, the sound has stopped, it is no more. It was in the future before it began to sound, and could not be measured because it was not yet. And now it cannot be measured because it is no more. It could only be measured while it was sounding, which is the only time it actually existed. But there was no resting point even then. It was in process of going by. Did that make it any more measurable? Is it the process by which it reaches over some length of time that we measure, rather than the actual present, which has no length?

Say that it is. Then what of this? Another sound begins, it goes on continuously sounding—we must measure it while it is uninterrupted, since it will no longer exist once it has stopped and no longer exists. We must measure while it is still sounding and say how long it lasts. But how can we say that, when the duration cannot be defined except from the beginning to the end. That is what we measure—the length of time from start to finish. So a sound that has not finished cannot be measured, making us able to say how long or short it was, whether equal to some other time, or twice or triple as long, and so on. But once it is finished, it will already no longer be—and what basis have we for measuring it then? We do measure time—but not, clearly, things which do not yet exist, or have no length, or no longer exist, or have no finish. Which means that we cannot be measuring the future, the present, the past, or the mere duration when we measure time—which is, nonetheless, a thing we do.

35. The hymn line [of Ambrose] *Deus Creator Omnium* has eight syllables, alternating long and short ones, the odd-numbered ones short, the even-numbered long, and the long ones take twice the time to pronounce as the short ones. I recite the line, and repeat it, and find this true, tested by the senses [which sound it and which hear it]. The actual soundings make it clear that I measure each long syllable by a short one, and find it twice the length. But since they sound one after another, first the short, then the long, how did I retain the short in order to apply it as a measure to the long, to establish that the latter has twice the duration of the former, when the short has to stop sounding before the long can begin? And while the long one is sounding, how can I measure that until it stops? But once it stops, it is in the past. So what is being measured? With what is it being measured? Where has the short one gone, and where the long? While the long is sounding to be measured, where is the short by which I measure? Both have been sounded, have flown off, they are in the past, and do not exist. Nonetheless I do measure, I can confidently say, as far as my trained senses can be relied on, that the long syllables take twice the length of time to pronounce as the short ones. I could not do this *unless* the syllables had been sounded out and ended. So those ended sounds are not themselves being measured, but something in my mind that they left behind them and that is still there.

V

TIME AS MENTAL PERDURANCE (*DISTENTIO ANIMI*)

36. So time is measured, my mind, in you. Raise no clamor against me—I mean against yourself—out of your jostling reactions. I measure time in you, I tell you, *because* I measure the reactions that things caused in you by their passage, reactions that remain when the things that occasioned them have passed on. I measure such reactions when I measure time. Time has to be these reactions for me to be able to measure it. Then how do we measure silence, enabling us to say that a period of silence has lasted as long as a period of sound? The mind must beat out the time taken by the silence as if listening to the sound, in order to establish the relative duration of silence and sound within the time being measured.

For we can run over in our mind poems and verses and speeches without speaking out loud, and can compare the lapse of time with other periods, just as if we were saying the words out loud. Suppose a person wants to give a long speech, and he decides beforehand just how long it should be. He has set the length in silence, and remembers what it should be. Then, once he begins speaking, he speaks on until he reaches the finish he decided on. Well, he does not quite speak on, but has spoken, or is about to speak, those parts of his speech that he has covered or is approaching. The mind reaches at the present to transfer things from the future into the past, what is still to be spoken shrinking as what has been spoken is swelling, until the future is canceled and there is nothing but the past.

37. But how can a future, something which is not yet,

be shrunk or canceled? And how can a past, something which is no more, swell up? Only in the mind can this be accomplished, because of three activities there—the acts of anticipating, of observing, and of remembering. What is anticipated passes through what observes it as it passes into what is remembered. Who can deny that what is to be is not yet? But what is to be is already in the mind, by anticipation. Who can deny that what has been is no longer? But what has been still is in the mind, by memory. Who can deny that the present has no length, since it passes with no pause? But the mind observes a present through which what is not yet runs into what is no longer. Thus a long future time is not really in the future, but is a present anticipation of a long time in the mind. And a long past time is not really in the past, which is no more, but is a present memory of a long time in the mind.

38.   Say I am about to recite a psalm I am familiar with. Before I start, my anticipation reaches to include the psalm in its entirety, but as I recite it, my memory reaches to take into the past each thing I shall be cropping from the future; so my soul's life-force reaches in opposite directions—into memory by what I have just said, into anticipation for what I am about to say—while simultaneously perduring in the present through which what was future is being shuttled into what is past. As I recite more and more of the psalm, anticipation is reduced in proportion as memory expands, until anticipation is canceled and the completed psalm deposited in memory. And the transition that happens with this psalm occurs also in each of its verses, even in each of its syllables, and the same occurs in the larger liturgy of which the psalm may be a part, or in the whole of a man's life, whose parts are his separate acts; or in the whole history of 'the sons of men,' whose parts are all the men there are.

39.   Since 'your pity superintends men's various lives,' behold how my life-force reaches in opposite directions. 'Your right hand has upheld me' in my Lord, the son of man, who mediates between your unity and our multiplicity (for we are multitudinous amid multitudinous things). Through him may I 'lay hold on him who has laid hold on me,' and be gathered out of my useless years by following the One, 'oblivious of the past,' not caring for future things that pass away but 'for things prior to them.' No longer reaching in opposite directions but reaching forward only—not with divided reach but with focused reach—'I seek the prize of your high calling,' where I may 'hear the song of praise' and 'contemplate your delight,' a thing not of the future or the past. But for now 'my years are passing amid sobs,' with only you to solace them, Lord, my everlasting Father. I, however, have been disarticulated into time, I cannot put the times together in my mind, my very thoughts are shredded, my soul unstrung—till I flow together into you, purified, to melt into the fires of your love.

40. Then shall I 'stand firm in the Lord,' unshakable, 'in my likeness to your truth.' Then will I no longer be troubled by the gibes of men whose spiritual dropsy makes them thirst for more than they can carry, those who ask what God was doing before he made heaven and earth, or when the whim took him to make something after not having made anything for so long. Grant them, Lord, the gift of reflecting on what they say, to learn that one cannot claim God did not make anything for so long, when there was no time to be long in. To say God did not act for so long is to say that he did nothing for a long [time], but time only began when he did make something. Let them stop talking nonsense and be drawn forward to the prior things, understanding that you are before all times, are of all times the eternal creator, that no times, no creatures, can be eternal with you, even if there are creatures [angels] of a special time.

41. How deeply infolded is your secret wisdom, Lord my God, and how far from it have I been thrust by the impact of my sins! Heal my eyes, to share the joys of your light. Were any mind so fraught with knowledge and foresight as to know everything there ever will be or ever was, just as this one psalm is known to me, it would be a mind of wonders, to stupefy one awed by it. Nothing ever enacted, nothing remaining in future years, would be veiled from it—any more than I forget what I have recited or have still to recite as I go through my psalm. Yet even my knowledge of the psalm is far, far from how you know everything that has been and will be, you the originator of the universe, and of all bodies and souls within it. Your knowing is deeply, deeply more astonishing, far deeper in its mystery. A person reciting or hearing a familiar psalm has reactions and sensations that are distracted as the psalm passes between anticipation of what is still to come and memory of what has passed—things impossible to you in an eternity that does not suffer alteration, for you are the eternal creator of all minds. Just as your knowledge of what you would create existed at the origin without any stages of your thinking, so your enactment of what was at the origin, creating heaven and earth, was not distracted between successive stages of your action. May the one who knows this testify to who you are, and the one who does not know it testify as well. You are supremely exalted, yet you 'house yourself in the humble person's heart.' For 'the crushed you lift,' and they cannot fall who dwell on your heights.

BOOK TWELVE

SON (FORM)

I

KNOCKING AT SCRIPTURE'S DOOR

1. My heart with all its poor resources is busied, Lord, as you knock at it with the words of your holy writings. The human intellect is full of its own emptiness, better at looking than at seeing. The petition takes longer than its fulfillment, and the hand that begs works harder than the hand that receives. Yet we have the promise, how can it fail? 'God with us, who can stand against us?' 'Only ask and you shall receive; seek, you shall find; knock and it will open to you. Each man who asks, receives; who seeks, finds; who knocks, has it opened.' The promises are yours, and who can fear their betrayal when it is Truth who promises?

"HEAVEN'S HEAVEN" AND FORMLESS "EARTH"

2. Let my tongue testify from its lowliness to your loftiness, how you created heaven and earth, this very heaven I see, this earth I tread, from which I derive the earth I wear, which you made. But where is 'heaven's heaven,' which we hear of in the psalm? 'Heaven's heaven for the Lord, but earth he gave to the sons of man.' Where then is this heaven above our perception, compared with which all that we see is earth? All corporeal reality, which is not entire in any of its parts, has a certain beauty even in its lowest parts, down to the very earth. Yet compared to your heaven, even our heaven is earthen, and it is not unreasonable to say that both our great physical realities, heaven and earth, are but as earth compared with that heaven beyond our knowing, which belongs to the Lord but not to the sons of man.

3. Admittedly, this earth was 'unseen and shapeless,' in the unknown depth of the abyss, which could have no light since it had no beauty of form. So by your direction it was written: 'There was darkness over the abyss.' This darkness was mere absence of light, since if light had been present, it would have been over the whole scene, pre-eminent and lustrous. But since it was not yet present, what could the presence of darkness be but the absence of light? So 'darkness was over' because there was no light above it—just as there is silence where there is no sound, and the silent place is the soundless place. For have you, Lord, not taught this mind that testifies to you, have you not taught me that before you gave form to this formless material and individuated its parts, there was nothing—not color, or shape, or body, or spirit? Or rather there was something—the mere formlessness, lacking all beauty of form.

4. What but some familiar phrase can bring this home to our sluggish intellects? And what can be found anywhere that could better suggest total formlessness than 'earth and the abyss'? By their low station they lack the beauty of form that takes and gives light. Is there any reason, then, not to find in 'earth unseen and shapeless' an expression fitted to our incapacity for indicating the unformed matter that you made, preparatory to making things with the beauty of form?

5. If we ponder this expression, to see what meanings we can reach, we say: This does not have intellectual form, like life or justice, since it is material. Nor is it sensibly material, since what can be seen or touched on earth that is 'unseen and shapeless'? When human intellect deals with such formulations, it must try to understand by not knowing, or else know by not understanding.

6. If I testify 'with tongue and pen' to all you have taught me, Lord, on the subject of this kind of matter, which neither I nor my [Manichaean] instructors understood, I did not think of it as formless but as deformed in many grotesque ways. My mind played with foul and disgusting forms, jumbling all categories. I called these formless, not because they lacked form but as if they had a form which, could I see it, would confound my senses with its unimaginable absurdity and overwhelm my human weakness. I was conceiving a thing not entirely without form, but with a form that seemed formless by comparison with fully formed things. Sheer logic told me I should extract all form from what I was considering if I were to treat it as literally formless; but I could not imagine it. I inclined more easily into thinking such a thing non-existent than to seeing it was midway between non-being and form—it was not nothing, though it had no form. It was formlessly *almost* not being.

At this point, my reason stopped consulting my imagination, stuffed as it is with images of corporeal forms, randomly multipliable or combinable. I looked rather at actual bodies, minutely observing how they change from what they were to something else that they were not. I entertained the hypothesis that this passage from one form to another went through an intermediate stage, not of nothingness, but of existing formlessness. But I still wanted real, not hypothetical, knowledge. Should my 'tongue and pen' testify to all the points I had to untangle on this subject, what reader would it not tire? Yet tireless is my heart in honoring you with songs of praise for what I am unable to convey. The changeability of changing things lies in their receptivity to the forms they take in this process of change. Yet what is this receptivity? It could not be mind, could it? Or body? Formable mind, or formable body? I would, if I could, call it a something-nothing, or a being that is not—though it must have some being, in order to receive visible and organized form.

7.   And whence could it derive even that sort of being but from you, 'the source of all beings' of any sort? Yet they are all unlike you to the degree of their distance from you—a distance not in space, since you are not at this or that point, in this way or that way, but yourself-in-yourself, yourself-in-yourself, yourself-in-yourself, 'holy, holy, holy,' Lord, the God all-powerful. At the origin, which you are, you made something of nothing in your wisdom, which is generated from your essence. Yet heaven and earth were made, not generated from you. Had they been generated from you, they would have been the equal of your Only-Begotten Son, and therefore equal to you; but it cannot rightly be said that anything is your equal that was not generated from you. Nor was there anything apart from you, God, triune Unity and united Trinity, that you could have used in creation. It was from nothing that you made heaven and earth, made all things great and small, since you have all power and goodness to make things good, the greater thing, heaven, and the lesser thing, earth, distinct things, one near to you, the other near to nothing, heaven than which nothing is higher but you, and earth than which nothing is lower but nothing.

8.   'Heaven's heaven' is for you alone, Lord, while 'earth, which you gave to men' is not what we now see and touch,

since it was 'unseen and shapeless,' an abyss with no light over it. 'Darkness over it' was more than we mean by a dark abyss. The abyss of deep water that we now see has some kind of light in its depths, visible to 'fish and serpents swimming' at its bottom. But that first 'earth' was on the verge of not being at all, since it lacked any form, though capable of being formed. 'It was from formless matter, Lord, you made the world'—which means that from nothing you made an almost-nothing, and from that you made great things, for 'the sons of men' to marvel at.

Marvelous indeed is the physical heaven, the canopy between the higher and lower waters, that you spread on the second day, after light was provided, saying: 'Let it be a canopy,' and it was. This canopy you called heaven, though it was only the heaven to land and sea, which you made on the third day, giving form to the formless matter you made before any of the days. For you had already made a heaven before any of the days, since it says 'at the origin you made heaven and earth'—meaning 'heaven's heaven' and the earth that was 'unformed matter, invisible and unorganized,' with 'darkness over its abyss.' From that earth 'unseen and shapeless,' from that formlessness, from that almost nothing, our changeable world subsists and does not subsist. Its changeability is registered in its times, perceived and measured, since time is produced by the alterations and alternations of the forms made out of the formless matter I have been describing, the 'unseen earth.'

9. For this reason the Spirit, who guided the writing of your servant [Moses], when he recorded that 'at the origin you made heaven and earth,' said nothing of time and named no days. Clearly that is because 'heaven's heaven,' which 'at the origin you made,' is a kind of intellectual creature—not, indeed, eternal as you triunely are, but approaching your eternity, arresting its changeability by a rapt sweet gazing upon you. Without falling back upon its own creatureliness, it holds so closely to you as to escape the fluttery oscillations of time. Similarly, formless matter, that 'unseen and unshaped earth,' precedes any days of creation. Without form

or sequence, nothing can arrive or depart in it, by whose motion days can be measured, or any temporal oscillations.

10. May truth, may the light in my heart, speak to me, and not my own darkness. Plunged as I was and blinded in darkness, out of it, even there, even from there I strove to love you. 'I remembered you in my straying' and 'I heard your voice behind me calling me back,' though I heard it only faintly through a clamor of those who know no peace. But see me now return, heaving and panting, to your fountain. May no one block my path to it, so I may drink of it, live from it. Let me not draw on myself for life—I lived wretchedly from my own resources. I was a death to me, and begin to live again in you. Direct your words to me, teach me. I have been drawing my belief from your books, from your words' deep mysteries.

11. By now you have told me, Lord, your voice resonant in my inner hearing, that you are eternal, the only immortal being, since you are altered by no form or movement, your decisions do not fluctuate with time—how could they be eternal if they decree now this, now that? This is evident to me, 'even as you view it.' Let it become ever more evident, I pray you, as I wait patiently for your further revealings, sheltered 'in the shadow of your wings.'

In the same way you have told me, Lord, your voice resonant in my inner hearing, this: All things that are, but are not you, are things you made. The only thing that is not from you is the human will moving away from you toward something less than you, and that movement is the definition of sin—yet no one's sin can damage you or upset the order of your rule, whether in the heights or in the depths—this, too, is evident to me, 'even as you view it.' Let it become ever more evident, I pray you, as I wait patiently for your further revealings, sheltered 'in the shadow of your wings.'

12. In the same way you have told me, your voice resonant in my inner hearing, this: 'Heaven's heaven,' your creature whose sole delight is you, did not begin with you, but inasmuch as it satiates its thirst from your pure springs, it will at no time and in no way yield to its own changeable-ness. Since you are always present to it, as the entire object of its attention, it has no future to look forward to, no movement away from a past to remember, no alteration to undergo, no temporal transition to pass through. Happy such a creature if it exists held close to you, 'for you dwell in it continually and illume it from within.' What other title could be better for this condition than 'heaven's heaven'? It is your dwelling place, contemplating the joy of you, with no impulse away from you toward anything else, with a mind in single and sweet 'accord with the blessed spirits, citizens of your city' in the heaven above our heavens.

13. Let me measure against that reality the thirst for you in a soul that has wandered far from you, subsisting on tears, hearing the daily taunt 'Where is your God?' as it prays and begs for one thing only, to 'dwell in your house for the rest of its life's days.' And what is real life but you, what a real day but your eternity, 'with no lapse of years, since you are always the same'? Let any intellect that can grasp it see how high you tower over time in your eternity, and that your dwelling, though it did not begin with you, suffers not the oscillations of time because it is held close to you, forever and without fail. This is now evident to me, 'even as you see it.' May it become ever more evident as I wait patiently for your further revelings, sheltered 'in the shadow of your wings.'

14. Change takes place in the last and least of your creatures through some kind of formlessness. If that formlessness is considered in it absolute deficiency, who can tell me that time exists in this formless substrate through which one form is changed to another, who but one whirled and twirled amid the frail wraiths of an empty mind? There is no time without the motion of forms, and the formless has no form.

15. Reflecting on these things so far as you grant me, my God, so far as you prompt me to knock and then 'open to my knocking,' I find two things that share timelessness, though they do not share your eternity. One [your 'heaven's heaven'] is so fully formed that, though changeable, it does not change—there is no break in its contemplation of you, no succession for time to register, so nearly does it approach your eternal changelessness. The other is so formless that it cannot of itself be changed from one form to another by any rest or motion time can measure. Yet you did not let this formlessness alone. 'At the origin,' before any days were created, 'you made heaven and earth,' the two things I have been discussing. 'Earth was unseen and shapeless, with darkness over the abyss.' The very words give some sense of formlessness, a partial expression for those who have trouble conceiving a pure formlessness, a privation just short of nonexistence. This is the stuff from which the lower [physical] heaven was made, and the earth that is both seen and shapely, and the beautiful bodies of water, and the rest of the universe recorded as having been created in a sequence of days, since they are capable of ordered alterations in form and motion, which are measured by time's oscillations.

16.   This, my God, is the present state of my understanding when I hear your Scripture saying, 'At the origin God made heaven and earth, an earth that was unseen and shapeless, with darkness over the abyss,' without specifying that this was done on a certain day. At present, then, my state of understanding is that by 'heaven' here is understood 'heaven's heaven,' the heavenly intellect that sees 'not in part, not murkily, in dim reflection, but entirely, with clarity, face to face.' This heaven's knowledge is not now and then, but all at once, not subject to time's fluctuations. And the formless 'earth unseen and shapeless' is also free from time's fluctuations, since it cannot be now-and-then since there is no form to be here-or-there. This, then, is my present state of knowledge on why in Scripture no days are mentioned for God 'at the origin making heaven and earth,' referring to the entirely formed and the entirely formless—that is, to 'heaven's heaven' and to 'earth unseen and shapeless.' Since it goes on to refer to another earth, it is clear which earth is first meant. And since it records that the canopy created on the second day was called heaven, it is implicit what heaven was meant before any days were mentioned.

III

DIFFERENT
INTERPRETATIONS

17. What stunning depths there are in your words, even on the surface, attracting simple people, yet what depths there are, my God, what stunning depths! We recoil when we peer into their depths, recoil with awe and tremble with love. 'Scripture's foes I hate with zeal'—'may you slay them with the two-edged sword' that makes them no longer your enemies. My love would have them die to themselves and live to you. As for some others, who do not mock the book of Genesis but praise it, they nonetheless make this claim—that the Spirit of God, who led Moses his servant to write this, did not intend his words to mean what I am saying, but something else that they are saying. Under your arbitrament between us, God of us all, I make this answer:

18. Surely you will not deny what truth itself, its voice resonant in my inner hearing, says about the eternity of the Creator—that time does not alter his reality, nor can he will something apart from his reality. He does not will now this, now that. His will is singly, simultaneously, sempiternally all that he wills, not willing now and then, on this or that. He does not will now what he nilled before, or nill now what he willed before, since that would show a changeable will, and anything changeable is not eternal, and 'our God is eternal.'

In the same way, can you deny what truth says, its voice resonant in my inner hearing, that the anticipation of a future happening becomes recognition when it arrives, and the recognition becomes memory when it passes, and such shifts in our focus, involving change, cannot be eternal? 'Yet our God is eternal.' Collecting and comparing these truths I come upon my God, our God, who did not need a new resolve in order to create, any more than he needed a shift in understanding.

19. What do you challengers have to say to this? Can you deny it? No? Then what follows? Can anything formed, or any matter capable of being formed, exist if not derived from the supremely good because supremely existent? You do not deny that, either. What follows? Do you deny that there is a lofty kind of creature clinging with such pure love to the true and the truly eternal God that, though not coeternal with him, it does not turn away from him and lapse into the alterations and alternations of time, but is content with the utmost contemplation of him alone, because you, God, reveal yourself to it, satisfy it while it loves you as you command, and therefore it does not turn from you to itself? This is God's dwelling place, made neither from the earth nor from the physical heavens, but immaterial and approaching your eternity, because it does not ever lapse from you. 'You have given it this standing for the ages, for all ages, setting up an ordinance without limit.' Yet, since it had a beginning, it is a creature and not eternal.

20. There was no time before its creation, since 'created before all things is wisdom.' This is not a reference to that Wisdom who is, as your Son, coeternal with you, our God, and your equal—the Wisdom through 'whom all things were created' when 'at the origin he made heaven and earth.' No, this other wisdom is created, an intellectual entity that becomes light by contemplation of the light. Though created, it is called wisdom. But the difference between Wisdom who creates and wisdom that is created is like that between a light that shines and that which is shone on by the light, or between the Just One who makes others just and the ones who are made just—in whose number even we are called justice, as a servant of yours wrote: 'That we may be in God his justice.'

There is, then, a wisdom that is before all other created things, though itself a created thing, the intellectual creature made to understand your pure city, 'our mother, which on the heights is free' and 'eternal in the heavens' (which heavens, but 'the heavens' heavens that praise you,' since they are 'the heavens' heaven of the Lord'?). We can come upon no time before it, it preceded time's creation, it is the first of all created things. Yet it was preceded by something—by its creator's eternity, from which it began, not in time (which did not exist) but in its unique status.

21. It is derived from you, our God, but distinct from you, not one with you. Nor can we come upon any time, not only before it but within it. It has the unique privilege of 'seeing forever your face,' from which it does not ever turn away, which preserves it from change. Yet it is capable of change, and it would darken and grow cold did it not cling to you with ardent love, receiving your 'noonday light' and warmth. Beautiful and shapely home, 'I have loved your decencies, where the glory of my Lord dwells,' who built you and resides in you. May my wanderings yearn out toward you, as I ask him who made you to let me, whom he made, become his in your habitation. 'Like a lost sheep I have wandered,' but I hope to be brought home to what he made 'on the shoulders of my shepherd.'

22. You challengers, whom I address, what answer can you give me, since you believe that Moses was a devout servant of God and that his books are a revelation of his Holy Spirit? Does this house of God exist, not indeed coeternal with God but with its own kind of eternity in the heavens, where you may search for the fluctuations of time and find none? It is not subject to the distensions and vacillations of time's different periods, 'its reward is its closeness to God.' They agree to this. Where then do they disagree with what 'my heart acclaimed before God' when my inner hearing responded to 'the sounding of his praise'? Is it over the unformed matter, which lacks all order because it lacks all form? But without order how could there be a sequence of times? And this near-to-nothing, insofar as it was not absolutely nothing, was the material from which things came to exist, in whatever form they exist. This, too, they do not deny.

23. I would continue to converse before you, my God, with those who grant as true what your truth resonates in my inner hearing. As for those who deny it, let them deafen themselves with their own barking. Still I will try to calm them, so they may by your Word find a way to you. If they refuse to respond, do not you, I beg you, my God, 'stay silent toward me.' Confide your truth to my heart, you who can alone speak it, and I shall turn away from those outside me, blowhards who puff dust into their own eyes. I shall 'go to my inner chamber' to sing of my love for you with 'moans on moans' for my wandering, 'remembering Jerusalem' with heart held high toward her, Jerusalem my fatherland, 'Jerusalem my mother,' and you her ruler, enlightener, father, teacher, spouse. There are pure and strong delights, trust-worthy joy, all goods beyond describing, enjoyed there at once, since you are the one true good. Let me swerve not, my God who has pity, until you collect all of me from my own dispersion and distortion, reforming me and reaffirming me in the peace of this dearest mother, where 'the first harvests of my spirit' are already lodged, and whence I derive all my certainty.

Some who honor the holy word of your holy servant Moses, while agreeing with us on its supreme authority, and not claiming that what I say is false in itself, still have grounds for disagreement with me. Those I would speak with, and may you, our God, judge between my testimony and their tenets. **24.** Their argument is this: What you say may be true, but it is not what Moses understood when he spoke under the Spirit's guidance, saying 'At the origin God made heaven and earth.' The heaven referred to was not a spiritual and intellectual creature forever contemplating the face of God. The earth referred to was not formless matter.

Then what were they? The answer comes: We can say what he had in mind, and what his words express. Namely? By 'heaven and earth' he meant to indicate in brief summary the whole visible world, whose makeup he would specify item by item under the different days, as the Spirit willed them to be named. He was addressing a crude and earthbound people, to whom he felt he could convey nothing but the visible works of God. But even they concede that 'earth unseen and shapeless' and 'the darkened abyss' could without contradiction refer to unformed matter, since from this it is later shown that all visible things, apparent even to crude people, are created and arranged day by day.

25. Are there other possibilities? One might be that 'heaven and earth' both refer in anticipation to unformed and jumbled matter, since from it the whole world of things taking visible shape is begun and completed, and that world is commonly referred to as 'heaven and earth.' Another might be that 'heaven and earth' are not improperly used of *unseen and seen* creatures, including in the two words everything that God made in his wisdom—that is, at the origin. Not that they were made from God's own substance. They were made from nothing. They do not have God's selfsameness. They possess the changeability of all created things, whether they are stable like the everlasting house of God, or they are unstable like the human soul and body. All things unseen or seen come from this formless matter, capable of form. 'Heaven and earth'—that is, everything created, whether unseen or seen—are indicated by the phrases 'invisible and shapeless' and by 'darkness over the abyss,' the former referring to physical matter before it received forms, the latter to spiritual stuff before its mutability was checked by the light of wisdom shining on it.

26. Or one might say, if you will, that where we read 'at the origin God made heaven and earth,' the 'heaven and earth' referred to are not their completed and final reality but an inchoate formlessness shapeable and separable into distinct forms, with existing potentialities not yet apparent in their forms and qualities, but destined to be sorted out into their appropriate identities—heaven, namely, and earth, the spiritual and the material.

27. After listening to all these possibilities, and pondering them all, 'I would not engage in quibbles, which can only confuse listeners.' The law is meant to be 'good for building up' when it 'works toward loving with a pure heart, a good conscience, and a sincere faith.' I realize that our master summarized all the laws and the prophets in two precepts. So tell me, my God, you who give my eyes an inner light, why should I care in this my testimony to you that different meanings can be found in Genesis, so long as they are true? Why should it bother me that another says that his meaning, not my meaning, is what Moses intended? Whenever we read an author, we try to uncover and accept what that author meant by his writings, and when we accept that he is truthful, if we think or suspect anything to be false, we have no right to believe that he was saying it. But if one is striving to arrive at what the author of the sacred writings was getting at, what is wrong with arriving at something that you, the light of every truthful mind, show him to be true, even if the writer he is reading, while writing the truth, did not intend that particular truth?

28.   Clearly it is true, Lord, that you 'made heaven and earth.' True that 'at the origin' refers to 'your wisdom, in which you made all things.' It is just as true that the visible world has as its major constituents 'heaven and earth,' an expression standing for all things made and given their own nature. True as well that anything changeable suggests to our inquiry a certain formlessness which can either receive form or undergo the change from one form to another. True also that time cannot affect formlessness, which is near-nothing. True also that a thing can by a figure of speech be named after the material it is made from, making it possible to use the words 'heaven and earth' for the formless stuff that heaven and earth were made from. In the same way, of all things having any form, 'earth and the abyss' can best be used of formlessness because nothing is nearer to that state. True that you, 'who made everything,' made not only the formed and finished creation but what was capable of being formed and finished, and that whatever was formed from formlessness was formless before being formed.

29.   These matters are accepted as true by those who have from you the inner eye to see them, and who accept unwaveringly that Moses, your servant, spoke 'out of the spirit of truth.' Compatible with these truths would be the opinion that 'at the origin God made heaven and earth' means that in his Word, coeternal with him, God made intellectual beings and sensual beings—that is, spiritual and physical beings.

Or the opinion that 'at the origin God made heaven and earth' means that in his Word, coeternal with him, he made the whole material substance of the world, with all the separate realities seen and recognized there.

Or the opinion that 'at the origin God made heaven and earth' means that in his Word, coeternal with him, he made the formless elements for both spiritual and physical creatures.

Or the different opinion that 'at the origin God made heaven and earth' means that in his Word, coeternal with him, God made the formless matter of all physical creation, wherein were still mingled the heaven and earth that would be separated out and given the forms of the physical cosmos that we see.

Or the opinion that 'at the origin God made heaven and earth' means that God began by making and ordering a formless material already vaguely formed into heaven and earth, whose forms would be brought out more clearly in all their distinct components.

30. As for the interpretation of the rest of the verse, compatible with the truths so far accepted might be the opinion that 'earth was unseen and shapeless, and there was darkness over the abyss' means that the physical reality God made was the formless stuff of corporeal objects, without order, and without light.

Or 'earth was unseen and shapeless, and there was darkness over the abyss' means that what we comprehensively call heaven and earth was the shapeless and dark stuff that would become the physical heaven and physical earth, with all the objects in them apprehensible by the senses.

Or 'earth was unseen and shapeless, and there was darkness over the abyss' means that what we comprehensively call heaven and earth was the shapeless and dark stuff that would become, on the one hand, the intellectual heaven (called elsewhere 'heaven's heaven') and, on the other hand, the physical earth, in which term is included our physical heaven (all physical realities, indeed, whether seen or unseen).

Or 'earth was unseen and shapeless, and there was darkness over the abyss' does *not* mean that heaven and earth are called formless matter. Rather, the matter was already there, under the description of 'unseen and shapeless earth and a dark abyss,' from which the preceding verse said that God created heaven and earth—namely the spiritual and the physical creation.

Or 'earth was unseen and shapeless, and darkness was over the abyss' means that there was some kind of formlessness from which the preceding verse said that God made heaven and earth, namely, the entire physical stuff of the cosmos, separated into its two major constituents, the higher and the lower, with all the things we encounter here and recognize.

31.   Some might feel impelled to question these last two views. If the unformed matter stands outside what is called heaven and earth, is there not something that God did not make, which he rather used in making heaven and earth? Scripture does not, after all, tell us of any such matter unless it is indicated by the words 'heaven and earth,' or just by 'earth,' in the sentence 'at the origin God made heaven and earth.' As for what follows, 'earth was unseen and shapeless,' Scripture admittedly means by that formless matter, but it does not stand apart from what is said in the preceding verse, that he 'made heaven and earth.'

Supporters of the last two positions listed above, or of one or the other taken separately, may respond when they hear these objections that they do not deny that God made the first matter, the God who after all 'made all things so that they were eminently good.' All they say is that there is more of good in what is fully created and formed, and less of good in what is merely capable of creation and formation—good though it, too, is in its measure—and that Scripture does not explicitly state that God made such formlessness, any more than it explicitly states that he made other things, cherubim and seraphim, for instance, or the 'thrones, dominions, principalities, and powers' specified by the Apostle, which God must have made. If all things are included in the verse 'he made heaven and earth,' what can we make of the waters over which 'the Spirit of God hovered'?

If the waters are included in the term 'earth,' how can that earth be formless matter when we find the waters called 'shapely'? Again, if heaven and earth are formless matter, why is it said that out of this formlessness the canopy was made and called 'heaven,' while it is not said that the waters were made? They could not still be unshaped and unseen when we find them flowing in fine shapeliness. Or were they formed when God said 'Let the waters under the canopy be gathered,' as if gathering were formation? Then what about 'the waters *above* the canopy'? Surely they could not have been unformed when they were given so high a position. Yet where does it say that they were formed?

We can see that if Genesis is silent about anything God made, this does not mean—as we know from firm faith and sound reasoning—that God did not make it. Our basic principles do not allow us to think that the waters were eternally there with God, simply because we find them mentioned in Genesis without explicitly being told that they were made. Thus when Scripture speaks of 'earth unseen and shapeless' and 'a darksome abyss,' we can follow truth as our teacher and realize that these too were made by God from nothing, and therefore cannot be coeternal with him, though we are not expressly told that.

IV

RULES FOR INTERPRETING

32. After hearing these arguments and testing them to the best of my fallible ability—to which I give you my testimony, my God, since you know it well—I find two kinds of disagreement are possible when something is presented to us by truthful people who nonetheless have to use the medium of words to convey it. One is a disagreement on the truth of what is being presented. The other is a disagreement over the intention of the one reporting it. Under the first head, we ask what really happened at the creation. Under the second, we ask what Moses, your devout attendant in the faith, wanted his hearer or reader to understand from his words. On the first head, why bother with those who are certain about the truth of what is, in fact, false? Similarly, on the second, why bother with those who believe that Moses spoke what is, in fact, false? But I do wish to share in you the company, Lord, and share the joy of those who 'find truth their grazing ground, where charity roams free.' Together let us approach the study of your Scripture, to seek out what you want us to take from what your servant [Moses] wanted to write as you guided his pen.

33. In the bewildering variety of true things that sincere inquirers discover in Scripture, who can be so bold as to say that he knows exactly what Moses knew and what he meant to say in this passage? Is it not easier to say what is the truth, whether Moses knew it or not? I can only 'serve you, Lord,' and make my offering of this book's testimony, as I pray that by your pity I may 'redeem my pledges' to you. I am bold enough to say that in your changeless Word you made all things, invisible and visible. But can I say as boldly that Moses meant this and nothing else when he wrote 'at the origin God made heaven and earth'? I am sure of what I hold, with the help of your own truth, but can I be as certain that I know what Moses was thinking when he wrote it? He might have thought 'at the origin' referred to the first act of creation. Or he might have thought 'heaven and earth' referred to the formless and inchoate materials for heaven and earth rather than to their full and final natures, whether spiritual or physical. In fact I can find truth in any such statements without being sure which of them Moses meant by his words. Perhaps this great man meant one of the things I have mentioned, or perhaps something else that has not occurred to me, while whatever he meant was true in itself and truthfully expressed.

34. 'No one should look for trouble' by saying that Moses did not mean what I interpret from him, offering a different interpretation. He might ask how I am so sure that Moses meant what I interpret him to mean. With equanimity I might reply with the arguments I have been giving, or with elaborations of them if he still doubted. But if he says that Moses did not mean what I say but what he says, but concedes that what we both say is true in itself—then, my God, boon of the poor, in whose breast there is no conflict, gently rain patience into my heart for dealing with such. They speak as if some mantic art let them read the mind of Moses, to know what he meant; but pride prevents them from knowing. They are less interested in Moses' meaning than in their own, not for its truth but just because it is their own. Otherwise, they would show interest in those speaking otherwise, so long as they spoke true, as I do in them when what they say is true. If it is true, it is not true because they speak it. If what they are after is truth, then their truth is my truth—and every man's who is seeking truth.

Thus, when they say that Moses did not mean what I say but what they say, I must part company, must not honor their claim. Even if what they said were true, the grounds for their assertion would not be patient study but brash crowing, the offspring not of insight but of bombast. 'Awesome, Lord, are your decrees,' since your truth is not mine, not this man's or that man's. You openly call all of us together into a communion of the truth, with a dire warning not to sequester truth lest we be sequestered from it. Whoever lays claim as his own possession to what you offer for everyone's benefit is driven away from others into himself—that is, from truth toward a lie, for the real lie of a liar is himself.

35. Support me, then, God, the highest judge and truth itself, support me when I answer my critic, give me your support. For I say this before you and before my fellows who 'use the law rightly for the sake of love.' Support me, tell me if you are pleased by what I tell him. I offer him an answer friendly and eirenic: If we both admit that what you are saying is true, and both admit that what I am saying is true, where do we find this truth we speak of? I do not find it in you, nor you in me. We both find it in something higher than our own minds, in the changeless truth. If we can come together in the light of the Lord our God, what keeps us apart from each other's minds? Those are harder for us to read than is the changeless truth. Even if Moses should come before us and aver, This was my meaning, we would not see into his mind, we would have to take his word for it. No one should 'go beyond what is prescribed, to puff one person over another.' Rather should we 'love the Lord our God with all our heart, all our soul, all our mind—and love our neighbor as we do ourselves.' Unless we hold that Moses acted on those two commandments in whatever he wrote, we 'make a liar of the Lord,' supposing that our fellow servant had a different thing in mind from what he wrote. It were foolish then, when a rich trove of true things can be found in his writings, rashly to claim which is the one he meant. Such destructive criticism violates the very love from which he wrote all the things we make a combined effort to understand.

36. My God, you height that calls me up from depths, you rest that calls me up from toil, hearer of my testimony and forgiver of my sins, since you order me to love my neighbor as myself, I cannot think that Moses, your faithful attendant, received less than I would have hoped and asked for, had I been born in his time and had you given me his mission—that through the medium of my heart and lips Scripture should go out to all future nations across the globe, with the highest authority for vanquishing all false and haughty teachings. Put thus in Moses' place (for all we humans are 'formed from the same stuff' and 'what is man but what your attention makes him'), I would have hoped, in performing the task of writing Genesis, for such power of expression and control over words that even those not yet able to grasp the mode of God's creation would not dismiss my words as too difficult to follow, while those who have reached some true conclusions about creation would not find that truth precluded by the words your servant was able to write on the subject—and that other conclusions, reached by other men in the light of truth, should not be excluded, either.

37. A spring of water, however limited its point of origin, distributes its flow through many rivulets over wider spaces than does any one of those rivulets, however far from its source it has gone over intervening territory. In the same way, the text of your attendant [Moses], though meted out in few words, sends out a strong stream of truth through many expositors, each drawing this truth or that according to his capacity, for dissemination in longer and more circuitous language. Some, when they read or hear Scripture's account, may think God made heaven and earth as a man might, or as an impersonal vast thing might if imbued with power— acting by a new and sudden decision on external bodies separate from him, with 'heaven and earth' as two vast bodies, higher and lower, containing everything else. They think, when they hear that 'God said let it be made and it was made,' that he used words with a beginning and end, their sounds rising up and passing away, and only when the words ended did the things he ordered into being come to be. This and similar notions they entertain because that is how things happen in our physical universe.

In these people, who are 'still little children' nursed with simple formulas like infants in their mothers' arms, a useful faith is instilled, enough for them to learn and accept that God made all the wonderfully varied things they see around them. But if one of them spurns this simple language of faith, and flings himself in high pride from the nest that protects him, so that he falls, poor thing—God keep the little fledgling from being 'crushed by the feet' of 'passersby.' Then 'send your angel' to take him back up to the nest, to stay there till he can fly.

38. For others, this bible passage is not a nest but a dense thicket. Glimpsing berries hidden there, they flit inside, merrily chirping as they spy the berries out and peck at them. When, our God everlasting, they hear or read the biblical account, they realize that you stand far above past and present time in your changeless continuity, yet everything temporally conditioned you have made. Your will, which is yourself, made everything, not from some new purpose or change of a prior one. You made it not from your own substance, in your all-forming likeness. You made it rather from nothing, which is unlike you in lacking all form. Yet it became like you when you gave it form, turning it back toward you in all its gradated potentials, assigned to each by its degree of being, so that 'all you made is good.' Some things are kept close to you, while others are kept at calibrated distances from you in space and time, revolving beautifully around you as they act or are acted on. Their beauty, seen in the light of your truth, delights those who contemplate them to the extent of their ability.

39. Another man studies the text 'at the origin God made' and interprets the origin as wisdom, according to the words of Scripture, 'Wisdom said . . . '

Another looks at the same words and takes 'origin' to mean the beginning of the creative process, taking 'at the origin he made' as referring to the first things he made.

Among those who think 'at the origin' means that 'in his *wisdom* he made heaven and earth,' one thinks 'heaven and earth' is a locution for the material from which heaven and earth can be made. Another thinks 'heaven and earth' refers to the fully formed creation. Another holds that 'heaven' refers to the formed spiritual nature, while 'earth' refers to the formless nature of physical matter.

Those who think both 'heaven' and 'earth' refer to unformed matter, from which both heaven and earth would be formed, do not agree on how this happens. One thinks this is the material for the perfecting of both intellectual and sensual natures. Another thinks it is the mass of matter containing in its deep womb only physical objects open to perception by the senses.

Those, moreover, who think 'heaven and earth' refers to completed and ordered nature have their own divergences, one taking this to refer to invisible as well as visible objects, while another thinks only of the visible, of the bright sky we look up at, and of the dark earth, and of all that is contained in either.

40. If, however, one takes 'at the origin he made' to mean 'the *first things* he made' he can do nothing but take 'heaven and earth' as referring to the *material* from which heaven and earth were made—that is, the whole cosmos, both intellectual and sensual. If he takes them as the *forms* of heaven and earth, he will rightly be asked what, if God made this first, he went on to make afterward. With the cosmos already formed, he will have to squirm under the question, How can this be first if there is nothing later? But he has a respectable position if he says that unformed matter was made first and then the fully formed matter later—if, at least, he is deft at distinguishing the four different meanings of *first*: that of eternity, that of time, that of preference, and that of origin.

> *Eternity* coming first is seen in God's preceding all things.
> A *time* coming first is seen in the blossom preceding the fruit.
> A *preference* coming first is seen in the fruit preceding the
>   blossom.
> An *origin* coming first is seen in the sound preceding a song.

Of the four, the first and fourth on my list are the hardest to grasp, the middle two the easiest. It takes a subtle mind and minute scrutiny, Lord, to see how your unchangeable eternity can produce things changing in time—and how it comes first only in that sense.

And what mind is clear enough to tell without exacting distinctions how sound precedes its song? The song is formed sound, so there must be something in existence that could be formed. In this way, prime matter precedes formed matter, coming first not as causing the form but as receiving it. This does not happen in temporal sequence. We do not first emit vague sounds without the song, and then shape and pattern them into the song. Sound is not the material of song as wood is the material for making a box, or silver for a cup. With those, the material exists before it is made into something, but sound does not exist before becoming song. It is only when the song is sung that the sound is heard. No formless sound was heard before its formation into song. If the sound came first, it would pass by before you could find something to shape artfully into song. The song exists only in the sound which is its matter, and the sound exists only in the song which is its form.

Only in this sense, as I said, does sound come first before being formed in song, not as producing the song, not as the shaper of its own material. Rather, the body produces sound that the singer's intelligence shapes into song. It does not produce it first in time, but at the same time. It is not first by preference—song is preferred to sound, since the song is not only a sound but a sound with song added. But it does come first as an origin, since song is not formed into sound, but sound into song. This is the parallel that lets us understand how matter can be at the origin, and be called 'heaven and earth,' since heaven and earth are made from it. The matter did not come first in time, since time is constituted by movable forms—thus matter is not perceived except in time, when united with its form. That is why it is impossible to describe matter without using temporal terms, since it comes before its form in logic, though it is the last of things in its worth (since form is nobler than formlessness), and it follows on eternity—the timelessness of God its maker, and the timelessness of nothing from which it is made.

41.   May truth itself bring these partial truths into harmony, God showing pity for us, that we may 'rightly use the law' as 'we are bid to do, for pure love.' If, observing that directive, I am asked which of these things was meant by your servant Moses, this book of mine would not really be a testimony if I did not testify: I know not. Yet I see the truth of these various views, except those of men who judge according to the flesh, on whom I have given my opinion—and even here the childlike people of hope need not be confounded by your Scripture, which is humble in its majesty, curt in its fullness. As for the rest, whom I recognize as knowing and speaking the truth, let us love each other, and love you, our God, truth's fountain, if truth and not self is what we are seeking. Let us revere, too, your servant, who mediated these words to us, so full of your Spirit that under your guidance, we believe, he intended what would best serve the light of truth and the benefit of readers.

42.   So when one man says Moses meant what *he* means, and another says Moses meant what *he* means, I think it is more in the spirit of our love to say: Why cannot both be true? And if a man finds a third view, or a fourth, or still another entirely new one, why should we not think that Moses intended all these meanings, since God, who is himself single, has suited his Scripture to readers who will find various truths when different minds interpret it? I affirm with all the strength of my heart that were I writing something so authoritative, I would want my words to accommodate any truth that might be found in them, rather than impose a single view as the obvious one, excluding others—I would exclude only views offending piety. I would not, therefore, be so brash as to doubt that your servant received this gift from you—that he meant as he wrote these words, whatever truths we can find in them, or any truths we have not yet found there, or not yet been able to find.

43.   Finally, Lord, who are God and not flesh and blood, if any man should see less than the truth in this passage, surely what you intended to reveal to future readers was not hidden from 'your favoring Spirit, who will lead me to the realm of virtue.' Perhaps even Moses, by whom the passage is spoken, had in mind only one of several possible truths. If that is the case, the truth he had in mind is more important than any others, and we beg you, Lord, make clear that truth or some other truth of your choosing. So disclose the truth to us—either what you revealed to Moses or what you meant us to find in the same words—that we may find pasturage in you, safe from all error.

See, Lord my God, how many words about few words I have written—see, I pray you, how many! At this rate, how much effort, how much time, would be needed to go through all your Scripture! Let me, then, limit my testimony to you, settling for just one truth you have prompted me to see, so long as it is firm and helpful, however many other truths may suggest themselves. Where so many can be considered, I make my testimony on the understanding that if I have identified what your servant meant, that is the best and highest truth, the one I was bound to strive for. But if I did not reach that truth, let me at least express what your truth willed me to take from the author's words, just as your truth willed what the author himself said.

BOOK THIRTEEN

SPIRIT (LOVE)

I

CREATION: GOD'S FREE ACT

1. You I call on, 'my God, who pities me,' who made me, and who did not forget me while I was forgetting you. I call you into my soul, which you are 'adapting to receive you,' from a desire you have first aroused in me. Desert me not, now that I call on you, you who 'responded before' I called. With increasing urgency, through various solicitings, you brought me to hear you from a distance, to turn back to you, calling you as you called me. You erased my 'acts deserving punishment,' the work of my own un-creating hands—just as you prompted all my acts deserving praise, 'the work of your creating hands.' For you existed when I did not, when I had nothing to which you could add existence. Yet here I am, by virtue of your goodness, which preceded anything of my own, or any of the elements that went into me. You could need nothing from me, I have no good thing that might profit you, my Lord and my God. No service of mine can relieve you of any burden, you will not be weaker for lack of my support. I cannot tend you as a farmer does his land, as if my neglect would leave you untended. No, I attend on you and serve you for the good that this does me, through you who made me capable of receiving good.

2. Out of the plenitude of your goodness comes your creation, a creation whose goodness cannot benefit you, nor be equal to you, though it can itself be benefited by your ability to create it. How can heaven and earth claim they deserved existence before the origin of things you made? How can all you created, whether spiritual or material, say it deserved existence before your wisdom formed

it, since it was already dependent in its most inchoate and unformed elements? Whether in the spiritual or material realm, those elements verge on formlessness and drift far off from resembling you—though unformed spiritual elements are superior to formed material ones, and unformed material elements are superior to non-being. All formless things depend on your Word, which alone can gather them into unity to be formed, becoming 'eminently good' only because the one supreme good makes them so. How, without you, could they have deserved to be even formless things, which without you can have no being at all?

3. How did physical matter deserve to be, even on 'the unseen and shapeless' level, when it could be nothing at all before you made it? Its very lack of existence made it unable to deserve existence. And how did the most exiguous spiritual matter deserve even shadowy indeterminacy like that of the abyss, so unlike you, if the Word had not turned it toward the Self-Same Word that gladdened it, made light shine on it, not as its equal, but as patterned on 'the pattern of one who is your equal'? With material things, to be is not the same thing as to be beautiful (or they could not conceivably be ugly)—so, with animate beings, to live is not the same as to live wisely (or they could *only* be wise). Thus 'should spirit cling always to you,' lest the turn toward light become a turn back toward darkness, sliding into a life like that of the dark abyss. For we, even though we are your creation in the spirit by our souls, 'were at one time darkness,' turned away from you, our light, and we flail with the aftereffects of darkness until we 'become your Right Order' in your only son. We are then like to 'the mounts of God' instead of what we were, 'your condemnation, like to a deep abyss.'

4. In your description of the stages of creation, 'Let there be light, and there was light' is best taken, I think, of the creation of spirit, for it had a kind of existence capable of illumination. It had no prior right to exist with that capacity, nor, once in existence, had it a prior right to be given the illumination. Its formlessness had nothing to recommend itself to you but that it could be your light, not merely by existing but by turning toward the light that illuminated it, and by clinging to it; and such life, such joy in living, comes only from your favor. By force of a better life it turns toward that which can never be better, never be worse—which you alone are, you who simply are, whose living and living in joy are the same thing, since you are joy itself.

5. What could you have lacked, were there no creation at all, or one that remained in an inchoate stage, since you create not out of need but from a surplus of goodness, giving things shape and definition, without any enhancement of your own satisfaction? Uncompleted things are at odds with your completion, so they seek to be completed and harmonious with you—but their incompletion is not a thing that, by being completed, can complete you. For your good 'Spirit hovers over the waters,' it is not rocked upon them to find rest. Where it is said that your 'Spirit rests on' people, he brings them to rest in him. For your will, forever undecaying and changeless, fulfilling yourself in yourself, hovers over the life you created, a life not synonymous with happy life, since it lived even when seething in darkness. It must be turned back to him who made it, taking ever more life from the fountain of life, to 'see in the light of his light,' to be completed, bathed in light, and glad.

II

THE SPIRIT OVER
THE WATERS

6. Here you give me 'in dim reflection' the Trinity that you are. For you 'made heaven and earth at the origin' of our wisdom, which is your wisdom, your Son, generated from you as your equal through all eternity. We have already spoken at length about 'heaven's heaven,' of earth as 'unseen and shapeless,' and of the dark abyss—dark with the incoherent diffusiveness of spiritual formlessness, until it turned to the source of what little life it had and in that light took on living form, to be that 'heaven's heaven' placed afterward 'between the water and the water.' I already recognized the Father in the phrase 'God made' these things, and the Son in the phrase 'at the origin,' and since I believed in a triune God, I sought what I believed in your holy pronouncements, and there it was—your 'Spirit hovering over the waters.' The passage contains the Trinity, Father, Son, and Holy Spirit, the maker of everything made.

7. I still wonder—may you answer me, you who are the assurance of truth, as I bring my heart to you, not trusting its own empty urgings, may you strike its darknesses aside and answer, I pray you through Charity the mother—I wonder why the Spirit is brought in by name only after the description of heaven, and the unseen and unformed earth, and the dark abyss. Could he not be introduced because he 'was hovering above,' and that could not be said of him until what he was hovering above had been specified? He could not, after all, have been 'hovering above' the Father or the Son, and could not be said to 'hover above' at all until there was something for him to be above. So the thing he would hover above had first to be mentioned, and only then could the one be introduced who 'hovered above.' But why should he not be introduced in other words than these of 'hovering above'?

8.   Here let the mind, if it is able, take its clue from your Apostle when he writes, 'Love floods our hearts from the Holy Spirit sent upon us.' Paul was instructing us 'in spiritual matters,' making clear that the way of 'love is supreme,' kneeling to you as an example to us, making us realize that 'the supreme way of knowing is the love of Christ,' a supreme love that 'was hovering over the waters' at the origin. To whom can I, in turn, express—how possibly express it?—the drag of human longing down toward the steep abyss, but also the updraft of love given by your Spirit, who 'was hovering above the waters'? To whom and how can I make clear that these are not physical places we sink into or soar to? Are they like them? The soul's tendencies are at issue, its loves—our longing for control driving us downward toward our filth, our longing for release letting your holiness lift us, to have our hearts on high with you, there where the Spirit is 'hovering over the waters,' so we may reach the supreme stability after our 'transit over the waters of pretense.'

9.   As the angel ruined down, so the soul of man ruined down—enough to consign the whole of spiritual creation to the pit's deep darkness, had you not said at the origin, 'Let there be light, and there was light,' on which light all the obeying intelligence of the heavenly city could remain fixed, finding stability in your Spirit, which hovers unchangeably above all changing things. But for that, 'heaven's heaven' itself would have been its own dark abyss, where now it is 'light in the Lord.' The sad instability of spirits ruining down, showing their dark nudity when no longer clothed in your light, is the measure of how noble you made your intellectual creatures, since nothing short of you can afford them stability in joy, or leave them any joy to be had in themselves— you alone, our God, 'will bring light to our darkness,' clothing us in it, making 'our darkness bright as noon.'

Make of yourself my gift, Lord, give me you. I love you— weak as my love is, I would make it stronger; but I have no way of measuring how far short my love falls of what it should be, if I am to run with all my energy into your embrace, not giving up until I am 'buried in the secret of your smile.' Of one thing only I am sure—that, apart from you, nothing I have or am can be good, and 'anything I gain is mere deprivation' if it be not my God.

10. Why could it not be said that the Father or the Son 'was hovering over the waters'? In fact, that cannot be said of the Holy Spirit, if it means that a body was hovering in space—only if it means that the supreme changelessness of the divine was above all changing things, and in that case Father and Son, as well as the Holy Spirit, did 'hover over the waters.' Then why is it said only of the Spirit, as if assigning him a physical place where there is no place? Well, why is it said of him alone that he is 'your gift'? In that gift we find our stability, there we enjoy you yourself. Our stabilization is our peace, so love tumbles us toward it, your Spirit's favoring will drawing our lowliness up from the portals of death. In that favoring will is our peace.

A physical object tends by its weight to find its natural level. It does not tend, necessarily, downward but toward whatever its natural level is. Fire tends up as a stone tends down. Their weight keeps them in motion till they find their own level. Oil poured out under water comes to the surface. Water poured out over oil sinks below it. Their weight keeps them in motion till they find their level. Out of their proper place, they are unstable. In their proper place, they are stabilized. The weight moving me is love. By your gift we are kindled and borne upward, we are set afire and we go, we 'ascend the heart's ascents' and 'sing the climbing song.' It is your fire, your fire for good, that burns in us as we go up toward 'our peace, which is Jerusalem,' since 'I take joy from those who told me, We are going to the Lord's house.' There your favor will give us our proper place and we shall wish for nothing but 'to stay there eternally.'

11. Happy the intellectual creation that knows nothing but that state. But it would not have been in that state were it not for your gift, hovering over all that changes, which snatched it up at the moment of its creation, not a second intervening, by your call into the darkness, 'Let there be light,' and it became light—unlike us, with our different stages, in which first 'we were darkness before becoming light.' Of the intellectual creation, by contrast, Scripture describes what might have been, had light not been given it—speaks as if it had a prior state of indeterminate darkness, in order to show the power that made it other than that, made it a light derived from 'the never-failing light.' Let those ask you for understanding who are capable of it. 'Why should they rely on me,' as if I could 'give light to anyone coming into this world'?

III

THE TRINITY

12. Yet who can understand the Trinity in all its power? All men think they speak of it, but do they? Rare the man able to say what it is he talks of. Some wrangle and contend over it, but the vision of it comes only in peace. The better course were to reflect each on our own inner threefoldness—not that this is the same thing as the Trinity; but even the extent of difference, I would suggest, is worth examining, testing, and experiencing. For I find these three acts in us, existing, knowing, and willing—I do exist and do know and do will. My existence is a knowing and willing one, and my knowledge is of a knowing and willing self, and my willing is for existing and knowing. Let anyone who is capable explore how inseparable in life are this separate existence, separate mind, and separate being, a separateness inseparable but still separate.

Each person has himself at hand to study, to observe and ponder and report what he finds. But in reporting his discoveries, let him not be so bold as to think he has discovered what is unchangeably above his own threefoldness—an unchangeable existing, an unchangeable knowing, an unchangeable willing. For who can glibly say whether these three things make up the Trinity, or whether each person in it has all three things, making each one threefold, or whether both things are true in some miraculous blend of singleness and multiplicity, of infinity defining its inner separatenesses, by an excess of unity unchangeably existing, knowing itself, and completing itself? What possible way is there to speak of this? Who ventures on a statement of any kind?

IV
"LET THERE BE LIGHT"

13. But forge on, faith, and testify! Say to your God, 'Holy, Holy, Holy,' Lord my God, 'in your name we were baptized, Father, Son, and Holy Spirit,' and 'in your name do we baptize, Father, Son, and Holy Spirit,' since through his Christ God has created a heaven and earth among us—the 'spiritual and earthly members' of your church. Our earth, too, before being formed by your instruction, was 'unseen and shapeless,' the darkness of ignorance covering us until you 'taught man in his ignorance' with 'judgments deep as the abyss.' Your pity did not abandon us in our pitiable state, since your 'Spirit was hovering above the waters,' and you said, 'Let there be light,' said, 'Repent, for the reign of God approaches.' This 'Repent' and thus 'Let there be light' were 'whirling our soul about,' and we 'harked back to you from the land of Jordan, from that mount [Christ] that is your equal though made lowly for us.' Our darkness distressed us, and we turned toward you, and there was light. 'We, once darkness, now are light in the Lord.'

14. In this state, however, it is a matter of believing, not of seeing, for 'our rescue is from hope' and 'hope that sees is not hope.' In this state, 'deep calls to deep,' though yours is 'a call of rushing floods.' In our state, even he who says, 'I cannot speak to you as to people having the Spirit, but only as to people in a natural state,' even he does not consider himself to have the prize, but 'abandoning all that is behind, pressing on to what is ahead,' he 'gasps under what weighs him down,' while his soul 'pants for the living God, as harts do for fresh springs'—he asks 'When will I arrive?' and longs 'to be in his heavenly shelter.'

Now he calls down to our abyss, 'Be not configured to this age, but reconfigure yourself to a new concept of yourself.' And: 'Be not childish in your understanding. Be children in innocence, but mature in mind.' And: 'Befuddled Galatians, who hypnotizes you?' Now, that is, he speaks not with his own voice, but with yours. Now you yourself have 'sent down your Spirit from heights,' through him who 'ascended those heights and opened the floodgates of his favor,' so 'river freshets would gladden your city.' The 'bridegroom's friend' [Paul] aspires to that city, 'harvesting the first growths of the Spirit' within him. He still pants within himself, 'in hope of full acceptance, with his body's resurrection.' He aspires to that city, as a member of the bride, but he is also protective of it, as a friend of the bridegroom. He is protective of it, not for his own sake or in his own voice, but 'in the voice of your rushing floods' that call out to the deep. He is protective 'from fear that, just as the serpent played a wily trick on Eve, their senses may be lured from the 'chastity that is in our bridegroom,' your only Son. Think of the beauty that will be revealed when 'we see him as he is,' all 'tears gone by that were once my diet day and night, when the daily question for me was, Where can your God be?'

15. I, too, ask, 'Where can my God be?' You are here, I have 'some surcease' in you as 'I pour my soul out in me' with 'the voice of one praising and testifying to you, with the noise that marks a festival.' Yet still 'my soul is sad,' since it falls back and an abyss opens—or rather I see that I am my own abyss. My belief, which you kindled 'to light my path through the dark,' tells my soul: 'Why, soul, are you downcast, and why are you whirling me about? Keep hope in the Lord.' His word is 'the light on your path.' Keep hoping and go forward, till night should pass, the mother of evildoers, 'till God's ire should pass.' We his sons were 'once darkness' and its taint we still bear in the body, 'mortal by sin's effect,' till 'daylight lives, scattering darkness.'

Keep hoping in the Lord. 'At daybreak I shall stand forth

and behold,' testifying to him forever. 'I shall stand forth at daybreak' and see 'what lifts my countenance toward my rescue,' my God, who will 'reanimate our dead bodies through the Spirit' infused in us, since he 'was hovering in pity over our interior seething darkness.' While still on our journey 'we have a pledge' that 'we have become light,' even as we 'live in hope of rescue,' we 'sons of light, sons of the daylight,' no longer 'sons of the night and darkness' as before. Only you, in this our darkling state of human knowledge, can distinguish us from the sons of darkness, since 'you test the heart,' you who separated 'light and called it day,' separated 'dark and called it night.' Who can make such distinctions but you, and 'what do we have that has not come from you,' who fashion 'from the same clay some vessels for honorable use, some for dishonor'?

V

THE CANOPY

16. Who but you have spread over us a canopy of authority in your divine writings? The 'sky will be rolled up like a scroll,' which is now 'stretched over us like a [parchment] skin covering.' Your divine writings are of more exalted authority, now that the mortals through whom you dispensed them have met their mortal end. You know, Lord, you know how you clothed humans in [animal] skin after they had become mortal by their sin. So did you give us the canopy of your Scripture, to serve like a broad skin covering, all your words fitted together in agreement to give us the shelter provided through your mortal instruments. At their deaths the solid authority of your writings, handed on to us by them, has been spread out on high, above all lower things, higher than when they were alive, when you had not yet extended the sky like a skin cover, and when you had not spread everywhere the fame of their martyrdom.

17. May we 'behold the heavens your hands made.' Clear from our eyes the cloud you wove over them. The heavens 'bear witness to you,' how 'you grant wisdom to lowly ones.' Now, God, 'complete the praise that rises from children, from babies at the breast.' No other writings, we know, can so conquer pride, so conquer 'the foe who excuses,' the man who will not make peace with you but excuses his sins. I myself have found no other words so cleansing, to make me testify to you, to supple my stiff neck to your yoke, to make me worship you freely. May I grasp those words, my favoring

Father, may I shelter under the strong canopy you provide for those sheltering under it.

18.   I believe that there are other and everlasting waters above that canopy, waters insulated from earthly taint. Let the angels of that high heaven praise you, praise your name. They do not need to look up at the canopy to learn your words by reading them, for they see you always 'face to face.' There they read, without sounding out syllables in time, what is your eternal will. They read, they heed, they accede. Forever they read, since what they read does not pass by. Heeding and acceding, they read what is unchangeable, your providence. Their book is never closed, nor their scroll rolled up. For you are their book, an everlasting one, since you have placed them above the canopy you spread as a shelter for the frailty of those below it. Those who look up at it find there your mercy, spelled out in time by you who made time.

For 'your mercy is in heaven,' Lord, and 'your truth is as high as the clouds.' The 'clouds vanish,' but heaven remains. In the same way, those bringing your words to us pass from this life to the next, while your word is spread out over the people till the end of time. 'Heaven and earth shall pass away, but not your words.' The 'parchment will be rolled up' and the 'grass shining under it will wither, but your word lasts forever.' At present, your word is seen by us in 'dim images of cloud reflected from the heaven,' not clearly for what it is. For neither is it 'clear what we shall be,' loved though we be by your Son. He 'looked through the lattice of our flesh,' he wooed, he inflamed us, we 'respond to the perfume,' and 'when he appears we shall be like him, for we shall see him as he is.' Seeing him 'as he is,' Lord—that is our prize not yet given.

19.   To know you through and through only you can do, since you exist unchangeably, know unchangeably, and will unchangeably. Your existence both knows and wills unchangeably, your knowledge both exists and wills unchangeably, and your will both exists and knows unchangeably. It is not right in your eyes for anyone who changeably receives light to know itself as you who give light know yourself. My soul is therefore like 'an arid desert in your eyes.' It cannot give itself life without you, cannot give itself fulfillment. For only 'with you is the fountain of life,' since 'in your light we shall see the light.'

VI

THE GATHERED WATERS

20. Who 'gathered men briny with spite' into one society? These all have one goal only, a happiness merely temporal and terrestrial. They do nothing except for this one thing, though many are the cares that toss them about in its pursuit. Who gathered them but you, who 'told the waters to gather themselves into one gathering' so that the land stood out, 'athirst for you'—for 'the sea is yours, you made it, and your hands shaped the dry land'? The sea here means the mass of gathered waters, not the clash of bitter men—but you also force together men's wicked desires, and 'set limits to them, how far the waters should advance,' that their waves might break back on themselves and become a sea by your imperious ordering of all things.

21. Other souls, however, who 'thirst for you and come before you,' you keep from the sea's salt margin and refresh from a sweet hidden spring, so their 'earth grows fruitful.' Their earth is fruitful at the command of its Lord and God— that is, our souls bring forth, 'each in its kind,' acts of mercy, showing love in the relief of others' needs, 'each seed bearing its like'—since we learn kindness from our very weakness, helping others 'as we would wish to be helped' if we were in the same plight—not just in small things, as 'grass germinates,' but with a tough resolution for giving help, as 'a tree bears fruit.' That means snatching the wronged person from the clutches of power, covering him with the protective shield of firmness in the right.

VII

LIGHTS IN THE HEAVENS

22. Let it be, then, I beg you, Lord, you who create, who give us our joys and our abilities, let it be that 'truth rises up from earth, and justice looks down from heaven,' and 'you fill the canopy with stars.' Break we then 'our bread with those who hunger,' share we our homes with the homeless, let us clothe the naked and 'treat no servant, who is our fellow human being, with condescension.' When these fruits grow from our earth, 'look on them and see that they are good.' May 'our brief light shine forth.' From the lower fruitfulness of this active life let us rise to the higher joys of contemplation, adhering to 'the word of life,' shining out as 'luminaries of this world,' woven into the canopy of your Scripture. You 'enter into discussion' with us through those writings, to separate things of the intellect from those of the senses, as you separate day from night; or, rather, you separate minds attuned to the intellect from those attuned to the sensual.

For though you alone separate light from dark (as you did before the canopy was made) in the depths of your supreme discrimination, yet may your spiritual creatures also, by the revelation of your favor around the globe, 'shine down on the earth' from their place high in the canopy, each with its own light 'to separate day from night and mark the times'— how 'the old order has passed, and things are made new'— for 'our rescue is nearer than when we first believed, the night advances, the day is near,' and 'you are blessing the year's completion.'

You 'send workers out to harvest' what 'others have been at pains to sow,' then you send others to a new sowing, 'for the final harvest.' Thus do you answer one who petitions you and 'bless the years of the just.' Though 'you are ever the same,' and you have 'no years to fail you,' you provide the barn for harvestings from years that pass. You provide things suitable for every time from your timeless design, working the will of heaven on earth.

23. To one the 'Spirit provides the gift of voicing wisdom.' This is like the sun's 'greater light,' to serve those taking joy in the clear light of truth, 'bright as the dayspring.' To another the same 'Spirit provides the gift of voicing knowledge.' This is like the moon's lesser light. Still others are provided with 'the gifts of faith, of healing, of working miracles, of prophesying, of identifying spirits, of speaking in different tongues.' These are like the stars. All are 'the work of one and the same Spirit, imparting what is fitting for each according to his decision,' revealing them as stars for the edification of mankind. The 'voicing of knowledge' is like the moon because it concerns the mysterious dispositions of providence, which vary according to the times. But the other gifts mentioned are like stars, as coming out at night, since their splendor is less than that of wisdom, whose joy, as was said, is 'in the dayspring.' These stars are needed by those whom your shrewd servant [Paul] could not 'address as spiritually formed, but as carnal,' while to 'the more advanced he voices wisdom.' The 'carnal man' is a 'mere child in Christ, a suckling incapable of solid food.' Until his eyes are strong enough to bear the light of day, he is not left with a featureless night, but has these stars and the moon to rely on. Thus you most wisely 'enter into discussion with us,' our God, in your Scripture, which is a canopy to cover us as we contemplate all things with awe, reading for now 'the signs and seasons, the days and years.'

24. In this discussion you tell us: 'First bathe and be cleansed, purge wrong from your mind and in the sight of my eyes,' that your 'dry land may appear.' 'Learn virtuous

conduct, champion the orphan, vindicate the widow,' that
the land may bear grass for grazing, trees for bearing fruit.
'Enter we then into discussion,' says the Lord, and your stars
will appear in the canopy, to give light on earth. The rich
man asked the 'good teacher what he should do to have eternal life.' The 'good teacher' (who had been taken for a good
man, and nothing more, though he was good because God)
answered that if he wished fully to live he should keep the
commandments, avoid the brine of 'thinking or doing ill'—
'kill not, nor commit adultery, nor steal, nor testify falsely,'
so 'dry land will appear' to bear 'reverence to his parents and
love for his neighbor.' He answered that he had done all that.
But if his dry land were fertile, why was it clogged with
thorns? Go and root out this dense thicket of greed, 'sell
what you own, enjoy a rich harvest by giving to the poor,
and your treasure will be in heaven.' Follow the Lord 'if you
would live fully,' be one of those to whom the Lord 'voices
wisdom,' knowing how to distinguish day from night and
sharing that knowledge with you, so that for you lights may
stand in the canopy of heaven. But this is only if your heart is
his, only if 'your treasure is with him,' as the 'good teacher'
taught the one whose land was sterile in regret, while thorns
choked the word.

25.   But you 'chosen ones,' who are 'weak in the world,'
who have 'left all behind to follow the Lord,' go after him.
'Stun the powerful' and 'foot it beautifully,' shine as 'luminaries in the canopy' so 'the heavens may tell God's glory.'
Separate the light of the lofty spirits (the not-quite angels)
from the darkness of the lowly (the not-quite abandoned).
Shine across the earth, let one day gleaming with the sun
pass on to the next day 'a message of wisdom,' and let one
night glowing with the moon speak to the next night 'a message of knowledge.' It is at night that the moon and stars
shine. It does not extinguish them, but is illuminated by
them 'according to the times.' For just as God said, 'Let there
be luminaries in the canopy of heaven,' so when 'the loud
blast came, as of a fierce wind whipping, tongues as of fire
appeared and settled, one on each,' and these became lumi-

naries in the canopy of heaven, 'with the message of life in them.' Race everywhere, then, you holy fires, fires glorious, you are the world's light, 'not hidden under a measuring container.' He you follow is raised on high, and high he will raise you. Race everywhere with news for all peoples.

VIII

FISH OF THE SEA

26. May even the sea grow fertile and bring forth your works. 'Let the seas engender sinuous things with living souls'—for you, 'distinguishing the precious from the worthless, are made the spokesmen of God,' who says, 'Let the seas engender' not the living soul formed from clay, but 'sinuous things with living souls, and flitting things above the earth.' These are your symbols, God, which through the actions of your saints went gliding, sinuous, through floods of worldly temptation, permeating the nations with the waters of 'baptism in your name.' In these floods are 'your great miracles' like huge sea monsters, and over the earth are your flitting heralds that skim the canopy of Scripture (the warrant for their flight, wherever winged). 'There is no language or discourse in which their voices are not heard,' as 'their utterance issues forth to the earth, their words to the earth's far ends,' since you, Lord, have 'multiplied them by your blessing.'

27. Can I fairly be charged with misleading, with mixing categories, with failing to distinguish the radiant expression of truths in heaven's canopy from material creatures in the wavering sea or elsewhere under the canopy of heaven? The meanings of the former are fixed and defined, and do not increase from one generation to the next, but have the clarity of wisdom and knowledge. Yet their exemplifications in the latter, in the physical world, are multiple and changing, as things 'increase and multiply by your blessing.' You have ministered to the sluggishness of our mortal senses by letting one meaning have, in the mind's expression, varied symbolic representations in the activity of your material

creation. 'The waters engendered' such activity, but only as
your Word intended. Such signs are engendered to suit the
mental limits of those still distant from your eternal truth,
but only as they serve your revelation. The need for these watery engenderings was man's briny resistance, but what produced them was your Word.

28.   Everything created is beautiful, since you made it
who are indescribably more beautiful than anything you
made. Had Adam not fallen, there would not have descended
from his loins the salt expanse of his descendants, a race
deeply transgressive, swollen with storm, restlessly roiled.
But for this, there were no need for the 'conveyers of your
mysteries,' working in 'the rush of waters,' to present your
words and acts in various material guises—symbols such as
the 'sinuous and flitting' things in my interpretation of them.
But men steeped in these physical symbols, given initial instruction in them, trained by them, cannot progress beyond
them unless their minds be spiritually raised to a higher
plane, carrying them 'beyond initial formulas as they press
on toward completion.'

IX

DRY LAND

29. According to your word the depths of the sea engendered 'sinuous things and flitting things with living souls,' but it was land dried from the brackish waters that brought forth 'the living soul.' The land that is dried no longer needs baptism as it did when covered with the water, or as pagans still do—for there is 'no entering heaven but by the entry you have established.' This dry land demands no miraculous wonders to constitute its faith, nor does its belief wait upon 'signs and prodigies,' since it is already a faithful land separated from the faithless waves' ill lavings. 'Speaking in tongues is not for believers but the unbelieving.'

This land you 'raised above the waters' has, therefore, no need of 'the flitting things the waters engendered' at your word. To the land 'you send your word' through your messengers. We celebrate their work, but it is 'your work effected through them,' and the effect is 'the living soul.' The land engenders this soul, since the land is what they live on, as waters caused the production of 'sinuous things and flitting things with living souls under the canopy of heaven.' These the dry land has no use for—except for eating the mystical fish [Christ] raised from the depths to 'that table you have prepared in the sight of believers.' He truly was raised from the depths for nourishment of the dry land.

Birds too are engendered from the sea, but they 'multiply' on land. In the same way, the preaching of the gospel must begin from men's unbelief, but as men become believers they are encouraged and blessed to multiply 'from day to day.' Thus, 'the living soul' takes even its origin on the land, which alone supports the baptized in their separation from worldly love, that their soul may be alive only with you, after the living death of pleasure, since pleasure is death-bearing if it be not the pleasure that pure hearts take in you.

30. Let your ministers work now on dry land, no longer in the waters of unbelief, where before they preached and explained by way of miracles, symbols, and mystical sayings. Ignorance, the mother of credulity, must be addressed through its fear of lurking powers. But though faith enters through this portal with the sons of Adam who have put you out of mind, 'hiding themselves from your gaze,' and become their own abyss, let your ministers now work on dry land, land separated from the maelstrom of the abyss. Let this dry land be 'a pattern of faith for believers,' lived out before their eyes, stimulating them to imitation. Not 'as hearers only but as doers' let them heed the words, 'Seek God and your soul will live,' and the earth will produce 'a living soul.' Therefore 'be not patterned after the world,' but shun it. The soul lives by fleeing what it would die by pursuing. Shun, then, the ravening beast pride, the easy surrender to sensuality, the 'knowledge falsely called such.' Let the wild beasts become gentled, the domestic herds become disciplined, the serpents become innocent. These are the soul's passions in symbolic form, but they are the passions of a dead soul—the elation of pride, the self-indulgence of sensuality, and the sting of transgressive knowledge. For the soul's death is not only at the end of life. It dies as soon as it turns away from 'the fountain of life,' taking on the imprint of the transient world, assuming its pattern.

31. This 'fountain of eternal life' is, God, 'your word that never passes away.' Our turning from God is checked by the word when it tells us, 'Take not your pattern from the world,' so that land, watered by the fountain of life, may 'engender a living soul,' a soul that, by your Word speaking through the gospel writers, chastely 'takes its pattern from those patterned on your Christ.' This action is 'according to its kind,' since 'rivalry is with one's like,' and our like tells us, 'Be then as I am, since I am as you.' The bestial natures in 'the living soul' will thus be gentled in their actions, for you have ordered us to 'complete your acts in gentleness, to be loved by all.' Domestic herds in the soul will be disciplined 'neither to abound by eating more nor to lack by eating less.' The serpents in the soul will be too innocent to sting, but wise enough to know, assessing temporal reality only so far as to let them see eternity shine through their 'understanding of created things.' The animal urges yield to reason when they are wrenched from their deadly course to live in a benign state.

X

MAN IN GOD'S PATTERN

32. Lord our God, you who create us, when our passions are wrenched from love of the world, from the life that was our death, when we adopt the life that makes 'a living soul,' then your word will be verified in us, according to the Apostle: "Pattern not your life on this world.' And that which you immediately added will follow: 'But take on a new form, based on a new mental pattern.' This is not done 'according to our kind,' as if we were conforming to some neighbor's example or some higher human authority, as if you said, Let man come to be according to his kind. No, you said, 'Let us make man to our own pattern and likeness,' that we might 'experience your will at work.'

That is why your minister [Paul], 'engendering sons in the gospel,' not wishing that they be always 'little ones nursed on milk' or 'tended by a nurse,' said, 'Take on a new form, based on a new mental pattern, that you may experience the Lord's will at work, how good it is, how benevolent, how complete.' You do not say, Let man come to be, but 'Let us make man.' And you do not say that this is to be according to his kind, but 'in our own pattern and likeness.' A man 'with a new mental pattern,' who sees your truth with understanding, has no need to prove that he follows 'his own kind,' since he 'experiences your will at work, how good it is, and benevolent, and complete.' For you make him capable of understanding the Trinity of your unity and the unity of your Trinity, from its being said in the plural 'Let us make,' followed by the singular 'and God made man,' and from its being said in the plural 'to our pattern,' followed by the singular 'to God's pattern.' Thus does man 'become new by knowing the God to whose pattern he was made,' and as a free spirit he 'puts all things to the test,' all things that submit to testing, 'while none test him.'

33. 'Putting all things to the test' refers to man's 'having dominion over fish of the sea, things flitting in the sky, herds and wild animals, all that move about on earth.' He exercises this dominion through the control of his intellect, 'understanding what is according to God's Spirit.' Were this not the case, 'man would have high status without corresponding intellect, and would resemble unreasoning beasts of burden, made in their image.' That is why in your church, our God, according to your favor shed on it, 'we who were fashioned by you to do good' exercise spiritual judgment—not only the leaders but those who follow them, since 'male and female you made them' and favored them as equal, 'no more male and female, Jew or Gentile, slave or free.' So free spirits in your church, whether leaders or followers, 'put all things to the test.'

They do not, of course, have jurisdiction over the disembodied intelligences that 'shine on high in the canopy,' which are too high for their reach. Nor do they put your Scripture to the test. Even though it has passages not easily understood, we submit our intelligence to it, acknowledging that even those parts impenetrable to our minds are proper and true, since man, even spiritual man 'becoming new by knowing the God to whose pattern he was made,' must obey the law, not judge it. Nor do they put their fellows to the test, separating the saved from the damned—though they lie open to your scrutiny, we cannot know 'the fruits of what they will do' as you, Lord, know them, you who in your hidden way singled them out and called them before the canopy was made. No matter how spiritual a man may be, he is no judge of people still caught in the riptides of time. How can he judge from the outside which man will reach by grace the final sweetness, which will welter on in the lasting brine of impiety?

34. Thus man, though you 'made him to your pattern,' cannot put to the test the luminaries of heaven, the hidden things of heaven itself, the dayspring or the coming of night, which you called up before the heavens' foundation, nor the 'gathering of waters into the sea.' But he has dominion over the 'fishes of the sea, flitting things of the air, all herds, and all the earth, and all animals moving on the earth.' He has jurisdiction, to approve as proper or reject as improper, over the administration of the mysteries by which those are initiated whom his mercy searches out in 'the rush of waters,' or by which the Fish raised from the depths and exposed for the sake of dry land is consumed. 'The spiritual man has jurisdiction' over the words used to interpret and expound the authority that reigns in your Scripture, where he acts like those messengers flitting under your canopy—finding meaning, sifting it, discussing, debating, blessing it and thanking you for it, shaping these judgments orally and communicating them so that 'people answer, So it is.'

The abyss of the world and the blindness of flesh block our vision of pure thought, making it necessary for these judgments to be expressed in physical sounds, which the ear must receive. That is why the messengers 'multiply above the earth,' though the need for them arises from the waters. The 'spiritual man has jurisdiction' to approve the proper, disapprove the improper, in the conduct and morals of the faithful—are they a fruitful earth in their almsgiving, is their 'living soul' gentled in its feelings by purity, by fasting, by devout assessment of what it perceives through its senses? Jurisdiction is also given him over things calling for correction.

XI

"INCREASE AND MULTIPLY"

35. But what meaning is to be puzzled out from the following verse, where, Lord, 'you bless them, to increase and multiply and fill the earth'? Are you signaling here something deeper that we should take in? Why did you not bless 'the light you called day,' nor the 'canopy of heaven,' nor the luminaries or stars or land or seas? It might be said, our God, that you wanted to confine your blessing to man, since you 'made us to your own pattern,' except that you 'blessed the fish and whales to increase and multiply and fill the seas,' and the 'birds to fill the skies.' I could say such blessing applies to things that reproduce 'after their own kind,' if I found it applied to trees and plants and land animals, but they are not expressly told to 'increase and multiply,' though they reproduce and maintain their own kind just as much as fish and birds and men do.

36. What, you light of mine, you the truth, am I to make of this? That nothing is meant here, it is mere verbiage? Not so, father of reverence, as I devoutly attend your word, never let it be so with me. If I miss the meaning of this passage, let better men have better views, those more intelligent than I, as 'you give to each his own degree' of understanding. All I can offer 'under your scrutiny' is my own testimony, and I testify to a belief, Lord, that you did not speak pointlessly. I shall declare what my encounter with these words brings to my mind, which is true in itself, and I see no reason not to find this truth in a symbolic reading of your Scripture, since I know that a single mental concept can have several material expressions, and a single material act can have several mental significations. See, for instance, how the simple idea of 'loving God and one's neighbor' is expressed in a wide variety of symbols, in countless languages, and in countless verbal turns in any one language—'increasing and multiplying' like the fish of your waters [the baptized]. Let any reader notice, as well, how the Scripture gives one simple expression in the words 'At the origin God made heaven and earth,' which nonetheless can be understood in many senses, not merely erroneous ways but variously true ones—'increasing and multiplying' like the offspring of man.

37. If we look to natural facts literally, not symbolically, 'increase and multiply' concerns only things propagated by insemination. But if we treat the words symbolically, which I find indicated in the fact that the blessing was singled out only for fish and men, we see that they apply to many more groups—to spiritual and material ones (symbolized as heaven and earth), or to the saved and unsaved (symbolized as day and night), or to the sacred authors who convey your law (symbolized as 'the canopy securely dividing upper from lower waters') and the 'gathered brine-bitter people' (symbolized as the sea). The labor of your people to bring 'mercy to the present life' is symbolized as the cultivated dry land where 'germinating plants increase,' and 'trees bear fruit,' and 'spiritual gifts shine for guidance' like 'luminaries in the sky,' and passions are tempered to bring forth 'the living soul.'

In all these cases we find multitudes and throngs that increase. But only when we take symbolically the physical descriptions of what 'increase and multiplies,' as expressing intellectual realities, do we see how a single thing can be expressed in many ways, and a single expression can be read in many ways. Sunk in our own deep carnality, we can interpret the increase of sea creatures as the signs expressed in material form. But because our reason bears offspring, we can interpret the reproduction of mankind as the generation of ideas from the mind. That is why we believe, Lord, you tell only fish and men to 'increase and multiply.' By that blessing I understand that you give us range and opportunity to express in different ways what we understand to be a single truth, and to understand in different ways what we read in a single obscure expression. Thus is our sea filled, where are no waves but the multiplicity of interpretations, and our dry land is filled by the reproduction of mankind, dry land labored by human toil and governed by reason.

XII

FRUITS OF EARTH

38. I would say what the next passage of your Scripture prompts in me, Lord my God. Forthrightly I revere your verity, in the verbal passages you wish me to expound. For no other guide, I believe, can assist me to expound verities but you, who are Verity itself, while 'every man is a deceiver,' and 'whoever lies reveals his nature'—which is why if I say anything true it reveals your nature. See how you give us provender 'from every sown plant on earth that propagates itself by seeding, and every tree whose fruit bears seed.' This is given to us, to the birds of the sky, and to 'the beasts and reptiles of the earth,' but not to the fish of the sea and the great whales. We noticed earlier that these fruits of the earth symbolize and are a type of charitable works, since food for the needy comes from the fertility of the fruitful earth.

Such an earth was the loyal Onesiphorus, on 'whose family you took pity because he often comforted' your servant Paul. He was 'not embarrassed by his imprisonment.' The same was true of Paul's brethren in Macedonia, who bore the fruit of good works by 'supplying what he needed.' Others, however, caused him anguish—trees not bearing the fruit that was his due—of whom he wrote: 'Under the first arraignment none came to my defense, but all abandoned me—count it not against them.' It is to teachers like him, who make the divine mysteries understandable to our minds, that we owe the services of nourishment. We owe it to them as to all men, but especially to them as 'living souls,' our models of temperate control. Beyond that we owe it to them as the flitting messengers whose blessings 'multiply' over the earth,' since 'report of them goes out to every land.'

39. Those who take in such provender find that it nourishes, though it gives no sustenance to those 'whose God is their belly.' And for those who furnish this provender, for them the real fruit is not what they give but how they give it. I understand entirely and share the joy felt by Paul, who was 'a servant of God, not of his belly,' and I share in his rejoicing. He received help from the Philippians, sent by way of Epaphroditus, but I notice what he took joy in. The joy that truly fed him he described with truth: 'I rejoice exuberantly in the Lord that the concern you once felt for me, of which you grew tired, has momentarily blossomed again.' Long weariness had withered them, dried up in them the fruit of good works. He rejoices that they were back in blossom, not that they were meeting his needs—because, as he said: 'I complain of no need. I have learned to deal with any situation I meet. I have experienced shortages and surpluses. I have been tempered by any and every turn—to eat well or go hungry, to have plenty or have nothing, since I can do anything so long as Christ is my strength.'

40. What is it, non-pallid Paul, that gladdens you? Where did you find joy, where graze, as a man 'given new form in acknowledgment of God, who made you to his own pattern'? Restraint made you 'a living soul,' and 'lips revealing mysteries' made you 'flit over the earth.' To such 'living souls' is this grazing reserved. What do you graze on but joy? I am alert as he continues: 'Despite all this [his sufficiency for any trial], you were right to take a share in my difficulties.' There is the real source of his joy, his nourishment, that they were doing the right thing, not that they had eased his trials—he prayed after all to you, saying, 'By trials you enlarge my scope.' It was in you, Lord, 'who gave him strength,' that he learned 'how to experience surpluses and to endure poverty.' He tells them: 'Philippians, you know how, from the early days of my preaching, after I had left Macedonia, you alone entered into my organization of alms collected and sent. Not once but a second time you sent me what was needed in Thessalonica.' It is their return to this spirit of giving that makes him rejoice, taking pleasure in their reflorescence, as from a barren field that bears again.

41. When he wrote, 'You sent me what was needed,' can we say that he was gladdened by having his need met? Surely not—for he goes on to say: 'I desire not a gift for me. The fruit for you is what I have at heart.' The difference between gift and fruit I have learned from you, my God. A gift is what one uses to supply a need—such things as money, food, drink, clothing, shelter, assistance. But fruit is the giver's proper motive in doing good. For our 'good teacher' did not simply praise 'one who welcomes a prophet,' but further specifies 'one who welcomes him because he is a prophet.' He did not simply praise 'one who welcomes a just man,' but further specifies 'welcomes him because he is a just man.' The one who has such a motive receives his due for welcoming the prophet or the just man. Similarly, he did not simply say, 'Whoever gives a cup of cold water to even the least of my followers,' but specified 'because he is a follower,' and then goes on to add: 'I say with authority, he will have his due.' So a gift is merely to welcome a prophet or a just man, or to offer a cup of cold water to a follower. But the fruit is in the intent of such actions, that they are done because he is a prophet, a just man, a follower. Elias was fed by such fruit, since the widow feeding him recognized that he was a man of God and acted from that intent. But when a raven fed him he received a gift only, since it was not the inner Elias that was being fed, but the outward man (who, even though a man of God, could starve unless outwardly fed).

42. Of this distinction I will say what is true in your sight, Lord, that 'ignorant and unbelieving men,' those symbolized as 'fishes and whales,' need to be taught and won over by beginners' rites and the wonder of miracles. Therefore, when they welcome your servants and provide them physical food or other support for the wants of this present life, they are not truly feeding them, nor are those servants being truly fed, since the givers do not know why or for what end they should be doing this. The givers do not act from a correct and holy motive, and the receivers can take no joy in a fruit that is not included with the gift. For the soul is gladdened by what gives it sustenance. That is why fish and whales cannot graze the produce of dry land, which bears fruit only after being separated from and kept unsoured by the sea's ill-laving waves.

XIII

"EMINENTLY GOOD"

43. You saw the entirety of your creation, Lord, that it was 'eminently good.' And we see it now as 'eminently good.' At the separate stages of your creation, after you had said 'Let it be made and it was made,' of each in turn you said only that it was good. Seven times by my count it is written that you saw that what you had made was good. But here, at the eighth mention, you saw all that you had made, that the entirety was not only good but 'eminently good.' The parts are good, but the entirety is 'eminently' so. The same is true of the animal body, which is more beautiful as a whole than are its members taken individually. Beautiful as the members may be in themselves, their harmonization into an articulated whole completes them.

44. I tried to discover from your words whether you had found your works pleasing by seeing them on seven occasions [separately] or on an eighth occasion [comprehensively]. As I considered things under your scrutiny, I could not understand the place of time in your looking on so many different occasions at what you had made. So I asked: Lord, surely your Scripture is true, since it comes from you, who are not only truthful but the truth. Then why do you tell me that your scrutiny is outside time, yet your sacred word tells me that you made things on successive days (I have counted how many), and then saw they were good? In answer to me—for you are my God, speaking forcefully into your follower's inner hearing, breaking through my dullness with your ringing clarity—you said: Surely you know, man, that what is said in Scripture is said by me. Yet it is said to those who exist in time, while time does not affect my own Word, which exists as my equal in eternity. What you see by the Spirit's action I also see, just as what you say by the Spirit's action, I say. But you see it in temporal sequence and I see it outside time, you say it in temporal sequence and I say it outside time.

45.   Hearing you, Lord my God, I am suckled on the sweetness of your truth. Now I can see why some people [Manichaeans] look on your works and find them not good. They claim you were acting under external compulsion when you made many of them, including even the layout of heaven and the placing of the stars, working not from yourself but upon pre-existing materials, supplied apart from you and from a different source. They say that after defeating your enemies, you had to grapple with these materials, fit them together, and make them interlock, to form out of them the ramparts of the universe, to repel with these fortifications any renewed assault from your foes. Other things they say you did not make at all, or even fit together—corporeal bodies, for instance, and insects, and plants 'whose roots lay hold on earth.' They say these were generated and given shape from the depths below by a malignant mind, with a nature not derived from you but opposed to you. They speak as men deranged, unable to see your works with the help of your Spirit, and therefore not 'recognizing you in them.'

46.   When people see your works with the help of your Spirit, you are seeing them through their eyes. If they see that they are good, it is you within them who see that they are good. If they take joy in them because of you, it is your joy they are feeling. Whatever by your Spirit delights us, it is your delight in us. 'What man knows the essence of another but that man's own inner spirit? In the same way, no one can know the essence of God but his own inner Spirit.' As he [Paul] tells us: 'We, who have not accepted the spirit of the world, have the Spirit sent us by God, that we may understand what God has given us.' This prompts me to say: If it is clear that 'no one knows the essence of God but God's own Spirit,' then how can we be said to 'understand what God has given us'? The answer is clear: If we know only by the help of the Spirit, that itself is the Spirit of God knowing in us. We rightly say, of those speaking by inspiration of the Spirit, that they are 'not speaking in their proper selves,' so we can say that those knowing the gifts of God know them not in their proper selves, but God's Spirit is knowing them. We can just as rightly say, to those who see in the Spirit, that they do not see of themselves, and if they see in the Spirit that a created thing is good, it is not their particular selves that see it. God does.

It is one matter to consider a good thing bad, like those [Manichaeans] already mentioned. It is another matter for a man to recognize the good in what is good—many, after all, take delight in your creation, seeing that it is good—but not to take delight in you, wanting to enjoy the creation apart from you. It is still a third matter for a man to see that a thing is good because you are seeing it in him. Then God is loved in the things he made, and he cannot be loved but through the Spirit he has given. For 'God's love permeates our hearts from the Spirit given us,' and in him we see that everything, whatever its degree of existence, is good, since it comes from him who has no degrees of existence but simply is the 'He Is.'

47. Thanks to you, Lord, we see heaven and earth—whether that describes the higher and lower orders of material creation, or the spiritual and the physical creation. We see its celestial adornment, whether of the physical universe or the entire cosmos, with the separation in each of day from night. We see heaven's canopy, whether it divides the higher spiritual waters from the lower material waters (the primal stuff of creation), or the space of air below the canopy which is called physical heaven, through which flit the roving birds between two forms of physical water—that which rises as mist and drops serenely as a dew at night, or the heavier flowing waters on earth. We see the shape of the sea marked by the gathering of its waters in a broad expanse, and dry land separated from it, either arid or cultivated in 'an order manifest,' with plants and trees drawn from it. We see the bright heavenly bodies—sun 'sufficient to the day,' moon

and stars 'comforting the night,' all of them 'spelling out
time and marking its passage.' We see everywhere a watery
element that nurtures fish and sea-beasts and birds. For
moisture in the air, drawn from the mass of water below,
holds birds up in flight.

We see the face of earth adorned with animal and human
life, the humans 'made to God's pattern and similitude,' and
holding dominion over animals by virtue of that 'pattern and
similitude,' its intelligence and reasoning power. And just as
in man there is one aspect that makes plans and rules, and
another aspect that follows the planning and is ruled, so does
'man rule woman' physically. She is the equal of man in her
capacity for intellect and reason, but she is subordinate by
the function of her body, just as the impulse to action is subordinate to a canny assessment of the proper course of action. We see each of these things that they are good, and we
see that all together are 'eminently good.'

48.   Your works praise you, prompting us to love you,
and we love you, prompting us to praise. Your works move
in time, passing from their beginnings to their ends, from rise
to decline, from start to finish, from definition to erasure.
Day alternates with night, passing through twilights to full
day or full night. They are created from nothing by you, not
from you, nor from anything alien or prior to you, since to
matter you instantly gave form, with no temporal lapse between the two acts. They are separate things—the matter of
heaven and earth, the form of heaven and earth—since the
matter you made from nothing at all, but the earthly forms
from shapeless matter. But you created them both at once, so
no matter would at any point exist independent of form.

49.   But symbolically, as we have considered, you willed
that creation be in a particular sequence, or be recorded in
sequence; so that we can see that each thing taken separately
is good, but all taken together are 'eminently good.' Each
particular is good, but the entirety is 'eminently good' in
your Word, your only Son, who is our heaven and earth—
that is, the head and body of the church, destined from eternity to have no dawn or dusk. When you began to fulfill in

time what was already planned, 'revealing hidden things' and gathering our scatteredness into form—for we were covered in sin and plunged in a dark pit far from you, till your 'Spirit should hover over the waters' and bring us rescue 'at the time foreseen'—the unjust you made just, and separated them from the evil, and spread the canopy of your book between the higher orders subject only to you and the lower orders subject to the book. You gathered the faithless into a single community with its own goal, that dry land might appear separate from it and be labored by the faithful, producing works of mercy as they deployed earthly means for reaching heavenly goals.

You lit the heavenly bodies in the canopy, your holy ones 'having the word of life' in them, effulgent with the high authority bestowed by spiritual gifts. Then for the initiation of unbelievers, you drew from formless matter symbols, miracles, the voices of those preaching from the canopy that is your Scripture, things helpful as well to the faithful. You formed in the faithful 'a living soul' with passions strictly disciplined. You renewed 'your pattern and similitude' in the mind subject to you alone and needing to imitate or follow no human model. You made rational action subject to presiding intellect, as woman is subject to man. You ordered the faithful to provide for the temporal needs of those who minister to their spiritual needs while on earth, services fruitful in the hereafter. All these things we see as good, 'eminently' so, because you see them in us, you who sent the Spirit by which we see them, that we may love you in them.

XIV

SABBATH REST

50. 'Lord God, grant us peace,' you who have given us everything, grant a peace of tranquillity, peace of the seventh day, a peace with no nightfall. This beautiful cosmos, made up of creatures 'eminently good' in their entirety, has an appointed course to run to its end—its dawn will have its dusk. **51.** But no dusk comes to the seventh day, its night will never fall, since you have made it holy to abide forever. You, who are always at rest, nonetheless 'rested on the seventh day' after completing your works—or so it is said in your Scripture, to signify that when we have completed our works, which were your works made 'eminently good' in us, we can rest with you on the eternal seventh day.

52. Then will you rest in us as now you work in us. Our rest will simply be you resting in us, as our work now is you working in us, though you, Lord, are ever at work, ever at rest. You see not temporally, work not temporally, rest not temporally, but you make us see in time, and see time itself, and see the release from time. **53.** We see the things you made because they are, but they are because you saw them. We outwardly see that they are, but see only inwardly that they are good, while for you to see that a thing should be made is the same as to see it made. At a certain point in time we were moved to good activity, as that was fostered in us by the Spirit, just as at an earlier point in time we moved ourselves to bad actions by turning away from you. With you, single in good, there is no break in your good action. Some of our actions are good, by your gift, but we do not perform good always. We hope after this to rest in your final sanctification of us. But you, a goodness in need of no added good, are always at rest, since your rest is what you are. What man can explain this to another man? What angel to an angel, or what angel to a man? Only to you can we pray, only from you can we hope, only at your door can we knock. Be it granted, be it fulfilled, be it opened.